Anonymous

Plumbing Problems

Fourth Edition

Anonymous

Plumbing Problems
Fourth Edition

ISBN/EAN: 9783744679053

Printed in Europe, USA, Canada, Australia, Japan

Cover: Foto ©Thomas Meinert / pixelio.de

More available books at **www.hansebooks.com**

PLUMBING PROBLEMS;

OR,

QUESTIONS, ANSWERS, AND DESCRIPTIONS

RELATING TO

HOUSE-DRAINAGE AND PLUMBING,

FROM

THE SANITARY ENGINEER.

WITH ONE HUNDRED AND FORTY-SIX ILLUSTRATIONS.

FOURTH EDITION.

NEW YORK:
THE ENGINEERING AND BUILDING RECORD.

1889.

PREFACE.

A FEATURE of THE SANITARY ENGINEER is its replies to questions on topics that come within its scope, included in which are Water-Supply, Sewerage, Sewage Disposal, Ventilation, Heating, Lighting, House-Drainage, and Plumbing.

Repeated inquiries concerning matters often explained in its columns suggested the desirability of putting in a convenient form for reference a selection from its pages of questions and comments on various problems met with in house-drainage and plumbing, improper work being illustrated and explained as well as correct methods.

It is therefore hoped that this book will be useful to those interested in this branch of sanitary engineering.

TABLE OF CONTENTS.

PAGES

DANGEROUS BLUNDERS IN PLUMBING:

Running Vent-Pipes in Improper Places—Connecting Soil-Pipes with Chimney-Flues—By-Passes in Trap-Ventilation, etc.—A Case of Reckless Botching—A Stupid Multiplication of Traps—Plumbing Blunders in a Gentleman's Country House—A Trap Made Useless by Improper Adjustment of Inlet and Outlet Pipes—Unreliability of Heated Flue as a Substitute for Proper Trapping—Need of Plans in Doing Plumbing-Work.... 17–38

HOUSE-DRAINAGE:

City and Country House-Drainage—Removal of Ground-Water from Houses—Trap-Ventilation—Fresh-Air Inlets—Drain-Ventilation by Heated Flues—Laying of Stoneware Drains—Requirements for the Drainage of Every House—Drainage of a Saratoga House—Ground-Water Drainage of a Country House—Ground-Water Drainage of a City House—Fresh-Air Inlets—The Location of Fresh-Air Inlets in Cities—Air-Inlets on Drains—The Proper Way to Lay Stoneware Drains—Risks Attending the Omission of Traps and Relying on Drain-Ventilation by Flues—The Tightness of Tile-Drains—Danger of Soil-Pipe Terminals Freezing unless Ends are Without Hoods or Cowls—Objection to Connecting Bath-Waste with Water-Closet Trap—How to Adjust the Inlet and Outlets of Traps—How to Protect Trap when Soil-Pipe is used as a Leader—Size of Ventilating-Pipes for Traps—How to Prevent Condensation filling Vent-Pipes—Ventilating Soil-Pipes—How to Detect Accidental Discharge into Trap Vent-Pipe—Why Traps Should be Vented.......................... 39–72

MISCELLANEOUS.

Syphoning Water through a Bath-Supply — Emptying a Trap by Capillary Attraction — As to Safety of Stop-Cocks on Hot-Water Pipes — How to Burnish Wiped-Joints — Admission to the New York Trade-Schools — Irregular Water-Supply — Hot Water from the Cold Faucet, and How to Prevent it — Disposal of Bath and Basin Waste-Water — To Prevent Corrosion of Tank-Lining — Number of Water-Closets Required in a Factory — Size of Basin-Wastes and Outlets — Tar-Coated Water-Pipe Affect Taste of Water — How to Deal with Pollution of Cellar-Floors — How to Heat a Bathing-Pool — Objections to Galvanized Sheet-Iron Soil-Pipe — To Prevent Rust in a Suction-Pipe — Automatic Shut-off for Gas Pumping-Engines when Tank is Full — Paint to Protect Tank-Linings — Vacuum-Valves not always Reliable — Size of Water-Pipes in a House — How to Make Rust-Joints — Covering for Water-Pipes — Size of Soil-Pipe for an ordinary City House — How to Construct a Sunken Reservoir to Hold Two Thousand Gallons — Where to Place Burners to Ventilate Flues by Gas-Jets — How to Prevent Water-Hammer — Why a Hydraulic-Ram does not Work — Air in Water-Pipes — Proper Size of Water-Closet Outlets — Is a Cement Floor Impervious to Air ? — Two Traps to a Water-Closet Objectionable — Connecting Bath-Wastes to Water-Closet Traps — Objections to Leaching Cesspool and Need of Fresh-Air Inlet — The Theory of the Action of Field's Syphon — How to Disinfect a Cesspool — Drainage into Cesspools — Slabs for Pantry-Sinks : Wood *vs.* Marble — Tests for Well-Pollution — Cesspool for Privy-Vault — Corrosion of Lead Lining — Size of Flush-Tank to deal with Sewage of a Small Hospital — Details of the Construction of a House-Tank — The Construction of a Cistern under a House — To Protect Lead Lining of a Tank, and Cause of Sweating — Stains on Marble — Lightning Striking Soil-Pipes — Will the Contents of a Cesspool Freeze ? — Bad-Tasting Water From a Coil — How to Fit Sheet-Lead in a Large Tank — Why Water is " Milky " When First Drawn — Material for Water-Service Pipes — Carving-Tables — Is Galvanized Pipe Dangerous for Soft Spring-Water ? — How to Arrange Hush-Pipes in Cisterns to

Prevent Syphoning Water Through Ball-Cock—Depth of Foundations to Prevent Dampness of Site—Where to Place a Tank to get Good Discharge at Faucet—Self-Acting Water-Closets—Wind Disturbing Seal of Trap—How to Draw Water from a Deep Well—Cause of Smell of Well-Water—Absorption of Light by Gas-Globes—Defective Drainage—Fitting Basins to Marble Slabs—Intermediate Tanks for the Water-Supply of High Buildings—How to Construct a Filtering-Cistern —Objections to Running Ventilating-Pipe into Chimney-Flue—Size of Water-Supply Pipe for Dwelling-House—Faulty Plan of a Cesspool— Connecting Refrigerator-Wastes with Drains—Disposing of Refrigerator-Wastes—Pumping Air from Water-Closet into Tea-Kettle as Result of Direct Supply to Water-Closets—Danger in Connecting Tank-Overflows with Soil-Pipes—Arrangement of Safe-Wastes—The Kind of Men Who do not Like the *Sanitary Engineer*—What is Reasonable Plumbers' Profit........ 73–134

HOT-WATER CIRCULATION IN BUILDINGS.

Bath Boilers—Setting Horizontal Boilers—How to Secure Circulation Between Boilers in Different Houses—Connecting One Boiler with Two Ranges—Taking Return Below Boiler—Trouble with Boiler—An Ignorant Way of Dealing with a Kitchen-Boiler—Returning into Hot-Water Supply-Pipe—Where Should Sediment-Pipe from Boiler be Connected with Waste-Pipe ?—Several Flow-Pipes and One Circulation-Pipe—How to Run Pipes from Water-Back to Boiler—Hot-Water Circulation when Pipes from Boiler Pass Under the Floor—Heating a Room from Water-Back—The Operation of Vacuum and Safety Valves—Preventing a Collapse of Boilers—Collapse of a Boiler—Explosion of Water-Backs —A Proposed Precaution against Water-Back Explosions—The Bursting of Kitchen-Boilers and Connecting-Pipes—Giving Out of Lead Vent-Pipes from Boilers in an Apartment-House—Connecting a Kitchen-Boiler with One or More Water-Backs—New Method of Heating Two Boilers by One Water-Back—Plan of Horizontal Hot-Water Boiler... 135–186

Hot-Water Supply in Various Buildings.

Kitchen and Hot-Water Supply in the Residence of Mr. W. K. Vanderbilt, New York—Kitchen and Hot-Water Supply in the Residence of Mr. Cornelius Vanderbilt, New York—Kitchen and Hot-Water Supply in the Residence of Mr. Henry G. Marquand, New York—Kitchen and Hot-Water Supply in the Residence of Mr. A. J. White—Hot-Water Supply in an Office Building—Kitchen and Hot-Water Supply in the Residence of Mr. Sidney Webster—Plumbing and Water-Supply in the Residence of Mr. H. H. Cook—The Construction of Turkish and Russian Baths.. 187–215

Form of Plumbing Specification for an Isolated Country House... 217–224

Appendix.

Text of Plumbing Laws and Regulations in force in New York, Brooklyn, and Boston... 225–236

Alphabetical Index.................................... 237–244

LIST OF ILLUSTRATIONS.

	PAGE
FIGURE 1.—By-pass around trap of basin.	17
" 2.—Overflow openings connected with soil-pipe and giving admittance to foul air.	18
" 3.—Trap-vent pipe used as urinal-vent and admitting foul air.	19
" 4, 5, AND 6.—By-passes around traps of water-closet, sink, and wash-basins.	20
" 7.—By-pass around trap of water-closet.	21
" 8.—Trap-vent and closet-bowl vent connected with the same pipe.	21
" 9.—Bath-waste connected with the heel of water-closet trap.	21
" 10.—Basin overflow connected with the crown of trap and admitting foul air.	22
" 11.—Ventilating opening in water-closet casing connected directly with soil-pipe.	22
" 12.—Safe-waste connected with heel of water-closet trap and causing a nuisance.	23
" 13.—Safe-waste connected directly with soil-pipe.	24
" 14.—Furnace drawing its air-supply from a drain.	24
" 15 AND 17.—Water-closet ventilator bringing foul air into a room.	25, 27
" 16.—Disgraceful plumbing in a Philadelphia house.	26
" 18.—Vent-pipe of a water-closet bowl connected directly with soil-pipe.	28
" 19.—Waste-pipe of wash-tub connected with outside of trap and admitting foul air.	28
" 20, 21, AND 22.—Chimney-flues used to ventilate plumbing-work, with mischievous results.	29, 30
" 23.—Typical defects in the plumbing of a Boston house.	31
" 24.—A case of reckless botching.	33

LIST OF ILLUSTRATIONS.

		PAGE
FIGURE 25.	—Stupid multiplication of traps under sink and refrigerator	34
" 26.	—Plumbing blunders in a gentleman's country house	35
" 27.	—The blunders remedied	35
" 28	—Basin-trap made useless by improper adjustment of inlet and outlet pipes	36
" 28A.	—Unreliability of heated flue as substitute for proper traps	37
" 29, 30, 31, AND 32.	—Plumbing and drainage (plans and elevation) of a Saratoga house	42, 43
" 33.	—Ground-water drainage of a country house	45
" 34.	—Ground-water drainage of a city house	47
" 35, 36, 37, 38, 39, AND 40.	—Various arrangements of air-inlets or foot-vents	50, 51, 52
" 41, 42, 43, 44, 45, 46, 47, 48, AND 49.	—Various arrangements of air-inlets or foot-vents in New York City	54, 55, 56
" 50.	—Plan of the drainage of the Pennsylvania Prison	63
" 51 AND 52.	—Deep and shallow seals in round traps	67
" 53.	—Syphoning water through bath-supply	74
" 54.	—Loss of trap-seal by capillary attraction	76
" 55.	—Irregular hot and cold water-supply	79
" 56.	—Hot water flowing from cold-water faucet	80
" 57.	—Automatic shut-off for gas pumping-engines	86
" 58, 59, AND 60.	—Position of gas-burner for heating ventilating-flues	90, 91
" 61.	—Disadvantage of connecting bath-wastes with water-closet trap	95
" 62 AND 63	—Detail of construction of house-tank	102, 103
" 64.	—Refrigerating coil giving bad taste to drinking-water	107
" 65, 66, AND 67.	—Steam carving-tables, with steam-pipes run over and under doors	111
" 68.	—Self-acting water-closet	116
" 69.	—Defective drainage and plumbing of an office	119
" 70, 71, AND 72.	—Fitting wash-basins to marble slabs	120
" 73.	—Intermediate tank for water-supply of high building	121
" 74 AND 75.	—Construction of filtering-cistern	123
" 76.	—Faulty plan of cesspool	126
" 77 AND 78.	—Methods of arranging refrigerator wastes	127, 128

LIST OF ILLUSTRATIONS. xiii

	PAGE
FIGURE 79.—Drawing foul air from water-closet bowl into tea-kettle	129
" 80 AND 81.—Arrangements of safe-wastes	131, 132
" 82.—Gas-stove and boiler for heating water	137
" 83.—Hot-water boiler and cisterns as used in Great Britain	137
" 84 AND 84A.—Saddle and dome-top boilers	138
" 85.—Saddle-boiler in position	138
" 86.—Dome-top boiler in position	139
" 87.—Complete English hot-water supply apparatus	129
" 88.—Hot-water boiler and cisterns as used in Montreal	140
" 89.—American method of fitting up ranges and boilers	141
" 90.—Auxiliary heater and boiler	143
" 91 AND 92.—Conical boiler with separate fire	143, 144
" 93.—Boiler with four couplings on top as used in Boston	144
" 94.—Double boiler used in New York City	147
" 95.—Reverse attachment	148
" 96.—Earlier substitute for reverse attachment	149
" 97, 98, AND 99.—Horizontal boiler's setting and connections	152
" 100.—Two boilers connected with a single water-back	152
" 101.—Boilers in different houses connected with the same range	153
" 102.—Two ranges on different floors connected with one boiler	154
" 103 AND 104.—Return circulation carried below the boiler	155
" 105.—Ignorant treatment of boiler circulation	157
" 106.—Return circulation connected with hot-water supply-pipe	158
" 107.—Several flow-pipes connected with a single return-pipe	159
" 108.—Plan of summer and winter kitchens and boilers	160
" 109.—Return circulation taken unsuccessfully below the kitchen floor	161
" 110.—Hood's diagram for hot-water circulations	162
" 111.—Combined vacuum and safety valve	163
" 112.—Collapsed boiler	165
" 113.—Pet-cock to guard against explosions of water-backs	167
" 114.—Bursting of water-pipes connected with kitchen boiler	168
" 115.—Bursting of lead boiler vent-pipes in an apartment-house	171

		PAGE
FIGURES 116, 117, 118, 119, 120, 121, 122, 123, 124, 125, AND 126.—Various methods of connecting several boilers and water-backs together.....173, 174, 175, 176, 177, 178, 179, 180, 182		
" 127.—Tucker's auxiliary apparatus for heating two boilers by a single back....		184
" 128.—Plan of a horizontal boiler near Boston.		186
" 129.—Kitchen in the residence of Mr. W. K. Vanderbilt..............		187
" 130.—Kitchen in the residence of Mr. Cornelius Vanderbilt...........		192
" 131.—Kitchen in the residence of Mr. Henry G. Marquand..........		196
" 132.—Kitchen in the residence of Mr. A. J. White.		198
" 133.—Hot-water apparatus and piping in the Duncan office building...		200
" 134 AND 135.—Kitchen in the residence of Mr. Sidney Webster.....203, 204		
" 136, 137, AND 138.—Details of the drainage, plumbing, and water-supply in the residence of Mr. H. H. Cook.... .....205, 206, 208		
" 139.—Kitchen in the residence of Mr. H. H. Cook......		209
" 140 AND 141.—Turkish and Russian baths in New York City.......211, 213		
" 142.—Needle-bath		215
" 143.—Design for trap and air-inlet		218
" 144 AND 146.—Arrangement of air-chamber on cold-water service....220, 224		
" 145.—Connecting lead to iron pipes...............................		223

DANGEROUS BLUNDERS IN PLUMBING.

RUNNING VENT-PIPES IN IMPROPER PLACES—CONNECTING SOIL-PIPES WITH CHIMNEY-FLUES—BY-PASSES IN TRAP-VENTILATION, ETC.

So many examples of curiously outrageous plumbing have come, in one way and another, to our notice, that we have decided to publish some extracts from our collection. The drawings show so plainly at a glance what is wrong, to one who knows something of plumbing, that comment would be unnecessary, except that many of our readers, not being plumbers, nor well posted in such matters, may want us to point out wherein the work is so bad.

A certain class of defects of very serious character, generally produced by an anxiety to do good work, without considering the relation several fixtures bear to each other, has been brought to light by the New York City Board of Health, under the name "by-passes." That is, when the waste-pipes of several fixtures are so connected that they have a trap common to more than one of the fixtures, the attempt to ventilate the traps may produce an open path around some other trap into a room. Figure 1, showing this defect, was a country job. The arrows indicate plainly enough that it was decidedly wrong, for study of the cut will show that both fixtures have a common trap—that, namely, in the course of the waste-pipe, which was intended to protect the bath. But by bringing the waste-pipe from the basin into the *inside* or *house side* of this trap, it followed when the traps were ventilated that an open course was made by way of the vent-pipe connecting the two traps, and

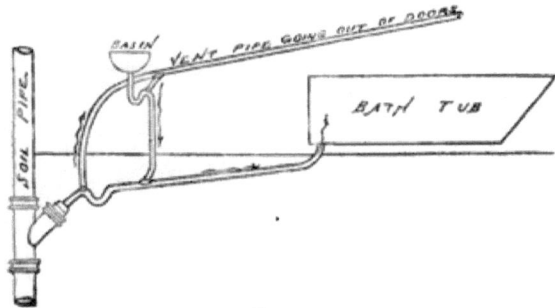

FIGURE 1.

then by the waste-pipe of the basin, around the trap which was supposed to cut the bath off from the drain, and the foul air in the house-waste system entered the bath-room through the outlet of the bath.

Figure 2 looks much like Figure 1, but is more stupid. It will be seen that there are no traps under any fixture except the water-closet, but the inventor of this system put a cowl on top of the soil-pipe, expecting to have an up-current always, and then connected the overflows of his basin and bath with a pipe leading to his soil-pipe, clearly supposing that he would always *draw air in* at the overflows, thus both preventing the escape of foul air at those openings and partially ventilating the room. But he forgot that no such constant upward current in the soil-pipe could be relied on, and when it failed the overflows became inlets for the foul air of the soil-pipe.

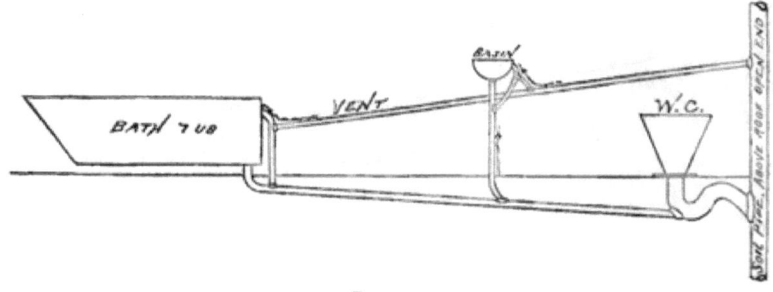

FIGURE 2.

In Figure 3 A and B represent the plumbing system in a New York building, where the value of traps was neutralized by attempting to use the trap-vent of one fixture as the ventilating-pipe of another fixture. B shows how this was done in the case of basins and urinals; A in the case of water-closet and urinal. In B a vent-pipe from the traps of several basins passed behind a row of urinals. The hood of each was connected with the trap-vent of the basins, which entered the soil-pipe. Of course an open way was thus provided for foul air through the urinal-hood.

In A the urinal was connected with the trap-vent of a water-closet, and the same mischief was done.

Mr. L. M. Hooper, one of the inspectors of the New York City Board of Health, has furnished additional examples of by-passes, as shown in Figures 4, 5, and 6. He explains them as follows:

"It seems hardly necessary to point out the objections to 'by-passes' from a sanitary point of view, when it is stated that a 'by-pass' is an arrangement of traps and air-pipes by which sewer-air passes around the trap and so out into the building, thus practically making of no avail the many other precautionary measures, such as tight joints, etc., taken to prevent its entrance into the dwellings. One simple rule, if followed, will prevent a by-pass of the ordinary type. Water should never pass through more than one trap in reaching the house-drain.

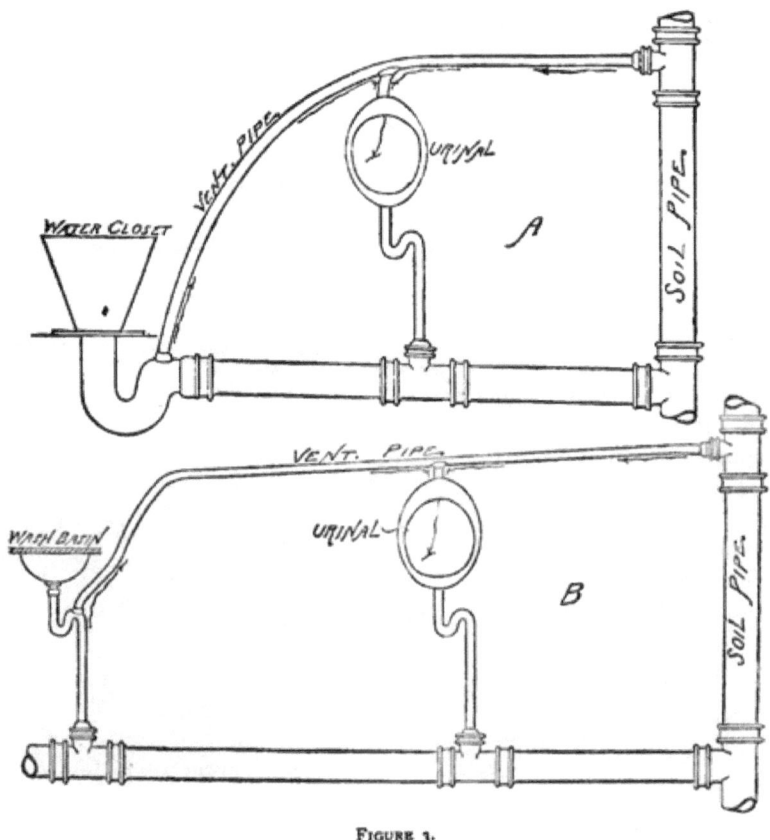

FIGURE 3.

If water after passing through the trap of its own fixture then passes through the trap of another fixture, and both traps are ventilated, there is sure to be a by-pass. One style of by-pass is shown by Figure 4. Here the water from the basin, in reaching the house-drain, passes through three traps, and the result is a double by-pass—one around the bath-trap and one around the water-closet trap. As a rule, there will be as many by-passes less one as there are traps through which one discharge has to pass in reaching the house-drain. If Figure 6 be examined closely it will be seen that the water from basin 2 does not pass completely through the trap of basin 1, but enters it just below the seal. In this case the danger is not so imminent as in the others; that is, the water, to make a complete by-pass, must pass entirely through the second trap. If it only passes half through —*i. e.*, enters it at its lowest point— the arrangement is not so dangerous. The greatest care should be exercised in overhauling old work. It is very common to hear the advice given, 'Well, trap that basin and ventilate it.' In nine cases out of ten it is the worst thing that could be done if nothing more is done. In almost every case in old work when the fixture is not already trapped, and often when it is, the trap of some other fixture will, upon examination, be found to act for it. The writer has one case in mind in which one water-closet trap answered for eight fixtures. A trap or vent-pipe should never be ordered for any fixture in an old house, without first tracing the branch waste-pipe and seeing that it does not connect with the trap of any fixture."

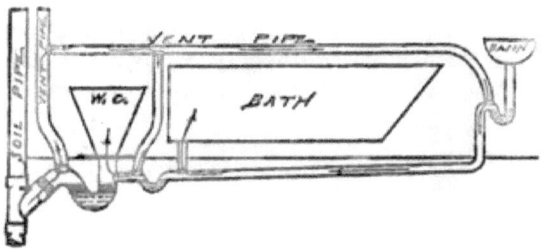

FIGURE 4.

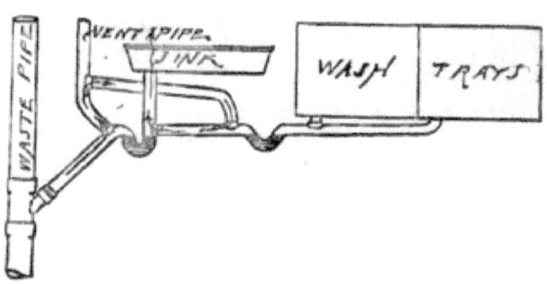

FIGURE 5.

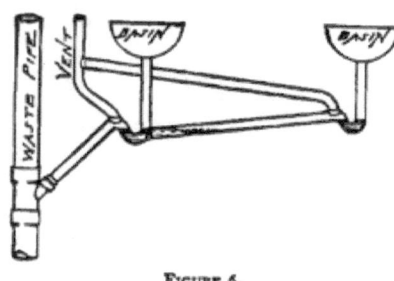

FIGURE 6.

A correspondent sends us a letter containing other illustrations of "by-passes." He writes as follows:

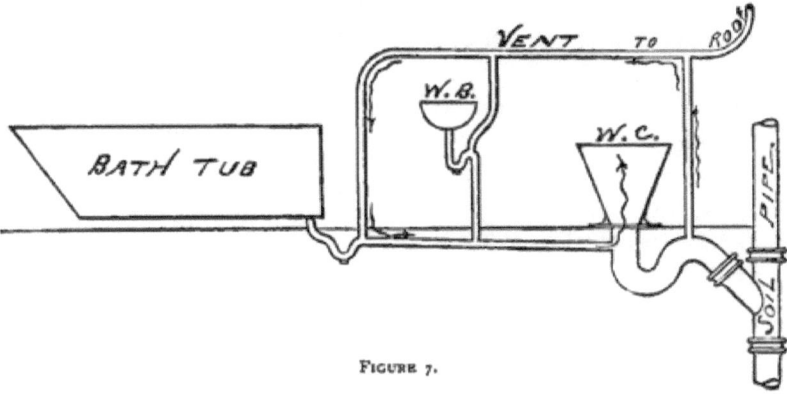

FIGURE 7.

"My attention has been drawn to some illustrations of defective plumbing, recalling to my mind several jobs of similar condition which I have seen while at work in buildings in this city. It is possible, however, that you have had illustrations of exactly the same defects as I now inclose you sketches of. In Figure 7 the original job had been done with but one trap—*i. e.*, that of the water-closet. On overhauling it had been air-piped, and the two remaining fixtures trapped and left in condition you see. In Figure 8 the hopper is made with side-outlet *a*, and the vent is run from it to the roof, a trap-vent on the same story connecting with it."

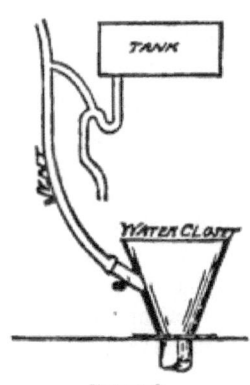

FIGURE 8.

Figure 9, from a town in Virginia, is a very good example of the mischief of connecting a bath-tub waste-pipe with the trap of a water-closet, for the evil was so manifest it could not be overlooked. The waste-pipe from the bath was itself untrapped, but connected with

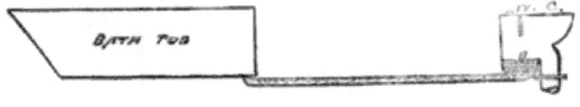

FIGURE 9.

the heel of the trap under the closet. The pipe was so nearly level that at all times it was full of the nasty fluids of the water-closet, and a discharge of the latter was pretty sure to throw part of this nasty matter up into the bath. It is a cardinal rule in plumbing that a bath and basin should always connect with the waste-system of the house separately from the water-closet, or at least that they should never connect with the trap of the closet, when their waste-pipes have to be nearly horizontal, as in almost every case they are. This illustration shows in an unusually forcible way the reasonableness of the rule.

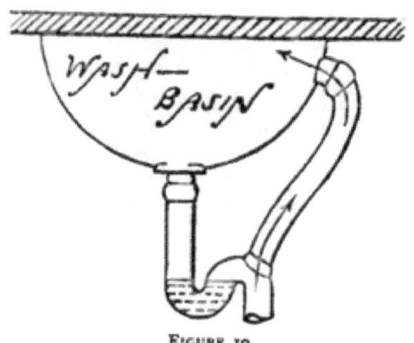

FIGURE 10.

The method of doing work shown in Figure 10 is an old acquaintance. This connecting of an overflow-pipe from a fixture to the waste-pipe in such a way as to make the trap of no use is forever turning up in different combinations. Sometimes, when it is not the overflow, it is a ventilating-pipe from the container of a closet, or some other pipe from a fixture which is perversely arranged to let in bad air. The wash-basin we show was found in a row of houses, whose plumbing generally was miserably done, in a town in Massachusetts. There was no trap on the house-drain, and hence gases from the sewer as well as from house-drainage system had free inlet through the overflow of the basin, which was connected with its waste-pipe *outside* of the trap-seal, as our illustration shows. Thus the trap was to all intents and purposes effectually done away with, and an open-pipe connection laid on to the sewer.

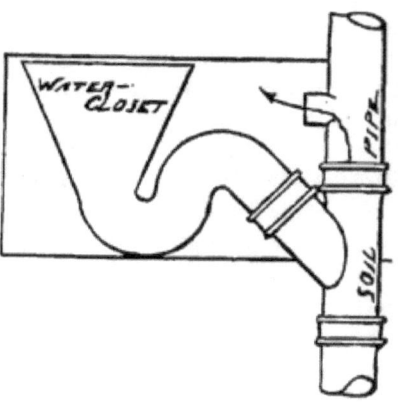

FIGURE 11.

In Figure 11, which should be compared with Figure 15, the workman tried to remove foul air from the casing around the water-closet with equal disregard of consequences. A short branch from the soil-pipe was carried through the casing and left open, with the idea that the up-draught in the soil-pipe would draw the air from the casing into the pipe, but the usual result followed. The soil-pipe air frequently came out of the branch into the casing and room.

Figure 12 shows what clumsiness did in a house on Second Avenue, in New York City. An old pan-closet, in a dark, unventilated central room, such as is common in many New York houses, had been filling the hall with a terrible odor for some time. Finally the owner of the house sent a plumber to fix it. The cause of the smells then became plain enough.

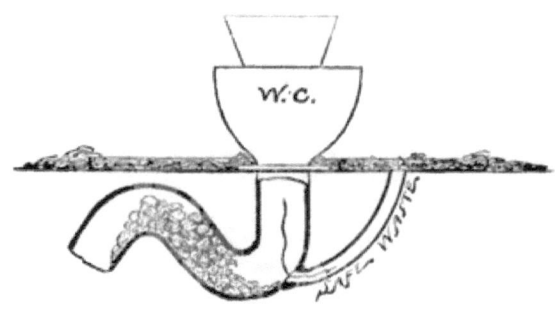

FIGURE 12.

Under the closet was a safe, and from this safe led a waste-pipe into the heel of the water-closet trap. The level of the safe was but little above the top of the trap, which had been partially clogged up by things thrown into the closet. The result was that every time the handle of the closet was pulled, the discharge from the pan caused a jet of filth to shoot up from the trap through the safe-waste into the safe. This was practically illustrated by the plumber who was sent to make repairs, and it had gone on until the safe had filled, overflowed onto the floor, and leaked down between the floor-beams. The whole space inside the closet-casing was a wet mass of nastiness, which had filled the upper floors of the house with foul smells for several weeks. Yet this so-called plumber insisted that the work in this house was a good job!

Figure 13 shows an arrangement even worse than the former. In this case the waste-pipe from the safe under the water-closet was taken directly into the soil-pipe, completely neutralizing the trap under the water-closet, and giving an opening for the foul air in the soil-pipe to enter the space within the water-closet casing, not shown in the drawing, whence it would readily enter the water-closet room and spread through the house.

Figure 14 was discovered by a well-known master plumber of New York City. It is drawn to represent the condition which he found

DANGEROUS BLUNDERS IN PLUMBING.

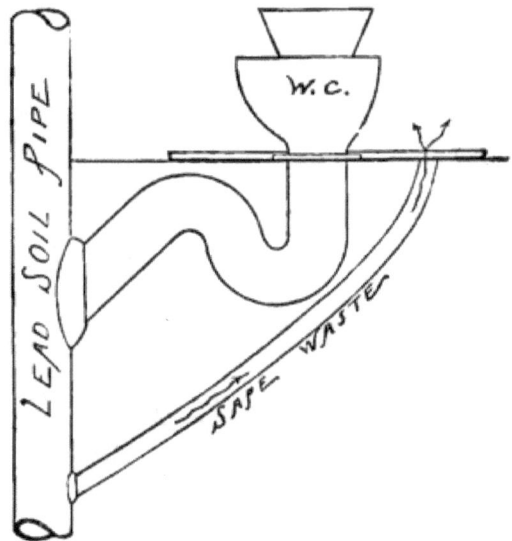

FIGURE 13.

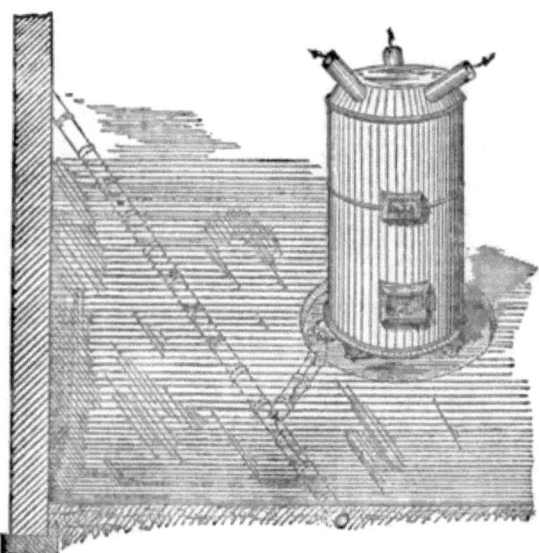

FIGURE 14.

when called in to discover and remove the cause of foul smells which permeated a residence in the fashionable quarter.

The house being built on a damp foundation, a drain to remove the ground-water had been put in, as shown by the dotted lines. This drain connected with the street-sewer directly without a trap, which, indeed, without some means of preserving its seal against evaporation, would have been of little use. The main line of drain not removing all the ground-water which collected in the ash-pit of the furnace, a branch drain was taken, without a trap, from it to the ash-pit. Mark the result. When the furnace was fired up in the autumn, a part of the air-supply was sucked, as by an air-pump, directly from the public sewer through the branch-drain, and these foul gases were distributed all over the house through the hot-air pipes. Unfortunately, this, though perhaps the worst, is not an isolated case of a furnace taking its air-supply from a drain.

Figure 15 is ingeniously bad. It was discovered by a journeyman plumber in the employ of one of the prominent plumbers of New York. By some process of reasoning the workman who did it had come to the conclusion that he could make one and the same ventilating-hood serve for his soil-pipe and for his water-closet room. He arranged it as shown in the drawing. From the top of the soil-pipe he took a vent-pipe to the

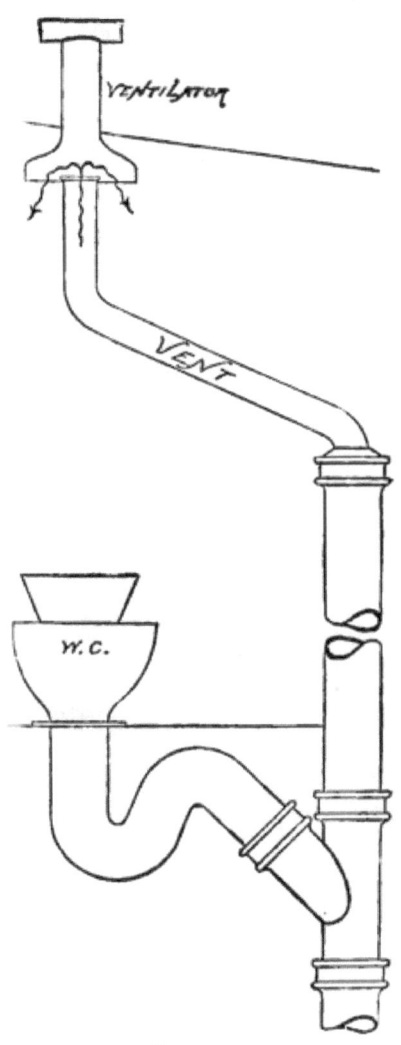

FIGURE 15.

under part of a ventilating-hood. This hood was open at the bottom to ventilate the room, and consequently there was produced a very good means of bringing the soil-pipe air first into the hood and then into the room, as the arrows indicate.

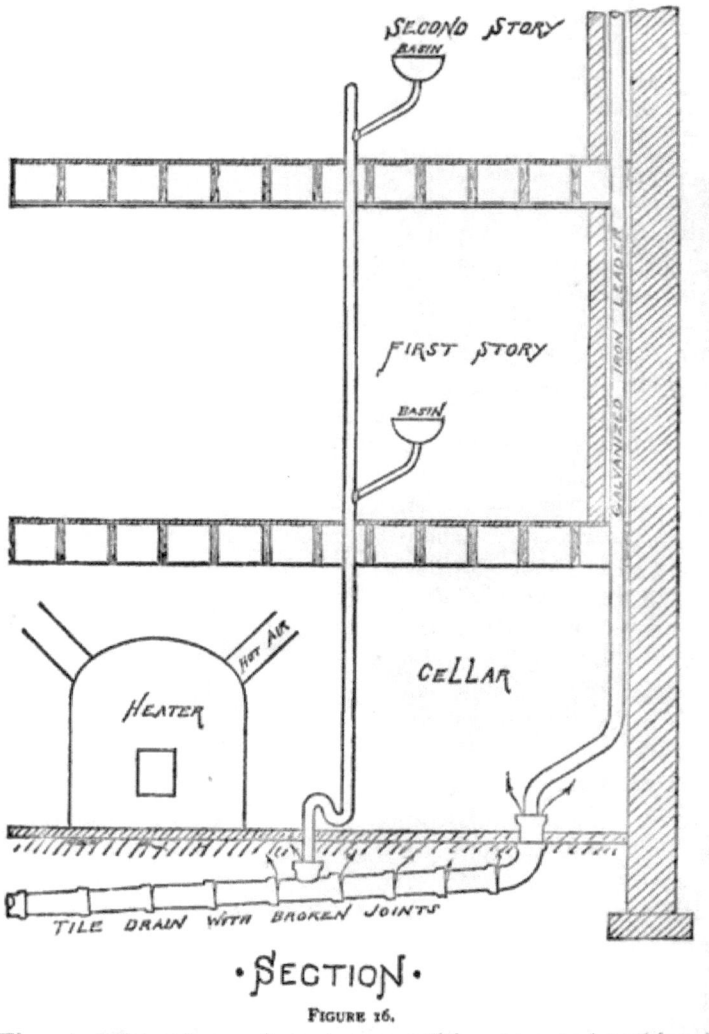

FIGURE 16.

Figure 16 shows how a dangerous condition was produced in a Philadelphia house by a somewhat different combination of causes. A tile-drain below the cellar-floor was broken and had imperfect joints.

Then into this drain was brought a galvanized-iron rain-leader from an extension. The joint where the leader entered a hub on the drain was imperfect; the leader itself was not tight, and was carried down between the wall and the studding, so that any foul air which passed into the leader from the drain found exit into the space behind the studding, and without much difficulty entered the house. At the same time the foul air of the drain was drawn from the imperfect joints and cracks into the heater as a part of its air-supply, and so sent over the house. Another clumsy feature about this job was the connecting of two wash-basins on upper floors with their waste-pipe without traps. The only trap between the basins and the drain was placed near the foot of the waste-pipe. Such an arrangement, of course, gave free access into the room of any smells from a long and dirty stretch of pipe, extending from the highest basin to the cellar, and having no trap to cut it off from the house.

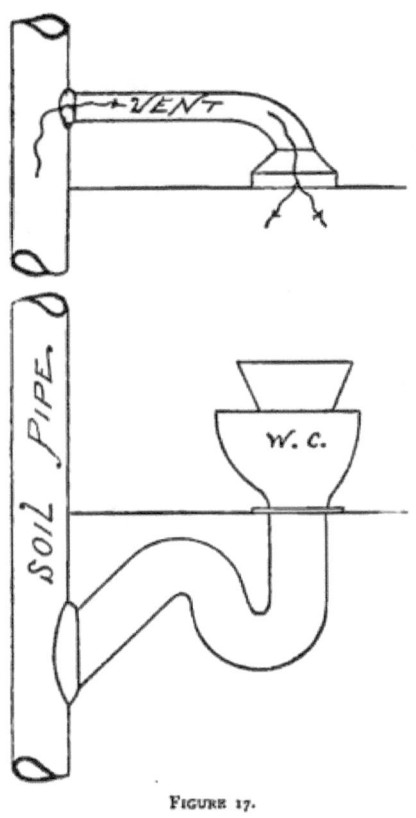

FIGURE 17.

In attempting to secure the ventilation of a water-closet room an economically inclined workman produced the condition shown in Figure 17. The soil-pipe running up above the roof with open end, it was plainly inferred that if the room was connected with it the room itself would be ventilated by reason of an up-draught, which was supposed to always exist in the soil-pipe. Accordingly a ventilating opening was made in the ceiling of the water-closet room, and a ventilating connection put between this opening and the soil-pipe. The result was, of course, that very often the currents of air in the soil-pipe were downward, and its foul air and smells passed into the room.

Figure 18 may be taken as a type of what has unfortunately been a common error. It is undoubtedly a good thing to ventilate the containers of pan-closets, if that is properly done, and that form of closet is used, but the container must then be connected with an independent flue or a pipe having no connection with the drainage system. Nevertheless, so-called plumbers take the "short-cut" method, and connect the container with the soil-pipe direct, or with the trap-ventilating pipe, which is equally bad, and so, of course, do away with the protection afforded by the trap of the water-closet; for the container vent-pipe offers a direct path for the soil-pipe air into the container, and there is no efficient protection to prevent its passage from the container into the

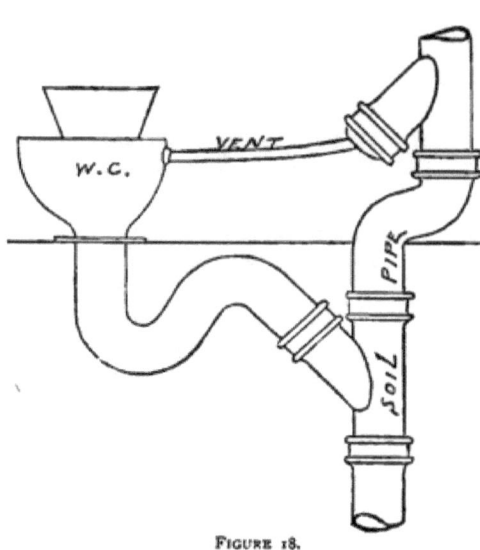

FIGURE 18.

house. This is the case with the work shown in the cut, where, it will be seen, a vent-pipe from the container of the water-closet connects directly with the soil-pipe.

Figure 19 contains its own explanation so clearly on its face that a definition is hardly necessary. One of the tubs of a set of wash-trays was connected into the *top of the trap*, which was common to all three. Of course, such a connection being outside of the trap-seal, an open course

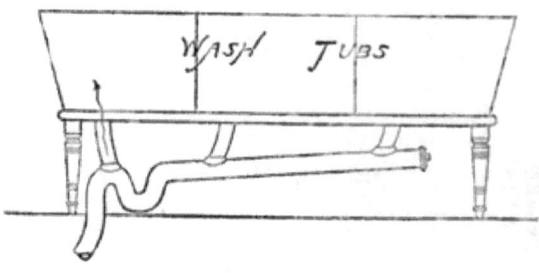

FIGURE 19.

was provided for the bad air from the drains into the kitchen by way of this tub.

DANGEROUS BLUNDERS IN PLUMBING.

Figure 20 shows a case where the soil-pipe terminated in a dead-end, and a branch-vent had been carried from it into a chimney-flue. It afterward proved that on this same flue was the fire-place of a lower room, and the result was that, the flue being seldom heated, foul odors poured from the drainage system out of the fire-place in such strength as to make the room uninhabitable. The job in which this occurred was in many respects a bad one,

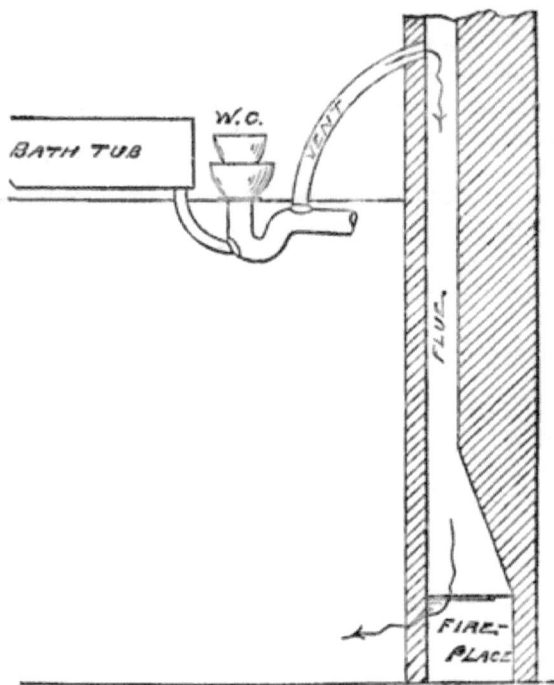

FIGURE 20.

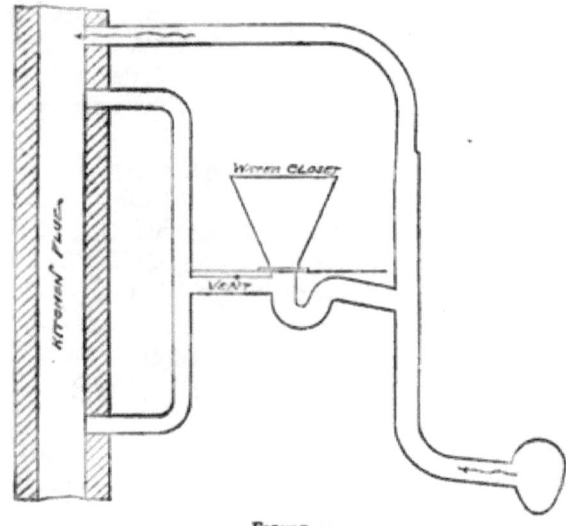

FIGURE 21.

but this feature was perhaps the most striking about it, and was a very good illustration of the whole class of work of this kind.

Figure 21 is an illustration of a part of the plumbing in a tenement-house. It will be seen that there is no trap between the house and the sewer; that the chimney flue is relied on to act as an efficient pump to always maintain a current from the sewer through the soil and waste pipes *outward*, and also to remove foul air from the hopper-closets which are connected with the same flue. The danger of the arrangement is apparent. Should the flue fail to draw for any reason, the connections with the hoppers serve as open roads for the passage of drain-air into the building around all traps, to say nothing of the possibility of escape of foul air through chimney-holes and fireplaces.

When the so-called plumber who did the job shown in Figure 22 designed it, he planned a variation on the ordinary chimney-ventilating system, which had disastrous results. There was ready to his hand, near the foot of the vertical soil-pipe, a joint into which a waste from a sink had once been inserted. By connecting a galvanized-iron pipe with this and with a chimney-flue he proposed to ventilate the plumbing-system of the house. The result, however, was that he converted the bottom of the chimney into a cesspool; for when the water-closet was discharged a part of the contents passed through the perfectly horizontal ventilating-pipe into the chimney, and there the matter gradually accumulated, until at the time of inspection the flue was filled nearly up to the vent-pipe. Yet the owner of this house, even when the state of things was shown to him, could not be convinced that the rational system of plumbing proposed as a substitute was necessary, and may have gone on using his chimney for a cesspool to the present time.

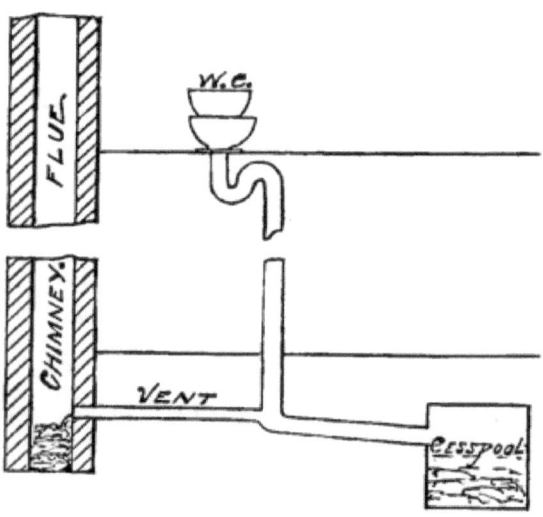

FIGURE 22.

Figure 23 shows a system of plumbing which was recently discovered in a row of houses in the vicinity of Boston, Mass. It forcibly illustrates the saying, "A little knowledge is a dangerous thing."

We wish to direct the reader's attention first to the 3-inch pipes above the upper water-closet. One of these, it will be seen, is the ventilating-pipe from the soil-pipe; the other is intended to remove bad air from the casing of the water-closet. Both terminate in a chimney-flue, and a few inches from each other. This flue was not heated. Of course

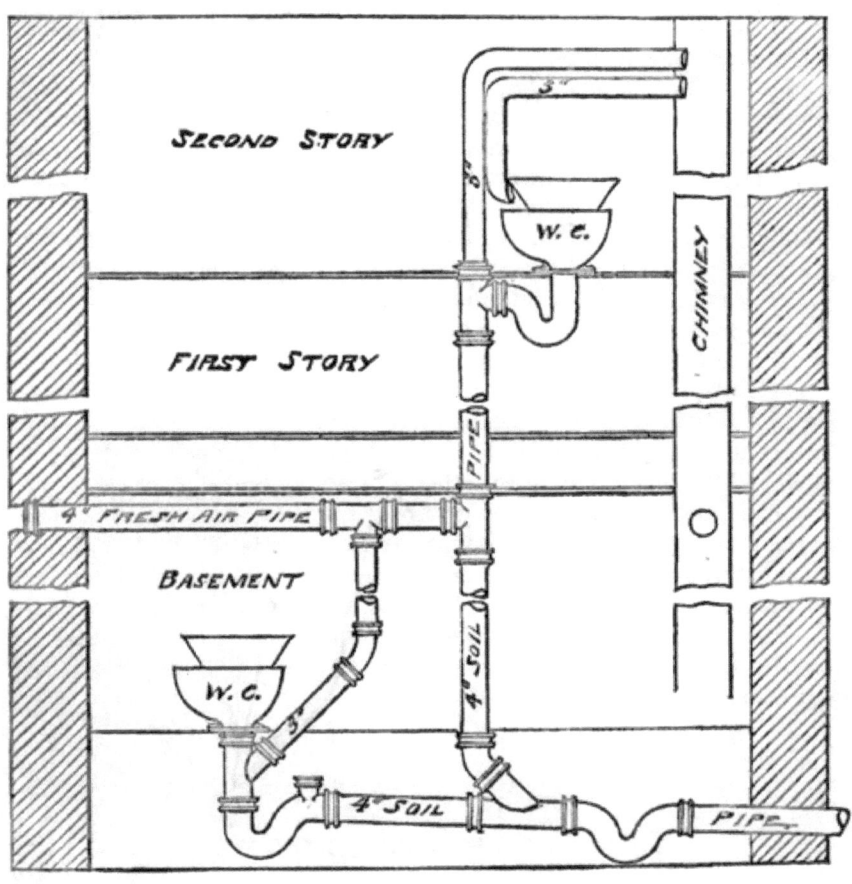

FIGURE 23.

the intention of the professed plumber who did this is plain enough. He expected to have a current of air through his soil-pipe and through his closet ventilating-pipe *outward and upward*, but it is almost a certainty that in some conditions of the atmosphere and wind a down draught in the chimney would result in carrying the foul air of the soil pipe back through the closet-vent into the casing and the room. And if a fire or stove in or near the water-closet room were drawing in air to supply combustion, there would be danger that a part of that air would be drawn from the soil-pipe through the closet-vent. Such an arrangement, as we have again and again pointed out, is unsafe and not to be tolerated.

It will be noticed further, that from the 4-inch fresh-air pipe to the left a 3-inch pipe is taken to ventilate the space between the pan and trap of the lower water-closet. Now, should the end of this air-pipe which goes out of doors be stopped up temporarily by a fall of snow, a mischievous boy, or by any other cause (and such temporary stoppages of air-pipes are of frequent occurrence), then the water, paper, and fæces from the upper closet, while falling through the upper portion of the soil-pipe, will drive the air in the soil-pipe before it and through the 4-inch air-pipe and 3-inch vent of the lower closet. The only obstacle to the passage of this air into the basement will be the shallow seal of the water-closet pan, which will break before either of the traps shown in the lower part of the drawing.

Finally, after a discharge from the upper water-closet has passed the 4-inch branch air-pipe, the air driven before it is compressed in the air-bound space between the two traps and the lower part of the soil-pipe, and the seal of one or the other trap will be probably forced. This would be prevented were there an air-inlet or foot-vent inside the trap at the lower right hand of the sketch. Indeed, this job shows at a glance one of the purposes of the foot-vent, while what has been said about the ventilating-pipe of the lower water-closet enforces once more the standing rule, that if receivers of water-closets, or spaces generally between fixtures and their traps, are to be ventilated, the ventilating-pipe must not connect with the drainage-system.

A CASE OF RECKLESS BOTCHING.

Q. I was lately called to examine a house, the occupants of which complained of bad smells, and in which I found one of the most expensive of the modern closets set, as in the accompanying sketch. The only ventilation to the soil-pipe was the 1¼-inch pipe D, which was branched out of the trap A, as shown. At B the waste-pipe from the basins was simply let into a hole cut in the iron pipe E, and an attempt was made to solder a joint at that point. You will also notice that the pipe C, which should extend independently out of doors, is branched into the apology for a continuation of the soil-pipe. Is it not high time that some one should have authority to stop men who commit such folly from working at the plumbing business?

A. We understand that the man responsible for this work is now dead, so as there is no danger that he will ever commit any more similar blunders, we may briefly point out the most glaring defects in this piece of botching for the information of such of our readers who do not fully comprehend the sketch. (1) The soil-pipe should be carried through the roof, the pipe D being of little benefit. (2) The pipe C, intended as a vent for the space between the water in the trap A and that in the bowl, should be extended out of doors, unless a convenient hot-flue could be used for that purpose. When it is connected to the continuation of the

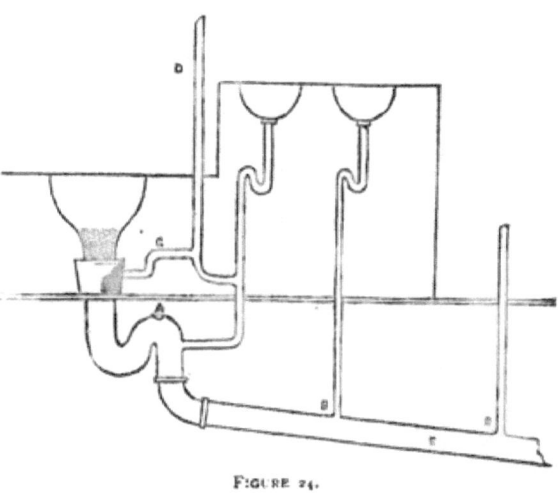

FIGURE 24.

waste-pipe, the benefits of the trap A are neutralized, and the drain-air is conveyed to the pot of the water-closet, and could gain an entrance to the house in the event of the water being out of the bowl. If the soil-pipe had been continued up through the house the two basins, which seem to have been located quite close to the water-closet, could have been drained into that pipe. Each of the traps should be ventilated, likewise the trap A under the water-closet.

The defects pointed out above might be attributed to gross ignorance, but the making of a connection of lead waste-pipe with iron soil-pipe in the manner described by our correspondent looks like reckless rascality. It is probably safe to say, what every plumber knows, that such a connection should have been into a Y-branch, with a brass or copper ferrule calked into it, on which the lead pipe should be properly soldered.

A STUPID MULTIPLICATION OF TRAPS.

A CORRESPONDENT writes a letter which may properly be inserted in this place. He says :

"I send you a sketch of some plumbing-work which came under my notice recently, as it was being overhauled. Originally the drum-trap (pot-trap) at kitchen-sink connected directly by a 2-inch pipe with the 6-inch earthenware drain below the cellar-floor. The refrigerator-trap also connected to drain by a 1½-inch pipe. Neither trap was ventilated. This latter was soon disconnected and made to discharge in an open pail, which was emptied every day. Eventually the house-drain becoming clogged with grease, the plumber advised putting in a grease-trap. This sketch shows the result of his labor. Not only did he put a grease-trap (not ventilated) on the sink-waste, but also added a drum-trap to the refrigerator-waste and discharged it into the grease-trap. This job has just been overhauled, a 4-inch vent carried from grease-trap to roof, and an open tray put on the line of refrigerator-waste, so as to entirely disconnect it."

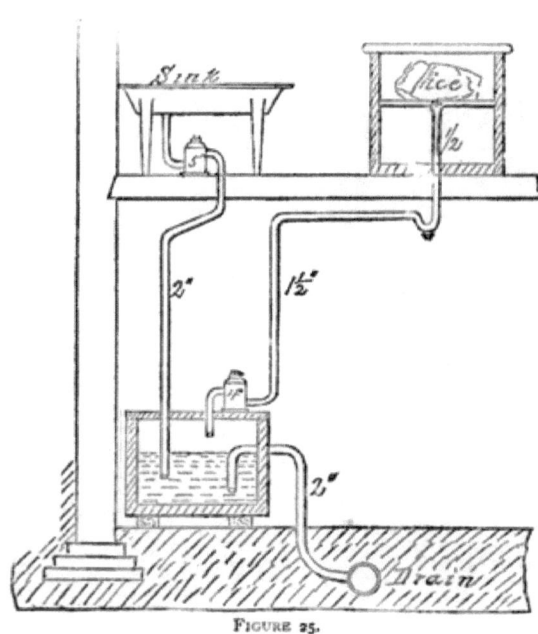

FIGURE 25.

The multiplication of traps with air-bound spaces between them here shown is a flagrant case of stupidity. No such duplication of traps should be allowed. The better way is to terminate the wastes that deliver into the grease-trap above the water-line.

PLUMBING BLUNDERS IN A GENTLEMAN'S COUNTRY HOUSE.

IT will be noticed that the man who did this work carried the vent-pipe A (Figure 26) into the continuation of the soil-pipe instead of out of doors, thus virtually neutralizing the benefits which the water-closet trap was intended to afford.

The ¾-inch pipe B also affords direct communication between the soil-pipe at one end and the bath-overflow and inlet at the other, which, under less favorable conditions, might produce serious results. This is only another evidence of how gentlemen, anxious and willing to pay for what is right in their plumbing arrangements, are the victims of ignorance and thoughtlessness. It also shows how much more important it is to have intelligent workmen than expensive appliances.

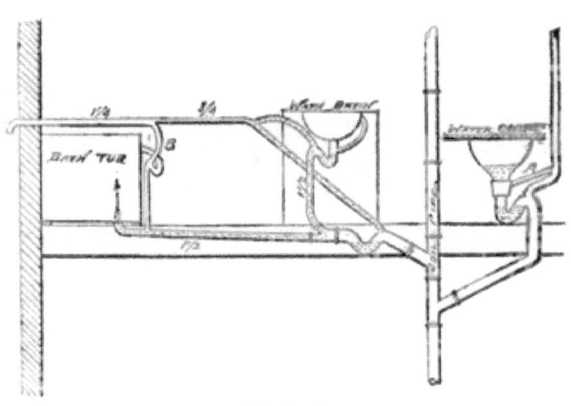

FIGURE 26.

Figure 27 illustrates the correct manner of arranging the traps and trap-ventilation. A reference to the previous sketch will indicate the points of difference.

It will be noticed, first, that the vent-pipe A from the receiver of the water-closet does *not* enter the soil-pipe, but leads independently to out of doors; secondly, the several traps are placed directly under the fixtures they are intended to serve.

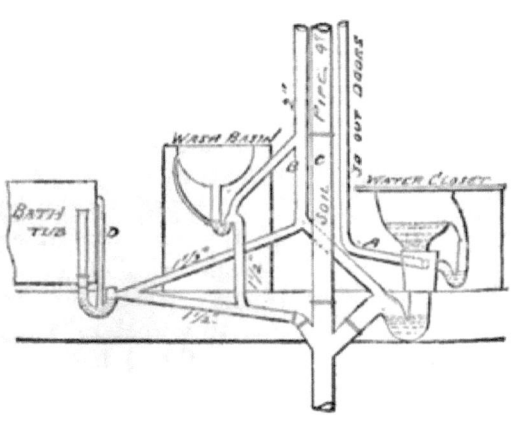

FIGURE 27.

The bath-trap is a half-S one, with a trap-screw close to the end of the bath and above the lead safe, the vent being close to it. As the least likely to get foul and offensive, we show a standing "overflow and waste;" if this is considered in the way and troublesome, then the overflow from the bath should be run as indicated by the dotted lines. The vent-pipe B, with which the vents from the several traps communicate, can run independently through the roof; but in this climate we should prefer to have it join the soil-pipe above, when any drainage enters the latter, the soil-pipe not being so likely to get closed by ice forming as the smaller pipe would be. The end of the soil-pipe should be without a bend or hood, as in this case there is no danger of articles being thrown down it.

A TRAP MADE USELESS BY IMPROPER ADJUSTMENT OF INLET AND OUTLET PIPES.

The accompanying drawing shows what was found in an up-town house in this city by a plumber who was called in to mend some leaky pipes. The pipe from the basin is supposed to extend down into the "round" or "bottle" trap, as is indicated by the dotted lines. The overflow-pipe entered the trap above the water-line, at the same level as the outlet, as shown, and the plumber who discovered the case and reported it to us stated there was a draught out of the overflow strong enough to blow out a candle. When our representative went to verify the matter he found the overflow closed by paper carefully pasted over it on the inside of the basin. This had been done by the occupants to keep out the smell, which was reported to be very bad.

Figure 28.

UNRELIABILITY OF HEATED FLUE AS A SUBSTITUTE FOR PROPER TRAPPING.

Q. The sketch which I send herewith illustrates a job of drainage and ventilation which I did in this city. I would like to have your opinion of the work. The pipe H in the heat-flue is of 4-inch wrought-iron, and is completely coated on the inside with sewer-slime, while the other, E, in the middle of the house, is perfectly clean. The work has been in use about two years and a half, and there is not a particle of smell anywhere about the house. I can refer you to the owner, who lives in the house himself.

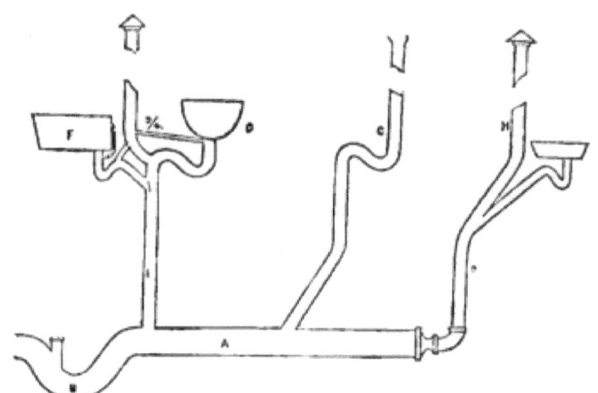

Figure 28.

A—Eight-inch terra-cotta pipe in the cellar.
B—Running trap.
C—Rain-water leader, with trap to prevent gas from corroding the leader-pipe.
D—Four-inch pipe to hot chimney.
E—Four-inch pipe.
F—Bath-tub.
G—A pan water-closet, with ¾-inch pipe from the container into the soil-pipe.

A. Judging from your sketch and description, we should say that the absence of any smell during the examination of the premises was due to the fact that such examination was probably made when the chimney was hot and the draught was down the pipe E, and through the pipe H in the chimney. In the absence of a constant heat in the chimney, we think the drain-air would be drawn through the ¾-inch pipe into your water-closet container, and from thence into your house. This pipe practically neutralizes the protection your water-closet trap is intended to afford, and we should advise dispensing with it; also should prefer an iron pipe inside the house to terra-cotta, and one not larger than six inches; in fact, with proper fall and flushing 4-inch is large enough and less likely to get foul.

In view of the foregoing, the propriety of the following, which was an editorial in the *Sanitary Engineer* of January 8, 1885, will be apparent:

NEED OF PLANS IN DOING PLUMBING-WORK.

The number of cases in which repairs to old plumbing-work have recently been found to result in mischief, by making open roads around the traps for foul air to enter houses, suggests the need of doing such plumbing-work especially by the aid of carefully-prepared drawings. It is often very difficult to foresee by simple inspection the result that ventilating the traps of old plumbing will lead to. The only safety lies in carefully tracing out the course of the piping as it is, and drawing the modifications on a sheet where the effect can be easily seen. When the alterations have been satisfactorily arranged and sketched the workman should be expected to carefully follow his drawing in making his alterations. We do not at all overstate the necessity for this course, as will appear by consulting the numerous illustrations we have published the last few months. Some of these have been seized upon by the opponents of trap-ventilation to bolster up their views, but we think any intelligent reader will see at once that the trouble is not in trap-ventilation, but in the botched way repairs are too often done. Our suggestion aims to substitute careful work for slipshod methods in this important matter.

What we have said of alterations suggests also the great usefulness of preparing working plans for all original work as well. It seems to us that this should be a duty in all plumbing shops. Plans of the piping, position of fixtures, etc., for all work, should be made, and after use filed away for permanent reference. Then any future changes in the work can be made with less trouble and disturbance, and with more certainty and safety. This is a matter which master plumbers should at once give attention to. Modern plumbing has become of too much importance to be done except as all other important works of construction are executed—namely, in accordance with carefully-prepared detailed drawings.

HOUSE-DRAINAGE.

CITY AND COUNTRY HOUSE-DRAINAGE—REMOVAL OF GROUND-WATER FROM HOUSES—TRAP-VENTILATION—FRESH-AIR INLETS —DRAIN-VENTILATION BY HEATED FLUES— LAYING OF STONEWARE DRAINS.

REQUIREMENTS FOR THE DRAINAGE OF EVERY HOUSE.

(From the Sanitary Engineer, September 1, 1879.)

In the light of present knowledge, the following seems to us the essential requirements for the drainage of every house. Time and further experience may suggest other features or modifications of these:

A trap should be placed on every main drain, to disconnect the house from the sewer or cesspool.

Every main drain should have an inlet for fresh air,* entering at a point inside the main trap, and carried to a convenient location *out of doors*, not too near windows. In places liable to unusual pressure from the sewer there should be two traps, with a vent-pipe from between them running up full size above the roof; or, where the pressure from sewer is only occasional and the rigor of climate will permit, this vent may be carried to the sidewalk or area, at a safe distance from windows. If the first trap is forced, the gas can gain easier exit through this pipe than through the second trap.

Every vertical soil or waste pipe should be extended at least full size through the roof.

No traps should be placed at the foot of vertical soil-pipes to impede circulation.

Traps should be placed under all sinks, basins, baths, wash-trays, water-closets, etc., and as near to these fixtures as practicable.

All traps under fixtures, wherever practicable, should be separately ventilated in order to guard against syphonage.‡ Such vent-pipes should not branch into a soil-pipe below where any drainage enters it. In some cases it is preferable to carry it to outer air independently.†

---

* This inlet will relieve the smaller house-traps from pressure occasioned by a descending column of water that would otherwise be likely to force the seals of these traps. The air drawn through this inlet to the lower part of the drainage-system assists the circulation within the drains, and is essential to insure the diffusion of the gases generated within them.

† The extension of soil-pipe, full size, through the roof is not a certain protection against syphonage of traps branching into it, and no protection when traps are on a horizontal pipe a distance from the vertical soil-pipe.

‡ And to permit the circulation of air through the drainage system.

Rain-water leaders should not be used as soil-pipes, and when connected with house-drains they should be made of cast-iron in preference to galvanized sheet-iron or tin, there being less liability of corrosion. Joints should be gas and water tight, to preclude possibility of drain-air entering open windows.

No safe-waste should connect with any drain, but it should be carried down independently to a point where its discharge would indicate the existence of a leak or any overflow above.

No waste from a refrigerator should be connected with a drain.

Unless the water-supply is ample, so that it will rise to every part of a building, insuring at all times the proper flushing of fixtures and traps, a cistern should be provided into which the water will rise at night, or into which it may be pumped. Said cistern should be large enough to hold an ample daily supply, be kept clean, covered, and properly ventilated. The overflow-pipe from it should *never* be run into any drain *under any circumstances*. The supply for drinking-water should not be drawn from it, but from a direct supply—*i. e.*, direct from the street-main.

Water-closets should never be supplied directly from street pressure or by a pipe from which branches are taken for drinking-water. Where the valve-closets are preferred to those that are supplied from a small cistern immediately over them, then the supply should be taken to a storage-tank, from which it can be conveyed to the valves on the closets, thereby insuring an equable pressure and securing more reliability in their working.

All drain-pipes within a house should be of *metal* in preference to stoneware, owing to the liability of the latter to crack, and the difficulty of keeping the joints tight. It is best to run them along the cellar-wall or ceiling, with a good incline. They should *never* be hidden underground, as then leaks will not be perceptible. In some places it is common to paint pipes white, so that any leakage will show itself to the most careless observer.

All drains should be kept at all times free from deposit; and if this cannot be effected without flushing, special flushing arrangements should be provided, so as to effectually remove all foul matter from the house-drains to the public sewers.

All horizontal drains should be laid in a straight line, with proper falls, and should be carefully jointed and made water-tight. No right-angled junction should be allowed, except in the case of a drain discharging into a vertical shaft.

No drain should be constructed so as to pass under a dwelling-house, except where absolutely necessary; and then it should be constructed of cast-iron pipes, with lead-calked joints, laid so as to be readily accessible for inspection, and ventilated at each end.

Whenever dampness of site exists, it should be remedied by laying subsoil drains, which should not pass directly to the sewer.

Water-supply and waste pipes should be concentrated as much as possible, and not scattered about a building. Horizontal soil and waste pipes are objectionable.

Plumbing-fixtures should not be hidden behind walls and partitions where their condition is never apparent. They ought properly to be open to view, and so situated that any leak would be readily detected. It is also well to have a plan of the plumbing of each house for the tenants' or owner's convenience and guidance in any emergency.

In planning house-drains they should be got outside the walls of the house as quickly as possible, so that there may be few joints of pipe, and the smallest chance of leakage from defects or accidents, taking precautions in locating to guard against freezing.

NEW YORK, April, 1885.

[In the light of the last few years' experience, we should say that there are few places where it would be desirable to use a double trap on the main drain. In other respects the requirements for the drainage of a house as formulated here seems to be as proper now as they were then, for most cities of the United States. And the plumbing regulations of certain leading cities, printed elsewhere, in the main very properly follow the lines here laid down.]

DRAINAGE OF A SARATOGA HOUSE.

Q. I AM building a country house at Saratoga, and inclose herein that part of the ground-plan of each floor which is to contain the proposed plumbing, also an elevation.

I have laid a 6-inch drain-pipe, which extends from the house through a sandy soil, at a good decline, some 700 feet, where it empties into the open air, in a low part of my place, from whence it readily flows into a neighboring marsh.

An ample supply of water is furnished by a ram, through a 1-inch supply-pipe, to a tank in the garret, thus giving an abundance of water at all times. The overflow from the tank runs to another large reservoir in the barn.

I desire to have your suggestions in reference to the best mode of connecting the plumbing with the drain and how best to provide for a thorough flushing of the drain without great expense. Also, whether it would not be better to connect the butler's pantry and kitchen sinks with the main drain by an independent drain flowing through a grease-trap; if so, where would you suggest putting the grease-trap, and how would you construct it, and where would you make the connection with the drain?

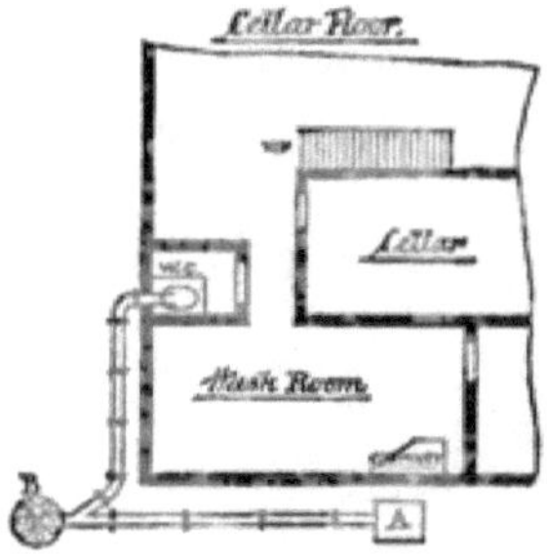

By referring to the cellar-floor plan, you will notice that it is my intention to connect the main drain with the sewerage-system of the house near the lower water-closet, which is almost under the slop-sink in the second story, which sink is under the tank, from which it would be possible to create a large flow of water to cleanse the drain. Would the water flowing through an ordinary faucet amount to more than a "driblet" for flushing, or would a larger stream be necessary?

A direct connection between the pantry-sink and the kitchen-sink would be difficult, owing to the chimney which projects into the room, as shown on the plan. Would you advise running a drain separately from each of these sinks straight down to connect with a drain underground on that side of the house? In that case would one large grease-trap be all that would be necessary?

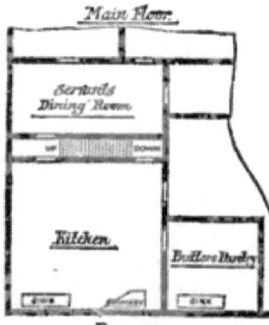

FIGURE 29.
A—Grease-Trap. *B*—Manhole.

FIGURE 30.

FIGURE 31.

A. There should be a vertical line or "stack" of 4-inch iron soil-pipe leading straight down from the water-closet in the bath-room to the basement story, and also up through the roof. In the basement story there should be in this pipe, directly under the ceiling, a ⅛-bend and a Y-branch with a clearing screw in the other hub of the Y. Thence the pipe can be suspended to the ceiling or attached to the partitions and pass with a good slope to the neighborhood of the water-closet in the basement story. Here three Y-branches should be inserted at suitable places, though two can be combined in one if convenient, to secure the drainage of the water-closet by a 4-inch Y, and the drainage of the slop-sink by a 4 x 2-inch Y, and the waste of the wash-tray by another 4 x 2-inch Y. The pipe can then pass out through the foundation-wall and some two feet beyond it, all of iron. Beyond this the pipe can be of 4-inch stoneware, with a Y-branch, to receive the overflow of the grease-collector, of the same size. The main trap, with its open T-branch, for the air-hole just above it, can be placed close below

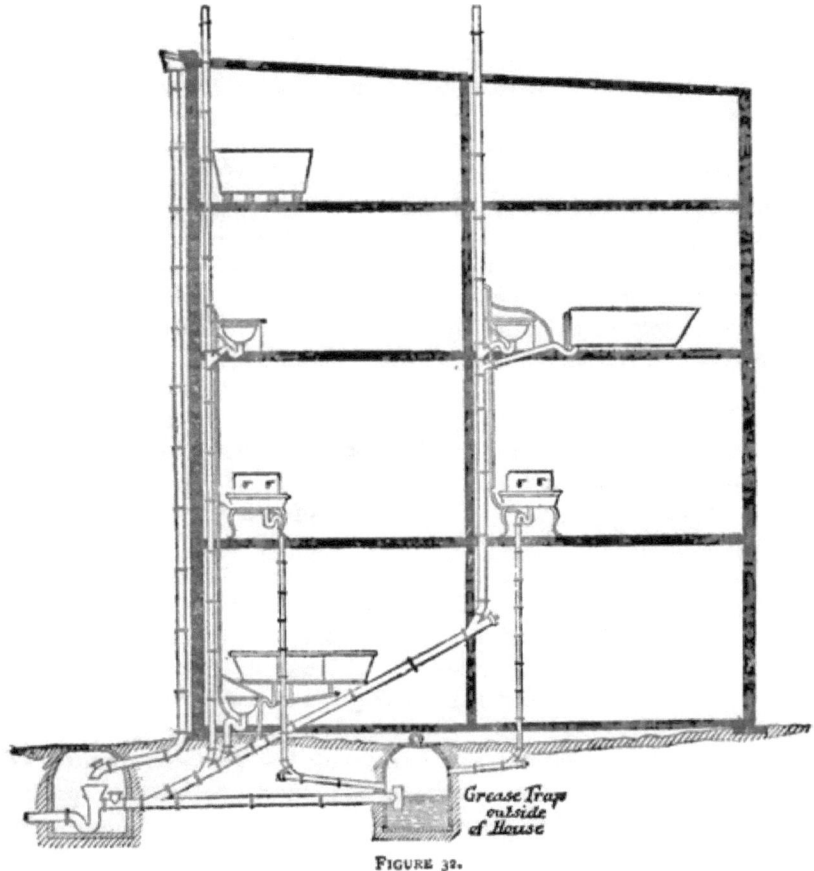

FIGURE 32.

this junction, and should be surrounded by a manhole, for getting access to it at any time. If possible, let the trap be at least six inches below the drain discharging into it, so the sewage will fall into the trap from above. It is also a good plan to lead a rain-spout into it by an open connection.

The branch-waste from the slop-sink should extend up through the roof, and should not be less than two inches in diameter above the roof and for two feet below it, though it should be larger, as hereafter explained, if the flush-tank is located in attic. The branch from the wash-trays may 1½-inch if of lead or 2-inch if of iron.

The waste-pipes from the kitchen-sink and butler's pantry should pass straight down to the basement story, and be provided with clearing screws, where they turn to discharge into the grease-basin. This should be outside and back of the chimney. It should be built of brick, and the overflow from it can be earthenware pipe, with its intake orifice at least six inches under water and joining the main drain just above its trap, as above described, opposite the corner of the house. But if the outlet be a T instead of a bend, it will be more readily cleaned out from above.

Of course, separate traps must be provided for the slop-sink, the bath-tub, the wash-trays, and the kitchen-sink, and for the butler's sink, and any other fixtures that may be provided.

The air-pipes from the traps at the cellar water-closet and the wash-trays and sinks over them can all join into one and connect with the air-pipe above waste of slop-sink, where a branch should be inserted for the purpose.

The air-pipes from the traps under the butler's pantry-sink and traps, and under the bath-tub and chamber water-closet, can also be combined and branch into the upper part of soil-pipe just above the water-closet trap.

Your proposed method of disposing of your house-drainage will inevitably make a nuisance in the "marsh." It would be better to distribute it on a field of grass, if you have one, where the ground would not become sodden and saturated with the water. But if you allow it to run in one place as it comes from the house it will certainly make a nasty place of it.

If you have a good fall, as we understand, it would be a good plan to make the discharge intermittent by building a small tank, to be discharged when it is full by some automatic arrangement just below the outside trap. Field's syphon will work well if applied with the clean water that overflows from the house-tank, and can thus be made to flush the whole drain below. The barn can be supplied by a part of this, and the rest used for flushing. The flush-tank can be placed in the attic alongside the supply-tank, if convenient, and thus flush the drain inside the house as well as outside.

In this case a 3-inch vertical pipe should be provided for the flushing, and it can receive the drainage of the slop-sink on the chamber-floor, and extend up through the roof. A flushing-tank of this sort should not be less than some fifty gallons capacity and the syphon not less than three inches.

No constant flow of water from a faucet will flush your drains. This can only be done by a sudden discharge of one or two barrels at once by a flush-tank, as we now recommend.

GROUND-WATER DRAINAGE OF A COUNTRY HOUSE.

Q. WILL you please illustrate the proper way to drain cellars, and the manner of connecting with the main drain leading to the sewer? What precautions should be used to prevent sewer-gas backing into the cellar, presuming that water passes from the cellar into the drain only during fall and spring—cellar being dry during summer and winter?

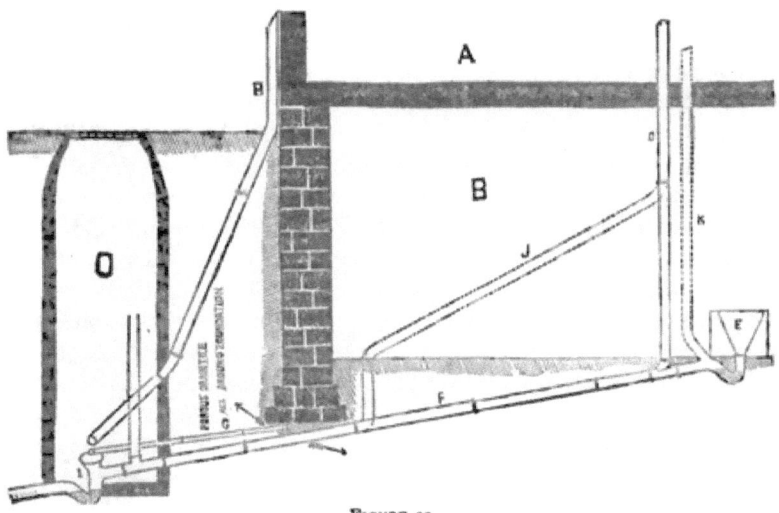

FIGURE 33.

A. The annexed cut shows how the ground-drainage can be delivered to the house-drain with little risk. It is supposed that the building stands by itself, and the ground-drain is to be laid quite around the foundation of the house. If so, it will effectually cut off all water that might otherwise make the cellar damp. It is also supposed that the soil-pipe extends up through the roof in all cases. This insures an *inward* draught at the vent-hole where the ground-water is admitted, so that the air from inside the house-drain is not likely to follow the ground-drain, which has no vent at its upper end. If rain-water is admitted into the trap as here shown, it keeps the trap flushed occasionally, and it is then better to provide an extra air-hole by a T-branch just above, as shown, so that the air-draught need not be in any way obstructed by a rapid influx of rain-water, as it otherwise might be.

If drainage-fixtures are needed on the level of the cellar-floor, the pipe draining them is laid below that level, as here shown; it should then be kept accessible by building dwarf-walls each side of it up to the level of the floor of cellar, where the trench can be covered with planks or flags of stone, so fitted as to be readily lifted, and not spiked or cemented down. If no water-closets, sinks, or similar fixtures are needed on the cellar-floor it is better to keep the pipe above that level, as shown by the dotted lines.

GROUND-WATER DRAINAGE OF A CITY HOUSE.

ON page 45 we suggested a plan for removing ground-water from a house standing alone. (See Figure 33.) We now give a plan for a house situated in a block, as ordinarily found in this city.

Where houses are built in continuous blocks, as in cities, the arrangement shown on the accompanying plan is appropriate. In this case the pipe under the basement or subcellar-floor should be of unglazed tiles, laid without mortar of any kind, so that the ground-water can get in at any joint, and as it is not a tight drain, but a porous one, for clean water only, it need not be made easy of access, but can be buried. In case a water-closet or other receptacle of foul drainage is needed at this low level, another pipe of iron must be supplied as shown in Figure 33.

Some people connect the ground-drain under the water-seal of the outer trap, but it is not so good a plan as the one shown in the cut, for the following reason: In that case the trap-water sets back into the ground-drain and stands there without circulation, except at such rare intervals as the ground-drain is in active use. This occurs so seldom that the opening where it discharges into the trap is liable to get closed up by fæcal matter and other substances which pass by the orifice, and the ground-drain has generally insufficient fall to enable its contents to crowd through such a pasty plug and clean itself. The longer this plug remains the more compact it becomes. Of course if the ground-drain discharges in the open air, as shown in Figure 33, page 45, this trouble is avoided. During the winter season, and as long as houses are heated by fires, there is always an inward pressure of air at all cracks and orifices near the basement, and the air which is in these ground-drains will at such times press upward through any pores and channels that can be found in the cellar-floor, gradually and surely working its way into the house. The ground-drain is deeply cov-

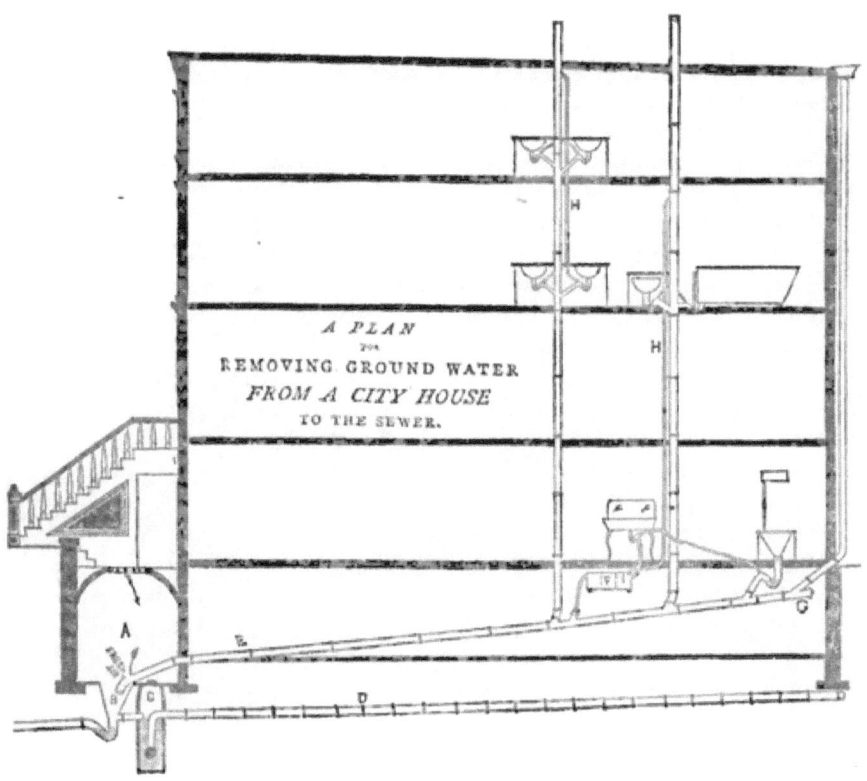

FIGURE 34.

ered and inaccessible, so that if by any chance it becomes defiled by sewage it is next to impossible to clean it. It is, therefore, *very* important that these ground-drains should be kept quite free from any possible contamination where connecting with the sewage-drain.

It is generally advisable to put the ground-drains as deep as two or three feet below the cellar floor wherever an outlet can be found at such a level, and this generally precludes the possibility of getting much fall where these ground-drains enter the main house-drain.

In consequence of this condition of things, a very slight obstruction in the house-drain trap, such as may happen from the deposit of a bit of cloth, a broken tea-cup or tumbler in any water-closet above, by a servant who thinks water-closets are made to hide such things, would serve to back up all the sewage of the house into the ground-drain, if care is not taken to prevent such an event.

If arranged as shown in Figure 34, a stoppage in the main trap would cause an overflow in the manhole, which should be inspected frequently and can be cleaned out when occasion requires. But if, as may often happen, it is not possible to get fall enough to prevent such a stoppage backing up the sewage into the ground-drain, some special safeguard must be applied in the shape of a mechanical valve. Such valves are not to be generally recommended in pipes where sewage flows, but this ground-drain is supposed to carry nothing but clean water. Under such conditions a valve may answer a good purpose. Metal valves, and even brass ones, are subject to corrosion, which would seal them fast to their seats if not often lifted.

A good form for this place is a rubber ball-valve arranged as in Bower's trap. But the trap should be specially constructed for this purpose, with a seal of at least twelve inches depth. The clearing-screw should of course be on top instead of at the bottom in this case, and should be examined for removal of sand or silt which the water may possibly bring in, especially during the first flow after the drain is constructed. The space around this trap where the water enters it should be well grouted with hydraulic-cement to prevent any back flow outside the pipe, in case of obstruction of sewage, while the valve in the trap will prevent it on the inside. Such a trap in such a position will hold its water for years, but *should be inspected at least twice a year, because it is of great importance to keep it free from sand and supplied with water.*

If the connection with the main drain were to be made beyond the trap in the latter, we should lose the additional safeguard of that trap against the admission of sewer-air, which safeguard it is best to retain.

FRESH-AIR INLETS.

Q. I HAVE read several articles recently wherein I see that, like myself, there are a great many plumbers who don't approve of the running-trap placed in the main sewer-pipe, and connected with fresh-air inlet on house side of trap, which seems to be the plan most generally adopted by most of your contributors.

I contend that when the pipe is flushed by a large discharge of water from slop-sink or other fixture, there will be a quantity of foul air discharged from the fresh-air inlet contaminated from contact with foul matter adhering to the inside of pipes, and likely to be carried back into the house through an open window or door. And then what would be the result? Another plumber would be sent for; he would condemn, or the house-owner would insist on its immediate stoppage. The trap it is likely they would let remain; then the discharge through the larger traps, not having free passage to sewer or cesspool, would overcome the water in smaller ones, and the air would be discharged into the rooms.

I believe in having the main trapped by all means if possible, but having it ventilated on a different plan, which others might not approve of, but one on which I would like to have practical opinion, and which I will try to explain.

I carry the soil-pipe full size through the roof. Trap all wastes as close to fixture as possible, using all-lead hand-made traps, which I consider best if properly made, excluding running-traps, which I don't think are reliable.

In the cellar, outside of all branches, place a half-S trap, branching the inlet in the back high enough so as to have a perpendicular fall of five or six inches to seal or outlet. Now, instead of carrying the upper part of trap outside through cellar-wall for fresh-air circulation, I return it back with 3-inch pipe through roof, and take a branch from all traps into it as close to the seal as possible, for vent to prevent syphonage and ventilate shorter branches. By not carrying this pipe as high as soil-pipe above roof, and being of different size and in the same atmosphere, they will be of different temperature, which, in my opinion, will insure a circulation at all times, materially aided by every discharge in the soil-pipe. I don't claim that I will have such a draught for my plan as by the former, but I do claim I will have a job that will stand the test of time much better.

This method I have adopted and found it to work well at all times and give entire satisfaction.

A. We have seen great numbers of fresh-air inlets, and have had them in use for years, but we never noticed the slightest odor from the cause suggested by our correspondent. As a matter of fact, a properly flushed and ventilated soil-pipe does not contain a very foul-smelling air. To guard against even such a possibility we have, in our early numbers, advocated that the fresh-air inlet should terminate in a vault with a perforated cover. This contains a sufficient quantity of air to dilute any occasional whiff produced by a reverse current.

The plan proposed of carrying a 3-inch pipe back and up through the roof, and using this pipe also to supply air to the separate traps, would be quite impracticable in our city-built houses. Besides the expense there would be considerable friction to overcome—in some instances quite enough to disturb the seals of the smaller traps down stairs when a water-closet was discharged upstairs. We admit that this 3-inch pipe is better than none at all, but we can assure our correspondent that his apprehension about offense from properly arranged fresh-air inlets are groundless.

THE LOCATION OF FRESH-AIR INLETS IN CITIES.

The following suggestions by L. M. Hooper, C. E., of New York, regarding the location of fresh-air inlets, are of interest:

"It seems to the writer that the location of the mouth or opening of the fresh-air inlet does not receive the attention due it. If the fresh-air inlet is an aid to the more thorough ventilation and purification of the waste-pipes, which is now generally admitted, its mouth should be so placed as to be always free from the danger of becoming choked.

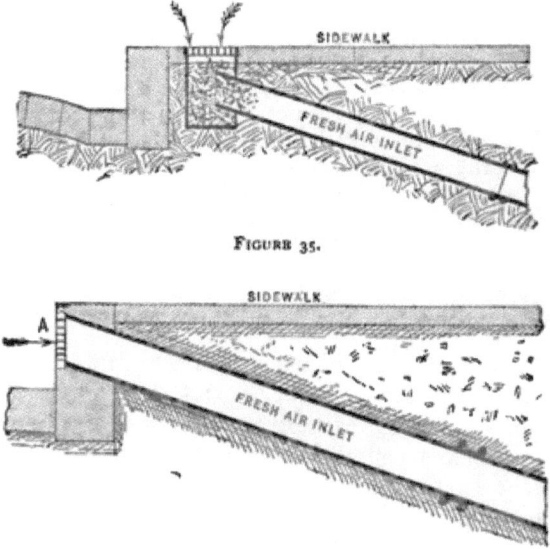

FIGURE 35.

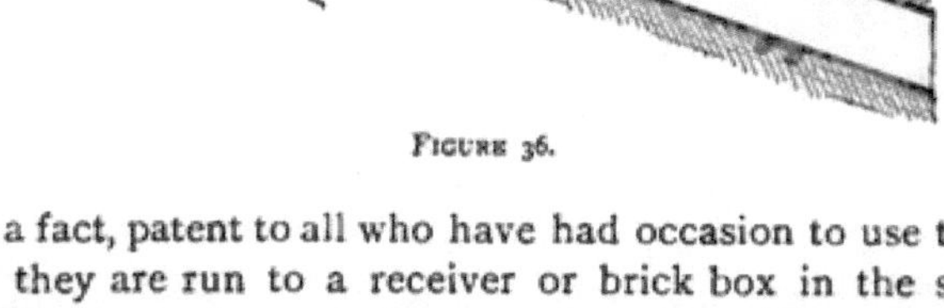

FIGURE 36.

"It is a fact, patent to all who have had occasion to use these inlets, that when they are run to a receiver or brick box in the sidewalk as shown in Figure 35, they soon become clogged and completely stopped up, and hence are worse than useless, as they give a false sense of security. When the fresh-air pipe is run to any point inside the stoop 'line, it is usually terminated by a 'return-bend,' cowl or grating inside of a stoop or house, and there is little danger of its becoming choked, except from snow, ice, etc.

"In most cases, however, it is impossible to carry it to a safe distance

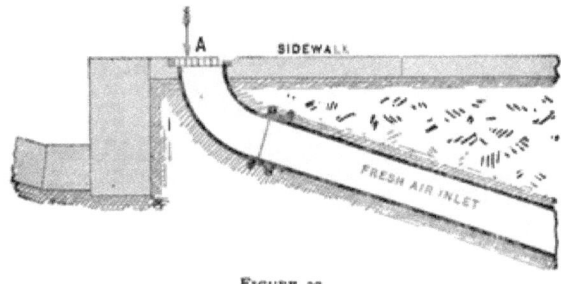

FIGURE 37.

from the house without taking it beyond the stoop line to some point on the sidewalk.

"When carried to the sidewalk the arrangement shown in Figure 35 is resorted to and the receiver (A) is sure to close up and thus become

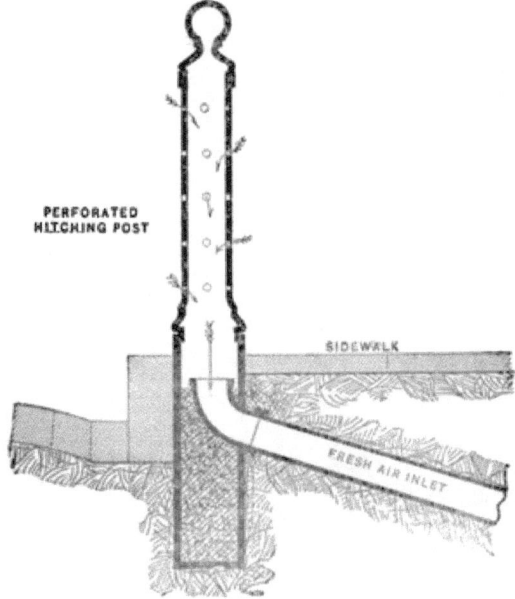

FIGURE 38.

52 HOUSE-DRAINAGE.

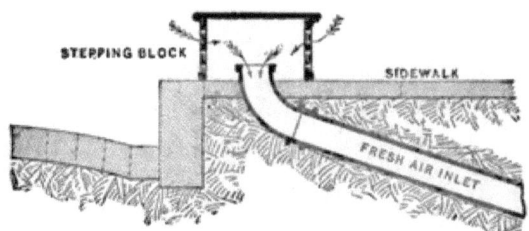

FIGURE 39.

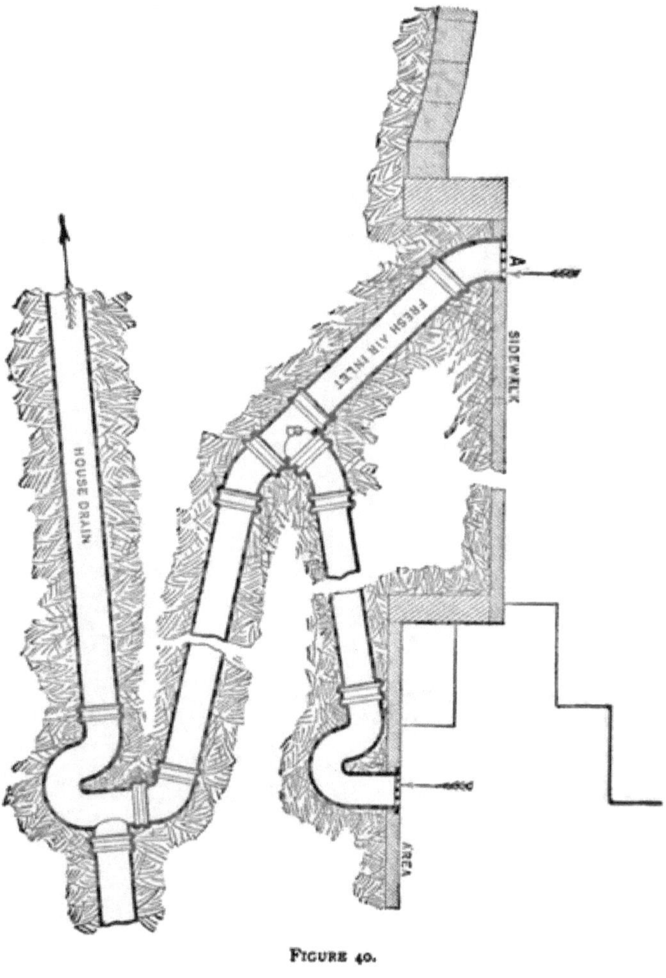

FIGURE 40.

inoperative. These receivers are difficult to clean, and seldom or never are cleaned.

"There are three general methods by which fresh-air inlets may be made self-cleansing:

"*First*—By keeping dirt out. This may be done by terminating the pipe under a perforated tie-post or carriage-block, as shown in Figures 38 and 39, or by extending it flush with the curb, as shown in Figure 36.

"*Second*—By giving to the pipe an inclination considerably greater than the angle of repose for dirt—say a little over 1 to 1—the dirt falling in will slide down into the house-drain. The mouth should be flush with the sidewalk, as in Figure 37. If arranged as in Figure 35, it will fill up no matter what the inclination is. When sufficient fall cannot be obtained from the curb to the house-trap to use the above method, the third method may be resorted to—*i. e.*, cleansing by water.

"*Third*—By cutting a small groove a few feet long on each side of the opening and parallel to the curb the wash of the sidewalk may be utilized to keep the pipe clean, or the water from the area may be carried into the fresh-air inlet, as shown in Figure 40. The fresh-air pipe from the opening to the point where the area-drain joins it should have sufficient fall to carry the dirt down to this point—*i. e.*, from A to B, Figure 40. From B, the fall need not be greater than one-quarter of an inch in one foot.

"If none of the above expedients are resorted to, it will be found convenient for cleaning to end the pipe as shown in Figures 37 and 40, as to clean it, it is only necessary to pour a pail of water into it. When arranged as in Figure 35, it is difficult to clean; even when the grating is removed and the accumulated dirt removed it is difficult to wash out the pipe itself."

FRESH-AIR INLETS.

DURING 1881, at our request Mr. W. G. Elliot, C.E., made sketches of various methods of arranging fresh-air inlets to house-drains. We give here several of them, with his description.

Figure 41, showing the inlet at the curb with a 6 x 12-inch cast-iron grating to protect it, can be seen in operation in many places, among which may be mentioned several houses on the south-east corner of Sixty-Second Street and Madison Avenue. This method is extensively practiced by one of our largest plumbers, and seems to give universal satisfaction.

Arrangement Figure 42 is quite common. The inlet should be located as far from basement-windows as possible, and not extend more than a few inches above the ground. The reverse action, however, takes place very rarely, if ever, and then only on a very hot summer day. A case of this kind can be seen at 125 West Forty-Third Street.

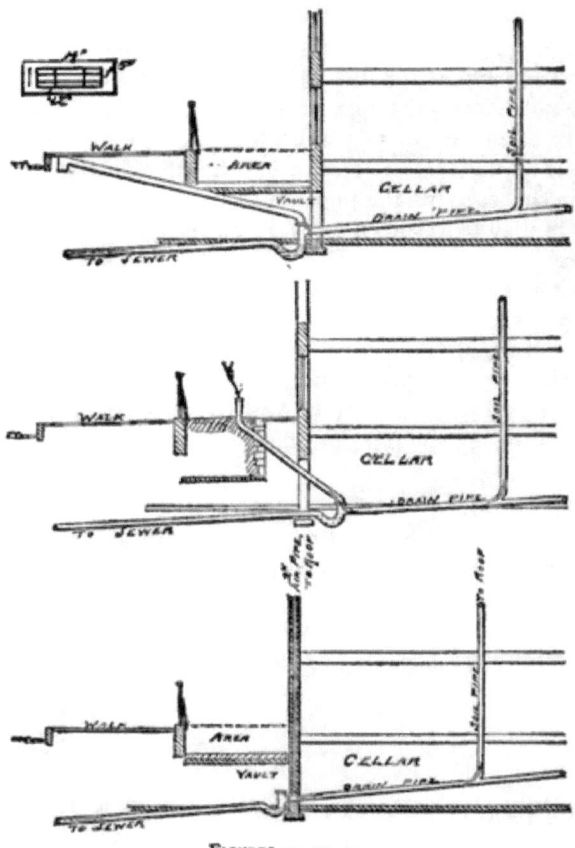

FIGURES 41, 42, 43.

Figure 43 is found at 31 East Fifty-Seventh Street. There are many disadvantages in the construction. Being carried up through the front wall of the building, it cannot well be over two or three inches in diameter, while to be effective in any case it should be the full size of the soil-pipe. In addition to this, its top is so nearly on a level with the top of the soil-pipe that the difference in the temperature of the air in the two must be very considerable to create a decided action. Beside these objections it has not even economy to recommend its adoption.

Arrangement Figure 44 is very common and effective. Examples can be found at Nos. 51 and 53 West Forty-Second Street, and 26 East Twenty-Second Street. It is second only to that of Figure 41.

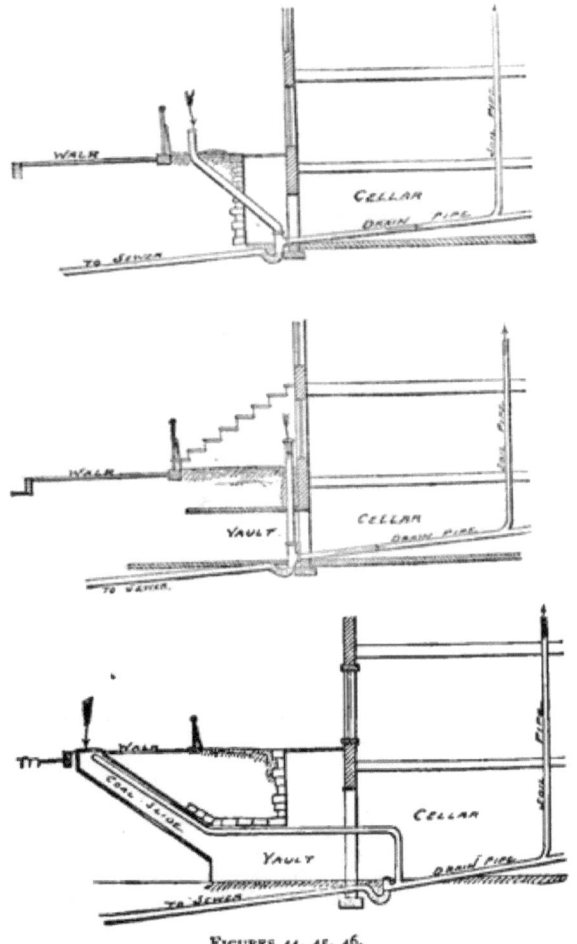

FIGURES 44, 45, 46.

Figure 45 has been found but in few cases, one of which still exists at 105 West Forty-Third Street, where the inlet-pipe opened in the corner of the area against the adjoining stoop, and hardly more than eighteen inches from the basement windows.

It was probably so placed from motives of economy, as it would have cost several dollars more to properly extend it, and the plumber must do the best he can under such circumstances.

A recent innovation in the location of inlets has been found only at 11 and 13 Waverly Place (Figure 46). The pipe extends from the trap along the side of the coal-slide near its top to within a foot of the cover, where it turns into the side wall of the coal-slide, and terminates

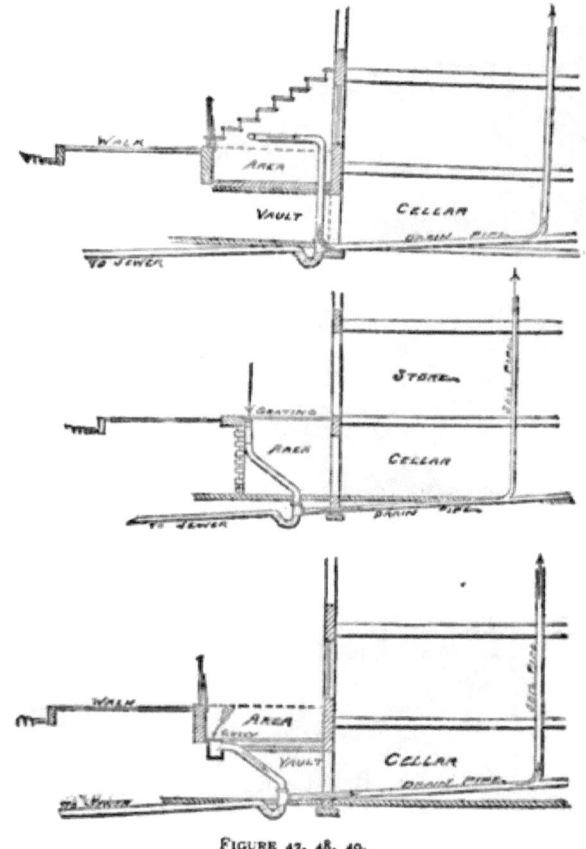

FIGURE 47, 48, 49.

in the side of a small gully provided with an iron grating, as in Figure 41. In plan, this grating is beside the coal-slide cover, and within a few inches of it. The arrangement would seem to be objectionable from its liability to obstruction by coal-dust, etc., from the frequent dumping and shoveling of coal necessary in a large building, but this is simply conjecture.

Figure 47 is employed in a number of instances, among which can be cited 310 Madison Avenue and 11 East Forty-Fourth Street. Another was found at 18 West Fifty-Seventh Street. There seems to be no especial advantage or disadvantage in its application more than a mere alternative where no other arrangement is found as economical under peculiar circumstances.

Figure 48 was adopted in the case of an apartment-house, with stores beneath, at Eighty-Second Street and Tenth Avenue, where it was introduced after the completion of the building, and where a large amount of blasting would have been required to extend it to the curbstone.

On being tested some weeks ago, after having been in operation several months, it was found that the draught was inward and strong enough to draw in the flame of a candle held near it, and extinguish it. The current was not reversed even for an instant when two water-closets were simultaneously discharged into the soil-pipe. A similar arrangement can be seen at 49 Wall Street.

Several cases of the arrangement shown in Fig. 49 have been seen, although no particular case can be cited. When the gully is located in the extreme corner of the area it would seem to offer all the advantages of Figure 44, the yard-washings and rain-water keeping it clean and free from obstruction.

With regard to the action of these air-inlets, there can be little doubt of their utility.

Popular opinion of them took its usual course, and the fact that they were new was for a long time sufficient to condemn them. Their rapid increase in number, however, proves conclusively that they are not only becoming popular with the better and more experienced plumbers, but that they rarely, if ever, give offense either to the occupants in the houses or passers in the street. Many have been tested by the writer, but have never been found doing their work improperly, except in one or two cases where they had been connected on the wrong side of the trap, and were freely ventilating the sewers.

AIR-INLETS ON DRAINS.

Q. IN the arrangement of the main drain in my house there is a good current of air in at the ventilating-pipe in the rear and out at the top of the soil-pipe; but one plumber tells me that we ought to have another just such current to ventilate that portion of the drain between the bottom of the soil-pipe and the trap in front, and wants to put in a ventilating-pipe just outside of the front wall of the house. Another plumber says that it is often found in practice that these ventilators work the wrong way, and bring a foul smell into the windows; he says he does not think any ventilator is needed in front, anyway—that it is of no consequence to have a current of air passing through the front half of the drain, and that he would rather not have it at all if he could not run it up to the very top of the house. He adds that the ventilator in the rear is dangerous, and ought to go to the top of the house. Now, will you please inform me, first, whether it is necessary to admit air into the front half of the main drain; and second, if so, whether it would be safe to use the usual short ventilating-tube?

I desire also to say that my bath-tub wastes run into the traps of the water-closets, but I have never known of any smell in the tubs, and on trying the tissue-paper experiment I could not perceive any tendency to blow it off when a full pail of water was dashed into the closets. My water-closet traps are ventilated by a special pipe running above the roof; is this why the paper was not blown off? And does the presence of this ventilating-pipe remove your objection to the arrangement?

One more thing. We are often very seriously annoyed by the behavior of the hot water at the stops over wash-stands. It comes at times in violent spurts, with a disagreeable noise, a tremor of the pipe, and such a splashing of the water as to drench your cuffs if your hand is under the hot water, and even to spatter all over your body. Sometimes the water runs smoothly for a minute before the spattering begins. Can it be remedied, and how?

A. A fresh-air inlet should be taken in at the front just inside the main trap. In our opinion it is important to have no dead ends in any part of the drainage-system—*i. e.*, air should be permitted to circulate through every part of it. If rain-water does not pass the house-drain there is no object in extending it behind where the waste from the kitchen enters it, and this pipe should extend through the roof unless the soil-pipe passes near these fixtures. Then if the traps are ventilated from their highest points there will be no "dead end" between the drain and these fixtures. The presence of a vent-pipe from your water-closet trap, doubtless to a certain extent, prevented the sudden compression of air when the water was thrown in your water-closet. This does not remove the objection to running bath-waste into water-closet traps, because this waste is liable to become foul, and it is a sanitary axiom to place traps as near the fixtures they are intended to serve as possible.

The spasmodic flow from your hot-water faucets complained of is doubtless due to the fact that air-traps have been formed in the hot-water pipes, caused by depressions or sags in these pipes.

THE PROPER WAY TO LAY STONEWARE DRAINS.

Pipes made of stoneware were used extensively in ancient Rome as water-conduits, and were introduced in this country over twenty-five years ago for drains. After a few years of experimental use, the advantages of the material over the old style of brick-drains were so obvious, and their cost so much less, that their manufacture and use has increased enormously. They have almost entirely superseded the use of brick. When properly made and put together no material is so good for drains, where buried in the ground outside of buildings. Their surfaces are indestructible for all ordinary service, only yielding to strong acids, such as may proceed from chemical laboratories or some kinds of manufacturing refuse. But the notion is very prevalent that any mason's tender who has begun to aspire to the use of the trowel can put them together well enough, and the result has been the wretched botching of by far the greater part of all the drains which have been laid in this material.

The natural result of this bad workmanship is the preference shown by the New York Board of Health, and other similar authorities, for iron pipes. The latter are generally put together with lead by plumbers, and these being also made in longer pieces than the stoneware pipes there is less chance of leakage at the joints. But iron is easily corroded, and it would be far better, provided good workmanship could be secured, to use the more imperishable material for all out-of-door drains, which after covering are necessarily difficult of access for repairs.

After many years of experimenting I have arrived at the conclusion that all stoneware pipes should be laid by none but first-class workmen, and even then the work should be tested by slight hydraulic pressure before it is buried deeply, so that defective joints can be readily seen and made good before filling up the trench.

The following specifications describe the method pursued in the sewerage of Princeton College and other places, which, if faithfully carried out, will insure satisfactory work:

SPECIFICATIONS FOR LAYING STONEWARE DRAINS.

Materials.—No pipes should be used which are not nearly cylindrical, a variation of over one-fourth of an inch in the different diameters of a 6-inch pipe being enough to condemn it.

The pipes should not have bells or hubs attached, as is now generally done, but should be formed in simple cylinders, the joints being covered by loose rings or collars of the same material, without glazing, to be broken in three or more pieces when applied.

The thickness should be uniform and not less than ⅝ and ¾-inch for 5-inch and 6-inch pipe, respectively.

The glazing should be "*salt glazing*," and not "*slip*" or *clay* glazing, and should extend throughout the whole interior, but should be omitted on the collars and on the outside of pipes for one and one-half inches at either end of the pieces. If the ends are glazed outside the cement used at the joints does not adhere well, and the joint may be leaky, even with good cement and put together with the best of care.

The clay of which they are made should, of course, be of good quality and well burned. Less trouble, however, is found in practice with the kind of clay than with the results of careless molding, such as oval, crooked pipes, with glazing applied all over the ends, for no better reason than because it costs some trouble to omit the glazing there, although it is a positive injury.

The cement should be of any good brand, of fair hydraulic properties, fine and freshly ground, and carefully mixed with not over its own bulk of *clean, sharp* sand. In all places where the sand is not clean (it should not soil the hands when rubbed between them) it should be washed thoroughly in a bed not over six inches deep with a copious flow of water, stirring the sand and water quickly with a hoe and allowing all the loam and clay to be carried off, till the water ceases to look muddy. The sand should be then dried and mixed thoroughly with the cement before applying any water. When wetting it for use, no more water should be used than is absolutely necessary to render the mortar plastic.

It should be wetted only in small quantities for immediate use. All lots left over an interval of half an hour, long enough to stiffen and begin to "set," should be thrown away and not "tempered up" as is generally done for indiscriminate use. Cement when rewetted after a partial set is sure to shrink and crack when it hardens, and is worthless for pipe-laying.

The ends of pipes and insides of collars should be wetted in warm weather before applying the mortar to these surfaces. If applied dry, the porous pipe absorbs the water so quickly from the mortar that it never hardens properly, and does not adhere to the pipe.

Workmanship.—Pipe should be laid with such good alignment that the inspector can see through every section, like a gun-barrel, from one manhole or lamp hole to another, or from house to sewer. This can readily be done with very little extra cost, if pains be taken to pursue proper methods.

Every piece of pipe should be bedded in cement-mortar through its middle portion as well as at its ends, leaving no voids longer than the inside diameter of the pipe between these bearings. The lower half of the pipe should be carefully aligned with its neighbor, by applying a straight-edge inside when bedding, to avoid offset at the joints, leaving slight inaccuracies in form to be developed at the top of the pipe, which is rarely wetted by the flow.

Through every piece of pipe as laid should be passed a cord, made fast where starting, and extending through every section of pipe laid, by means of which a wiper, or rubber disk between two smaller wooden ones, can be pulled through the whole section before leaving it for a night. Of course, the mason is expected to see that every joint is clean as laid, but human nature is fallible, and cannot be trusted to remember this, the consequence of such neglect being often a total failure of the drain.

Every section should be covered about three inches with fine earth, and tested by some two or three feet of water-pressure, when the defects will be seen, and may be remedied before filling the trench. The best masons will be astonished to see how many leaky joints they make unawares, and which may never be detected in any way but this.

The back-filling should be applied with care, packing the material around the pipes without moving them on their beds even a hair's breadth. The trench may be puddled with water if it is at hand, taking care not to wash the cement when applying it.

No good drain can be laid on a yielding foundation. No matter what the material may be, it will break and make leaks when settlement occurs, for though the drain itself is light, the material over it is heavy, and crowds it down as it settles. All drains on newly-filled land should be treated as temporary works, to be replaced when the settlement is finished.

There may be places where the difficulty of getting proper workmanship and proper materials will render it advisable to use iron pipe between the house and sewer, and New York and Brooklyn may be such places; but wherever it is used, it is subject to corrosion, and becomes so incrusted with tubercles inside, after a score of years, that it cannot serve as a self-cleansing sewer. It is necessarily always foul when incumbered with rust, for the flow of water does not cleanse it. It is then a sewer of deposit, open to all the objections that attach to cesspools or other foul sewers.

When used inside of houses it is accessible, and can therefore be readily inspected, both inside and outside, and readily repaired or replaced in case of need. But if buried in the ground, it is out of sight and out of mind, and should therefore be made of imperishable materials.

RISKS ATTENDING THE OMISSION OF TRAPS AND RELYING ON DRAIN-VENTILATION BY FLUES.

Q. I would like to have a few questions answered on the following plan. It is proposed to build a new wing to the county jail here, and according to the plans there are no traps on any of the hoppers, nor is there any vent-pipe from the top of soil-pipe, where the upper hoppers connect. There is to be one vent-pipe at back of building, where the rain-water pipe acts as another. Then in the front there is a 20-inch cast-iron smoke-stack, and on the inside of that is an 8-inch cast-iron pipe for vent-pipe. Now, I would like to know if the 3-inch outlet from the hoppers is not too small; also, if they should not be properly trapped? Or does the vent-pipe that goes up inside the smoke-stack take all the foul air down and up it, without letting any smell back in the cells? I wrote to the architect in Baltimore, and he says that they are not to have any traps, and that the 3-inch soil-pipe from hoppers to the large pipe is large enough. I contend that it ought to be 4-inch, and that all the hoppers ought to be trapped; and I also think that the pipe ought to continue up through the roof.

A. The system of drain-ventilation described above is similar to that carried out by Dr. Kirkbride some years since at his hospital, and in some respects similar to the device of Mr. Rand, in Philadelphia. The principle is briefly this: To create by help of a fire-heated flue a constant upward draught in a pipe which is to be connected to the house-drain, and to stop all the holes which might supply air to the drain, except those by which the drainage itself enters. Then all traps are dispensed with, except that on the main drain outside the house, and air enters the drain at every water-closet, sink, etc., to supply the vacuum created by the aspiration in the heated flue.

When this flue is kept well heated, and all parts of the apparatus are well proportioned, according to the circumstances of the case, it may work well. But if the fire should be allowed to go down, or if not perfectly adjusted, the draught will be insufficient to maintain the excess of inward pressure at all points, and if it fails at any point we have trouble at once. If the draught is weak, some of the inlet-holes will supply the whole—viz., those nearest the point where the suction is applied, while the more remote ones will not get any. This experiment was tried some time ago at the Danvers Asylum, in Massachusetts, and failed on account of the inefficiency of the draught to serve the remote openings.

We notice an unnecessary and foolish complication in the basement, where an air-pipe is arranged so that air can pass quite around the outer trap, thereby dodging it entirely. Why not omit this outer trap, and the air-pipe also, and save their cost? If the trap is really needed to stop the air from passing that point, why put in the by-pass to give it a chance to go just where it might if no trap were there?

We notice, also, that 3-inch pipes are applied as branches from water-closets to main soil-pipe. If such pipes could be made perfectly smooth, and without any offsets or inside ridges at their joints, such a small size might possibly be advisable. But with the ordinary imperfections at joints, we do not think it safe to provide less than 4-inch pipes, although the orifice at the base of a water-closet may safely be

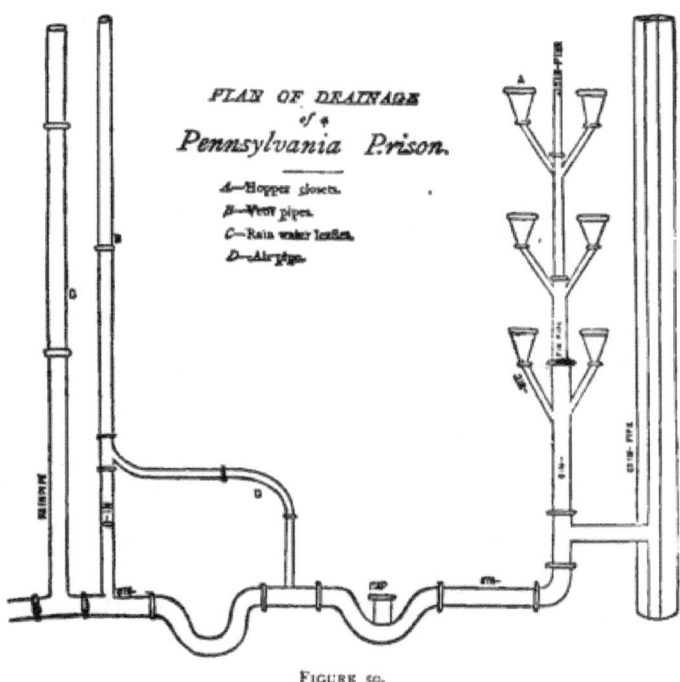

FIGURE 50.

restricted to three inches, because whatever is obstructed there is within reach and can readily be removed.

In any such system which depends upon fire draughts to keep the house free from drain-gas, we must remember that the constant presence of a sufficient fire is an essential part of the scheme, and we must keep that fire burning all summer, night and day, Sundays included. In case such a fire is needed for steam-power, or any other such purpose, it may do very well; but the maintenance of a fire for this special purpose would be rather irksome, and might sometimes be neglected, with very unpleasant results. Moreover, the adjustment of the power of the draught to the sum total of all the inlets is a problem which must be worked out by actual trial in every separate case, and would vary very largely in different conditions of wind and weather, so that an apparatus which would work well during one week might be quite inefficient the next. We should not consider such a system safe, unless a large surplus draught were sure to exist at all times from a fire maintained for some purpose that *rendered it positively sure to be constant and unfailing*. The use of traps under each sink and water-closet would be entirely inconsistent with this system of ventilation, which demands open orifices.

THE TIGHTNESS OF TILE-DRAINS.

Q. IN laying some tile recently we came in contact with several small springs in line of the trench, which tile empties into the bed of a rapid mountain stream. There are springs walled in on both sides of the stream above, within 200 yards of where the tile was laid.

Some days after the work was done water began running from the inside. There has been no connection with any fixtures. The tile was good vitrified drain-tile, laid in cement, each joint being carefully made.

Perhaps it would be well to state that the above is to convey the waste from a bath-house containing nineteen tubs, two closets, one swimming-bath, and a few bowls. Is it not *probable* that some of the tile is not thoroughly glazed and allows seepage? Also, please state if you consider it detrimental or objectionable to leave it as it is. Water turned in from the upper end of the waste passes off promptly and *perfectly* free.

A. We should not consider the probability of the water soaking through imperfect glazing so great as that of its coming through imperfectly-closed *joints*. Few masons who put pipe together are aware how difficult a thing it is to insure the tightness of all the joints. Whenever a test is applied the number of leaks developed is astonishing.

If imperfections in the glazing exist to a sufficient extent to account for the flow above reported, they will be likely to be silted up and stop the flow after a few months. We would advise having your pipe tested by applying a tight rubber plug at the lower end, and filling it with water. If any bad joints exist they can be found readily in this way. Of course, there should not be much earth filled over the pipe where such a test is made. Leaks often occur by breaking down the pipe, and splitting the bells or hubs open with the load of the trench-filling, for lack of good continuous bearings. The pipe should be bedded in cement the whole length of every piece, to insure good support.

The objections to using a leaky pipe for drainage are these—viz.: Whenever a dry time occurs the sewage will flow out through the leaks and pollute the soil. The importance of such pollution is entirely a local question. Moreover, the escape of the more fluid parts of the sewage through leaks would, perhaps, lead to trouble for lack of flushing the inside of the drain-pipe, and allow it to accumulate solid matter.

DANGER OF SOIL-PIPE TERMINALS FREEZING UNLESS ENDS ARE WITHOUT HOODS OR COWLS.

Q. During the recent cold snap I was called up-town to investigate the cause of escape of sewer-gas into the house of a well-known gentleman of this city. I knew the house-drains were thoroughly ventilated, and was at a loss to locate the cause. Upon examining the work we found it apparently all right, but in spite of that fact, when we lifted the plunger of the water-closet, the traps immediately syphoned out, and on going to the roof, thinking something was wrong there, imagine our astonishment at finding the ventilating-cap frozen solid. Other houses in the same row were found to be in the same condition; the damp vapor rising through the sewer had struck the upper or dome-like portion of the cap and gradually frozen its way down like an icicle, and finally closed it tight. In our climate this is liable to happen at any time during the winter, and, in my opinion, calls for an air-cap of a different pattern. Upon examining the present air-cap you will wonder how the sewer-gas escapes from it, as the dome falls down over the lower or straight part at least one-fourth of an inch, while it really ought to stand clear above it at least $1\frac{1}{2}$ or 2 inches. This would also prevent its freezing, as the space would not be so confined, and would be more difficult to fill up with ice, as there would be no support.

Either remodel the hood or dispense with it entirely, and leave the end of the pipe open to the air. This, I know, would be open to objections, as malicious persons would probably drop obstructions down the pipe.

A. We think this letter of great importance. We have hitherto preferred the open pipe or a properly constructed hood to a return-bend or cowl, as we consider the latter liable to be closed by ice during very cold weather. From our correspondent's experience it appears that the hoods were so constructed that ice readily formed and closed them, while return-bends were found open. After this experience we should advise that open pipes be used, and, if it is necessary to prevent articles from being thrown down the pipe, our preference would be an open-mouthed pipe sufficiently high to be beyond the reach of children, and properly supported.

A similar experience to that of our correspondent was brought to our attention also about that time, and on frequent occasions since we have expressed our objection to the return-bends or hoods of this description for this climate, and even the wire-basket, in localities north of this, we should apprehend, would close up and become a ball of ice, unless the mesh were large.

OBJECTION TO CONNECTING BATH-WASTE WITH WATER-CLOSET TRAP.

Q I HAVE for some time past been troubled with a bad odor which comes from my bath-tub, the waste of which runs into the trap of a pan-closet, which is on the other side of the partition. The soil-pipe runs full size through roof and is in full view in its course through the house, and is provided with foot-ventilation outside. Three times I have applied peppermint as described in a late issue of your paper. Twice I stopped up the roof outlet after putting in the peppermint there; also the pipe at the foot in the yard. The other time I left them open, but in neither case could I find the slightest traces of peppermint.

I am confident that the soil and waste pipes are perfectly tight, yet the smell continues.

Will you be good enough to inform me through your journal what I can do to remedy the trouble?

A. It does not follow because the soil-pipe is run through roof and provided with foot-ventilation, and that all pipes are perfectly tight, that a pint or quart of peppermint would be sure to disclose the evil arising from this particular as well as many other cases of bad plumbing. We have repeatedly pointed out the danger of connecting bath or other wastes with water-closet traps.

To make the matter plain to our correspondent, and for his benefit, and in order to satisfy others who, like him, think it is all right to go and do a job like the one in question, we ask them to take a piece of tissue-paper, wet it and place it over a bath-waste—connected like the one above described—then pull up the closet handle, or empty suddenly a pail of water into the closet, and it will be noticed that the paper has been blown off by the rise of water in the trap, which displaces a portion of the foul air in the waste-pipes into the room.

If our correspondent will call in a respectable plumber, and allow him to put a trap under the bath with a vent-pipe from same and connect the waste-pipe directly with the soil-pipe, no more bad odors will emanate from the bath.

HOW TO ADJUST THE INLET AND OUTLETS OF TRAPS.

Q. PLEASE give me your idea on this subject: A claims that the pipe *b* in trap in Figure 51 should be as high or even higher than shown. He says that a current of air passing through pipe *a* will syphon out the trap.

On the other hand, B claims that in trap Figure 52, pipe *b* should be as low as shown, or even lower. Now, if the water comes down pipe *b* and goes out pipe *a* with a rush, it will not have a chance to syphon out. Who is right or wrong?

A. The ability to resist syphon-action is not in this case affected by the location of the pipe *b*, since this does not affect the amount of water in the trap, the depth of seal being apparently the same in both. It should be borne in mind that to syphon out the trap there must be a partial vacuum in the pipe *a*—*i. e.*, a part of the air has been withdrawn by the descending column of water, so that the atmospheric pressure is less on that side of the water-seal than at *b*, in which case the atmospheric pres-

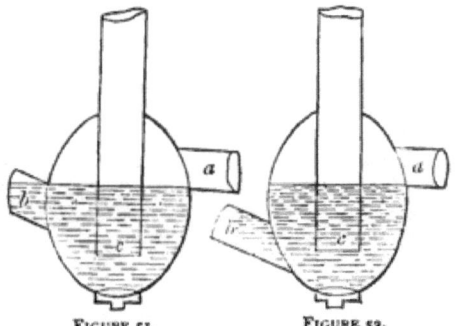

FIGURE 51.   FIGURE 52.

sure at *b* will force out the water until it supplies the vacuum, or what is lacking at *a*. To accomplish this the water would be forced out at *a* until it fell below *c*, so the air could pass through and make the atmospheric pressure the same on both sides. It is for this purpose that traps are vented, so that the vents may supply the air and not oblige the taking out of the water so as to get the air from the other side of the water-seal. So far as the inlet of *b* in Figure 51 is concerned, it is too high to be of much service to the fixture it is presumably intended to serve, since a slight lowering of the water-line will open direct communication between *a* and the fixture at the other end of *b*. In fact, it is not good practice to use one trap for two fixtures; each should have its own trap wherever practicable.

HOW TO PROTECT TRAP WHEN SOIL-PIPE IS USED AS A LEADER.

Q. WHERE a water-closet or other fixture is connected with soil-pipe also used as a leader, is there any way of securing the trap on the water-closet from syphoning when the leader is gorged with rain; or would it be preferable to disconnect it entirely? The water-closet is on an upper floor, say twenty-eight feet from the roof. The leader is 4-inch, and the water-closet trap has no separate ventilation.

A. A vent-pipe, not less than three inches in diameter, should be taken from the highest point of the trap to above the roof. In this case it should not branch into this soil-pipe.

SIZE OF VENTILATING-PIPES FOR TRAPS.

Q. WILL you be kind enough to inform me through the columns of your paper on two points which I have no means of deciding—viz.:

First—What proportion should the area of a pipe, ventilating a trap, bear to the area of the pipe on which the trap is located?

Second—Is the placing of a gully with trap, at level of yard, the best way of breaking connection between a rain-water leader and the main house-drain? Would frost injure its efficiency?

Being somewhat of a novice in sanitary engineering, an answer with the weight of authority your paper carries with it will greatly oblige.

A. The size of a pipe used to ventilate a trap, should be as near the size of the trap as practicable and depends largely on the distance such a pipe has to go to reach air. Moreover, if the climate is a frosty one, say above a latitude of 40 degrees in the United States, the part of the pipe extending through the roof should not be less than four inches in diameter in any case, to prevent its being filled up with ice from condensation.

Second—The gully with strainer on a level with surface of yard with a trap below is a good method of breaking the connection of rain-water leaders with drains, provided the trap is supplied with water by some more reliable source than the rain; otherwise it might dry up and leave the trap inoperative; also, provided the water in the trap is protected from freezing, which is purely a local question, depending on climate and exposure.

HOW TO PREVENT CONDENSATION FILLING VENT-PIPES.

Q. WILL you please advise me what means plumbers in your city take to prevent condensation filling vent-pipes and making them no good? It is not always possible to give them a steady pitch.

A. They are so arranged that there are no pockets or traps in them, and so that the water of condensation can flow back to the waste-pipe in some way. It sometimes requires considerable ingenuity to accomplish this, but that should be exercised every day in the plumbing business.

VENTILATING SOIL-PIPES.

Q. IS IT more desirable to ventilate soil-pipes upon the roof or into a heated chimney-flue? Also, is there any objection to making a storehouse for ice under a corner of a house in the country; can the ice be stored there without creating dampness in the vicinity, and will it keep as well as if stored in buildings for the purpose? What is the best plan of construction?

A. Soil-pipes should always be extended to the open air, either through the roof or at a proper point on the side of the building, in as direct a line as can be found above the upper fixtures by which drainage is admitted. The objections to having them enter a chimney-flue are as follows: The flue may not *always* be heated. Even kitchen-flues are sometimes cold in summer, when temporary stoves are used in some outer room for cooking. At such times the draught is very apt to be downward, bringing the air from the soil-pipe directly back into the house. Moreover, the joint where a metal pipe enters a brick flue is never a tight one for any length of time. The iron pipe is changing its length with every change of its temperature, working back and forth, and crumbling the mortar away around it. Such joints have given out a very unsavory smell in certain houses where the writer has seen the experiment tried.

If the soil-pipe is extended up inside the flue quite to its top and three feet above it, there may not be as much objection. But such a position renders it difficult, if not impossible, to repair it without taking down the chimney, while the gases given off by burning coal are quite corrosive to cast-iron, so the pipe will not endure so long in a chimney as if outside of it.

While upon this subject, it may be well to refer to the need of securing a permanently open end for the soil-pipe in the open air. The severe weather of last winter gave rise to considerable accumulations of ice at the openings of such pipes. It arises from the condensation of the watery vapor that always comes up from the drains below, and which freezes to the side of the pipe as fast as it condenses. An inspection of a number of roofs in Boston has shown a collection of ice in all the pipes so examined, from half an inch to an inch in thickness. Where cowls or caps of any kind are used, the openings are sometimes entirely closed. Straight open ends of four inches diameter are the safest.

Ice should never be stowed under a dwelling. Its constant drainage and condensation of vapor from the surrounding air keeps everything damp. Ice is found to keep best when packed in masses above ground, and surrounded by a double-boarded frame, filled with sawdust or shavings, to check the circulation of air. The roof should also be double, with a confined air-space between the sheathings.

HOW TO DETECT ACCIDENTAL DISCHARGE INTO TRAP VENT-PIPE.

Q. I HAVE had a case of plumbing brought to my notice, where the pipe from a sink stopped up between the trap and the soil-pipe. How long it had been so no one seemed to know, as the water that should have passed down the waste-pipe passed over through the vent-pipe, and found its way into the soil-pipe through the vent-drip. What is the usual way in your city to prevent this?

A. When the vent and soil pipes are carried in a recess back or near the sink, introduce your Y-branch into the vertical line of vent-pipe, half-way between the bottom and the upper edge of the sink, or other fixture. This will cause the water to show in the sink should the waste-pipe be stopped beyond the trap, but will not allow the sink to run over.

If the pipes are all below the floor, arch the vent-pipe up behind the sink sufficiently high to raise water into the bottom of the sink, but not high enough to run over.

WHY TRAPS SHOULD BE VENTED.

"THE writer of this letter recently submitted a bid on the plumbing-work of an eight-story and basement building, having water-fixtures on all stories. There are fifteen stacks of cast-iron pipes extending through from cellar to roof (eight of 4-inch and seven of 2-inch pipes).

The fixtures consist of 159 wash-stands, fifty-five water-closets (cistern), about the same number of bath-tubs, together with other fixtures. One of the features of the specifications is that the traps of the water-closets alone are all the traps which are required to be back-vented in the building. Many of the other fixtures, particularly the wash-stands, are remote from the upright pipes into which they discharge. One 2-inch pipe receives the waste of fourteen, and two other 2-inch pipes receive the waste each of twelve wash-stands. The specifications state that no back-vent pipes are to be put on these wash-stand traps, and no other means are devised to preserve an equilibrium of pressure between the inside of said pipes and the atmosphere. The writer suggested that the lead-safe pans, four pounds per square foot, be changed to three or two and one-half pounds per square foot, making a saving of nearly two tons of lead, the value of which could be applied toward back-venting fixtures. The suggestion was not favorably received by the architect. The proprietor of the building is desirous of having the best class of work. The writer will be pleased to read any criticisms on the above, or any recommendations you may think called for."

The above letter has a somewhat melancholy and discouraging effect upon all who have been laboring to convince the public that it is useless to expect traps to serve any good purpose when placed on such small waste-pipes as two inches, unless every trap is vented to the open air by a pipe as large as the waste itself. The experiments of Messrs. Philbrick and Bowditch proved this most conclusively. We can only regret that such an architect as is above referred to should have neglected to read that report to the National Board of Health. No one who had read the clear statements contained therein could fail to appreciate the risks incurred by placing traps under fixtures on 2-inch waste-pipes with no air-vents. Such traps are mere "man-traps" and not water-traps, for they give a sense of security to the owner or occupant of the building when in reality none exists. If the plumbing should be executed in the manner above described by our correspondent, it will not be many weeks after occupancy before the traps can be found empty for about half the time under the wash-basins and the whole length of their waste-pipes ventilating into the rooms which they are intended to serve. No better contrivance can be devised for supplying foul gas in a constant stream to the interior, after artificial heat is applied in winter, than the methods above proposed. The large number of basins draining into single lines of pipe will add to the risk by the frequent draughts of air which will rush down, gurgling through the traps of these wastes to supply the vacuum created by the discharge of other bowls connected with the same line. The remoteness of some basins from the vertical lines constitutes another element of danger, as every plumber will appreciate who has had occasion to open and clean out the horizontal waste-pipes used in such cases. The 2-inch wastes used in such lines, under the flows, will soon become nearly filled with a putrid, slimy lining, which by its constant fermentation will supply gas enough to contaminate a whole block. We hope the proprietor of this building will be invited to read the record of the experiments alluded to on this subject, even if the architect he employs does not find time to do so. In these days of cheap printing the great trouble is to know how much to read and what selection out of the plethora of current literature. But however difficult it may be for all proprietors of buildings to keep well posted on such subjects, there is less excuse for the architects, who should at least be able to attend to the specialties connected with their professions and make proper use of the facts placed before them from reliable sources.

MISCELLANEOUS.

SYPHONING WATER THROUGH A BATH-SUPPLY.

Q. The writer, while repairing the connections to one of the many styles of bath-tubs which admit the water at or near the bottom, noticed that when the tub was filled, and the water shut off at the stop and waste in the cellar, upon opening the cocks in the tub the water syphoned back through the stop and waste. This is, in his opinion, a fault with tubs of that kind, or rather in connections of that kind, and one which, in the judgment of the writer, might be easily remedied. Let the manufacturers see to this, and further improve a good thing.

A. It is not clear how manufacturers can guard against such a contingency. As a practical question, we imagine such an occurrence as that cited must be uncommonly rare, though we recently heard of a case where a small service-pipe conveyed water under a light pressure to a bath, and below it to a pantry-cock and sink. On one occasion, when the bath-cock was open and a person was bathing, the pantry-cock below was also opened and speedily began to discharge dirty water, because there was not sufficient pressure to deliver at both points, the water being drawn from the bath and discharged below.

If baths are to be supplied in this way, the inlet should be above the usual water-line, though in such cases the special object of the end-supply is lost, since it is used to avoid the steam from the hot water running in. If the bath-supply were taken from a tank, there would be no risk of such an occurrence, but if, as in the case cited, the bath-cock is supplied from the same pipe that supplies several cocks below it, the opening of one or more of these lower cocks would draw the water back from the bath, providing its cock were open. We should, therefore, when the bottom supply is used, either rely on tank-supply, or be sure, if it is from street-pressure, to have the supply-pipe of sufficient size to permit water to flow at the bath, even if all the taps below it were open. In any case, it is another instance where the judgment of the plumber must be exercised.

Mr. Stephen H. Terry, of London, relates his experience as follows with regard to the foregoing :

"I will state my own experience, which goes to prove that water may be so sucked into the service-pipe, and delivered (mixed with water from the cistern) at taps below, the only requirements necessary to fulfill these conditions being that the tap or taps at the lowest level shall be open and capable of discharging (cognizance being taken of the difference in head) slightly more than the orifice of the service-pipe at its junction with the supply-tank.

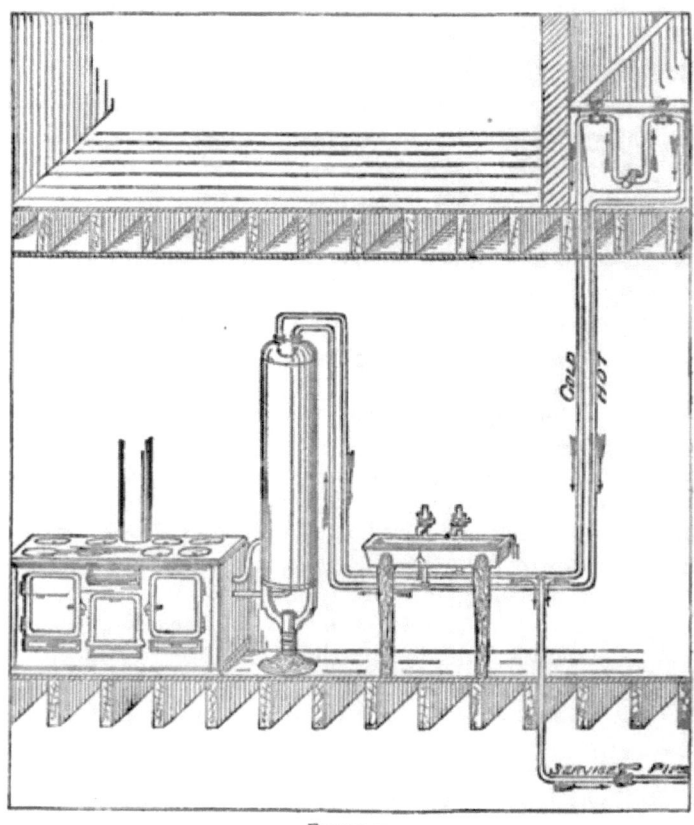

FIGURE 53.

"I have a cistern at the top of my house which holds about 500 gallons; this is on the third floor. On the second floor is a bath-room, closet and draw-taps. On the first floor is a lavatory and closet, on the ground-floor is a closet, and in the scullery a ¾-inch screw-down draw-off cock. About five weeks since, wishing to clean out my lead cistern, I commenced by running off the water, for this purpose opening the scullery and lavatory draw-off cocks, and fixing the pedal of the basement-closet open. Water was plentifully discharged from all of these. I then proceeded to open the draw-off taps in the bath-room on the second floor, about ten feet lower than the water-level in the tank (the tap from which the water was running being about thirty-six feet below the water-level). To my surprise, instead of water coming out, air was sucked in, with much gurgling sound. On going up to the tank overhead, I found there was still two feet deep of water in it, while air and water were being discharged below with considerable noise.

"I may mention that the service-pipe is a small one, one inch in diameter, and this is slightly—very slightly—throttled at the place where it is soldered into the bottom of the tank.

"From the above description it is evident that all that is necessary for the suction of bath-water, or other even more objectionable liquid, into the service-pipe, is that the supply to bath or sink, or, for that matter, closet, should discharge below the level of the water in such bath, sink, or closet, and such conditions, unfortunately, are not difficult to fulfill. A bath may be left full of dirty water at a time when the cistern above is nearly empty, the supply-cock may be open, the taps in the basement may be opened, and in that case the whole of the bath-water might be syphoned out through the supply-cock, as soon as water comes on from the main to start the syphon. Sinks and closets may become choked with tea-leaves or thick paper, and other material which should not be thrown in.

"The lesson to be learned from this is that the regulations of the Metropolis Water Act, 1871, framed partly to prevent waste of water and partly for purposes of promoting public health, should be attended to. I quote Regulation 26:

"'In every bath hereafter fitted or fixed the outlet shall be distinct from and unconnected with the inlet or inlets; and the inlet or inlets must be placed so that the orifice or orifices shall be above the highest water-level of the bath. The outlet of every such bath shall be provided with a perfectly water-tight plug-valve or cock.'"

We are glad to record this further instance of the risks incurred in a supply to a bath entering below the water-line, especially as our attention has been called to another case, in which, as in the one cited above and in those which we have before cited, the mishap seems to have been due to insufficient size of main supply-pipe to the various fixtures. The risks of direct supply to a valve on a water-closet without the intervention of a cistern are also above forcibly illustrated.

EMPTYING A TRAP BY CAPILLARY ATTRACTION.

Q. I was requested a few days ago to investigate the cause of a terrible stench, similar to that found in a sewer, which filled the bath-room (which also contained a water-closet) almost to suffocation, during the early hours only of each morning, and until the water-closet had been used or the bell-pull lifted. The cause for this terrible stench was found to be a most peculiar one indeed—viz., a large 4-inch P-trap being syphoned by capillary attraction.

The entire plumbing-work was carefully examined, but no leak or other defect was visible. Yet the trap under the water-closet was found to contain very little, if any, water for several consecutive mornings. Then a series of the usual but most severe trials or attempts were made to syphon this trap (there is a similar bath-room above this one, and *all* using the same soil-pipe), all of which failed.

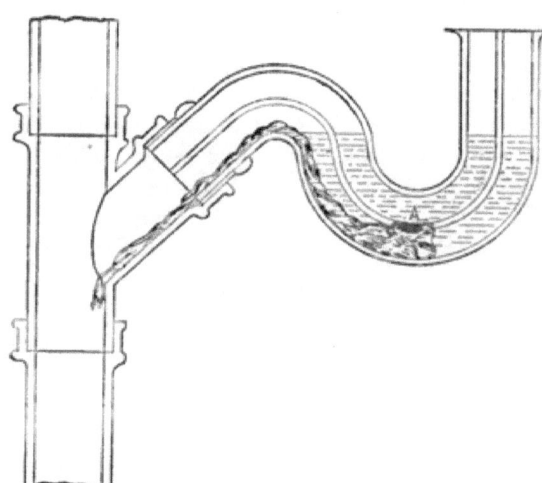

FIGURE 54.

Then the water-closet, etc., was removed, and the following was found—viz.: The trap was found to be a hand-made, soldered, side-seam one, made of sheet-lead. In soldering the seams some of the hot metal had been permitted to protrude beyond the *inner* side of the trap, and thus formed a projecting "peg," on which a large cloth had caught in attempting to pass. As the closet necessitated the use of a considerable quantity of water, the effect was to attempt to carry the cloth out of the trap, but the actual result was to firmly retain one portion of the cloth at the lowest point (nearly) of the trap, and carry, in a continuous line, the remaining portion up and out into the soil-pipe, thus completely syphoning the water from the trap during the night hours, when the water would not be replaced at short intervals. A similar circumstance was found in the trap of a kitchen-sink almost two years since. However, in this case the trap had first caught some shreds of cloth on the rough edges of the trap-screw, the result being almost identical with the above. I send you herewith a sketch of the first described trap, which you are at liberty to use in such manner as you deem proper.

A. The trap described above was an old-fashioned one, such as is not made nowadays. Yet the imperfection seems to have served a good purpose in this case in drawing attention to the cloth in the trap. If it had been washed through it would have been very likely to make a dam at some other point less accessible than this one, and render it necessary to cut the pipe open to get it out. If the water-closet had been a simple hopper with accessible trap there would have been no need to remove it, for any one could have reached the cloth in a moment.

Moral—Avoid complicated fixtures, and preserve all textile fabrics for paper stock instead of putting them down the drains.

We believe that a few months ago a New York plumber had his attention directed to this same capillary action, and made several experiments upon it, which satisfied him that, under some circumstances, it could and did cause the loss of seal where other explanations failed to account for it, all of which enforces the moral cited above.

AS TO SAFETY OF STOP-COCKS ON HOT-WATER PIPES.

Q. Is it safe to put stop-cocks on the hot-water pipes from a boiler, so that in case of bursting pipe, or other reason, water can be shut off? If not, what is the reason, and how can precautions be taken?

A. It is safer to have no stop-cocks on hot-water pipes. If the stop-cock on the cold-supply pipe to the boiler is closed, there would be no pressure on the hot-water pipes, which pipes could be emptied by opening the hot-water faucet over the sink.

HOW TO BURNISH WIPED-JOINTS.

Q. I have just finished the fitting-up of a double boiler, and while I work with fine metal and am particular, the owner recommends burnishing the joints. Can you give me any information how to do it? He wants them to look like silver.

A. You may burnish a joint with any smooth and round steel burnisher, first carefully removing any roughness with a rasp and file. If you succeed in getting a smooth, bright surface, which is exceedingly difficult on such soft metal, you may then coat it with white varnish to prevent tarnishing. On the whole, we do not think it will improve the appearance of your work, while it may convey the impression the plumber was not capable of wiping a good joint, and that he trimmed it into shape.

ADMISSION TO THE NEW YORK TRADE-SCHOOLS.

Q. I have read so much about plumbing apprenticeship in your valuable paper that I would like to know under what conditions I could get into the Trade-Schools. If you would be kind enough to inform me I would be ever so much obliged to you.

A. No examination is required to be passed in order to enter the schools. The management prefers that the pupil should not be too old to begin learning a trade, nor too young to appreciate the instruction—say not under sixteen nor over twenty-five at most. But no hard-and-fast rule exists, and doubtless any one who showed that he was capable of improving himself would be admitted. The charge for instruction in the New York Trade-Schools is $3 a month, or $10 for the full course. We would advise our correspondent by all means to call at the Trade-Schools and see the manager. A personal interview will in a few minutes give him all the information he needs, and he can then decide for himself what he will do. The schools are located on First Avenue, between Sixty-seventh and Sixty-eighth Streets, and are open until ten P. M.

IRREGULAR WATER-SUPPLY.

Q. The water-works in my house act so singularly that I would like very much to have the opinion of some of your readers versed in such matters as to the real cause of the trouble before I attempt to do anything to remedy it. I inclose a sketch of the boiler and kitchen-sink, with its hot and cold water-supply, which I hope will be of service. The difficulty is :

First—The water rises to the second floor only for a short time during the night, although the houses on each side of me have it all day on that floor.

Second—On opening the *cold-water* faucet of the kitchen-sink the water runs cold for an instant, then hot for a little time, and then cold again ; and this thing goes on as long as the faucet is open.

Third—The *hot-water* faucet delivers a strong stream at first, then reduces to a mere dribble, then strong again, and so on.

You can imagine how annoying this is, and if you can do anything to solve the problem you will greatly oblige.

A. The conditions of your house-plumbing presents a singular combination, noticeably as respects the second and third difficulties.

In answer to your first point, the pipe from the street (if it is the same apparently as your neighbor's) must have at some part of its length a greatly reduced area, so that when there is a decreased pressure in the main (in the day-time) enough does not force through to give the required head within the house when a lower faucet is opened, or there is any steady drain, such as a leak, between the house and the contraction.

The second difficulty is a result of the first. When you open the cold faucet the water within the pipe (cold) runs out; then in consideration of the very small passage in the pipe, the head of water which has accumulated in the pipes above the boiler runs back through the boiler and through the cold faucet. When the water has thus run down to the top of the boiler, cold water will come again slowly in the intended direction; but it will not again repeat the operation unless the pressure within the service-pipe is subject to fluctuations, which are not likely to take place during the day, and which only can be accounted for on the supposition that you and your neighbors — one or both — are branched from the same tap, and that *you alone* have a stoppage inside the junction with their branch. The explanation just given applies also to the third question. The hot water flowing downward from the pipes in the house, passing through the boiler a little strongly at first until the head is gone, then reducing to the amount of water which will pass the obstruction—fluctuations being attributed to the same cause as before. If there is sufficient pressure in the street-mains to raise the water at all times in the house, as indicated by your neighbor, large piping will cure the trouble with a tap to yourself.

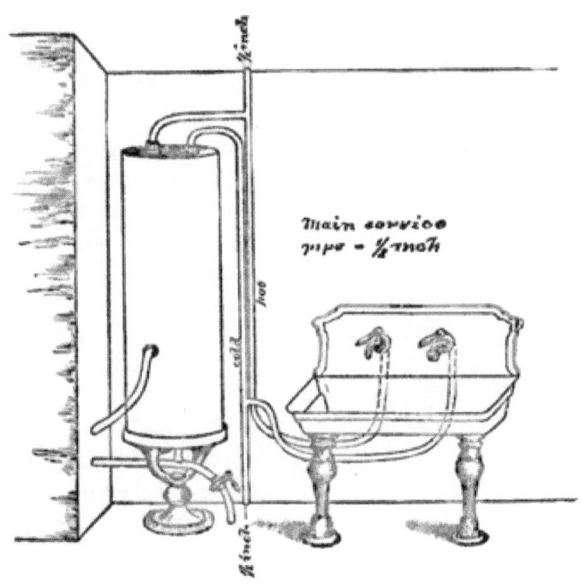

FIGURE 55.

HOT WATER FROM THE COLD FAUCET, AND HOW TO PREVENT IT.

A GENTLEMAN from Brooklyn writes to confirm our views in reference to the preceding question, particularly the answer to the second difficulty, which he also experienced and which our hint set him to investigate intelligently:

"The inclosed diagram, which I believe is a correct copy of the plumbing of a great part of the small brick residences which are being built in this city (Brooklyn), represents the principal features of the hot and cold water-supply of my house.

"You will notice that for cold water to enter the boiler it must flow past the cold-water faucet at the sink. If, now, some one opens the hot water faucet at the bathtub or one of the washbowls upstairs, and some one else goes to draw cold water at the sink, say to rinse his hands under the faucet, he is likely to take them away with a start, and for a moment think he is scalded, and that he has opened the wrong faucet, but upon further trials he will find it is the faucet intended to be the cold one, and upon trying it again he is treated to a similar experience.

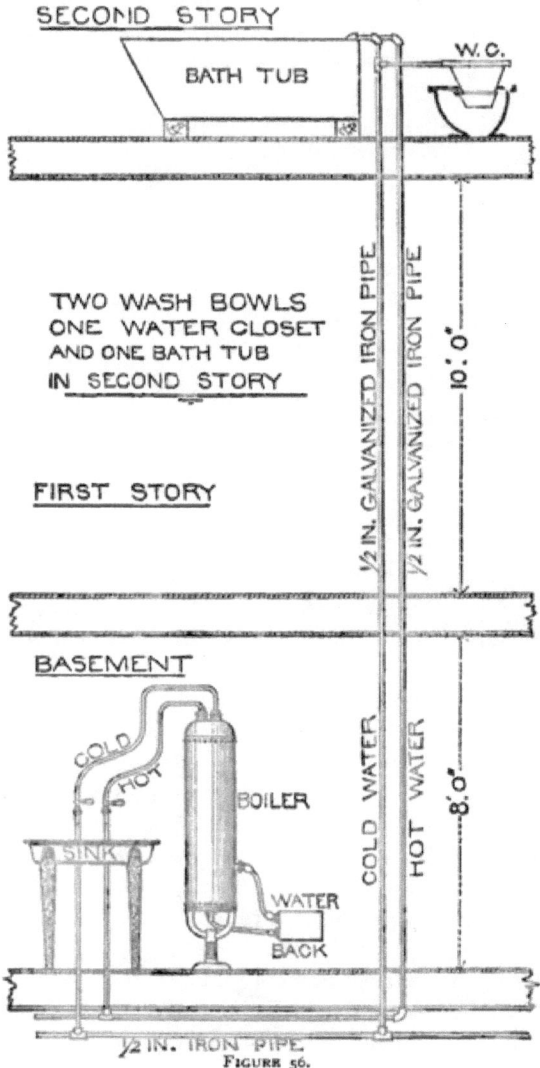

FIGURE 56.

This I could not always repeat before I saw your answer, and when I brought persons to try my geyser I was generally disappointed, but now when I want to show any one how to draw hot water from the cold faucet I send one of my children to open a hot-water faucet upstairs.

"The reason of it is plain to me now. The ½-inch pipe from the street is not large enough to send water to the upper floor when cold water is being drawn down-stairs at water-closet or wash-tubs, and the accumulated head of water in the hot pipe running upstairs flows backward (the pressure being reduced) into the boiler and over through the cold pipe and faucet until the water finds its equilibrium somewhere between the top of the boiler and the second floor.

"This can be repeated continuously, and one hand may be placed where the word *cold* is and the faucet manipulated with the other, when hot and cold water will be found to pass back and forth with each increase and decrease of pressure."

DISPOSAL OF BATH AND BASIN WASTE-WATER.

Q. As a personal favor, will you tell me if there can be any harm in allowing waste-water from bath and wash-basin to run into an open-side cesspool (covered at top), such cesspool being in gravelly ground? Water-closets and wash-tubs will be connected by a separate pipe to cemented cesspool. House is in the country, and open-side cesspool would be 100 feet from house.

A. Such a cesspool will contaminate the soil about it quite as surely as if receiving the drainage of water-closets, though perhaps not quite so rapidly. It is better to distribute the refuse on or near the surface. A collection of waste-water from bath-tubs and wash-bowls will become as foul as any other refuse from the house, and differs only from other refuse in being diluted by a greater bulk of water.

The disposal of house-sewage in suburban residences is a very troublesome question, especially where a public water-supply is afforded without sewers—a state of things which is not compatible with public safety. Distribution *on* the surface is the simplest method; but this requires at least an acre about every house, in order to make it free from offense.

It can be distributed in porous tiles about ten inches *under* the surface on smaller house-lots if the conditions are favorable—viz., a well-drained or porous soil.

Whether on the surface or beneath it, there must be slope enough to allow the sewage to flow by gravity from the bottom of the cesspool to the place of distribution, otherwise pumping is necessary, which is of course onerous. When distributing in pipes beneath the surface, it is usual to lay 2-inch unglazed tiles, with joints at least one-quarter of an inch open, in trenches ten or twelve inches deep, graded with a uniform fall of not over an inch in ten feet at most, and sometimes not over half this amount. Sufficient ramification and length of pipe must be provided to give a capacity of at least one-half that of the cesspool or tank to be discharged; the other half is generally soaked away during the flow. It is important to secure an intermittent flow in the tiles. If a constant driblet flows into them they will always be choked in a short time. When on a larger scale, as for hotels and public institutions, Field's flush-tank is used with success to secure this periodic or intermittent flow, but it does not operate so well for small cesspools. If the water-supply is limited to what is pumped by hand in the house, the discharge can be made by means of a stop-gate laid in the outlet-pipe leading from the bottom of the cesspool, and operated by hand when required, as described in Philbrick's "American Sanitary Engineering," page 93. The tiles adapted for this purpose are readily obtainable.

TO PREVENT CORROSION OF TANK-LINING.

Q. We have a tank lined with copper and supplied with water from a well. There is some substance in the water that causes the solder to corrode. Can you inform us of anything with which we can cover the inside of the lining that will prevent the action on the solder?

A. We think that a coat of "black varnish," put on when the tank is perfectly dry, would prevent the water from coming in contact with the solder, and consequently prevent the corrosion.

NUMBER OF WATER-CLOSETS REQUIRED IN A FACTORY.

Q. In putting in water-closets for a large factory in an Eastern city, employing in one large building perhaps 300 hands, about one-half of whom are women, the question arose how many water-closets would be needed. Will you please inform me whether sanitary engineers have adopted any ratio for such or similar cases? I have thought that perhaps your city Board of Health may have considered the question in connection with your densely-populated tenement-houses, and if so, would like to know their regulations in the matter. Also, whether under such circumstances, as all the closets will be on one soil-pipe—*i. e.*, arranged directly over one another in a shaft or annex, and will be flushed with 2-gallon flushes from cisterns—a 5-inch drain-pipe, iron, running some distance, with a fall of one in forty, will be sufficient to take care of the wastes and occasional foreign bodies thrown in by carelessness, without risk of obstruction.

A. We think you would require at least sixteen water-closets—eight for each sex. The pipe proposed is large enough. It should be provided with hand-hole screws to admit of the removal of obstructions. You do not state how many operatives will be employed on each floor. Our rule would be to provide at least one closet for each twenty operatives on a floor.

SIZE OF BASIN WASTES AND OUTLETS.

Q. What do you consider the proper size for wash-hand basin waste-pipes? Is it well to have so great a difference as is common between the outlet of the basin and the trap? Would not the latter be more thoroughly flushed and kept cleaner if the hole in the bottom of the basin and the coupling connecting it with the waste-pipe were of the same size as the latter? Do you approve of bars or strainers over the outlet of basins and baths, and of the ordinary plug attached to a chain? Is there any way of doing away with the latter without using a patented device?

A. The outlets of basin-plugs could with advantage be larger. It is necessary to have the strainer to keep articles from dropping in and choking up the trap. The ordinary Boston waste-cock is not patented, though the fact of a device being patented should be no objection to its use.

TAR-COATED WATER-PIPE AFFECT TASTE OF WATER.

Q. I desire to use some 8,000 feet 3-inch tar-coated cast-iron pipe to convey water from a mountain spring. Is there any danger of there being any taste of tar in the water?

A. There is no danger of the tar imparting a taste to the water if it is properly applied to the pipe. When water is first introduced it is better to let it run to waste for a few hours.

HOW TO DEAL WITH POLLUTION OF CELLAR-FLOORS.

Q. LAST winter the water-pipes and the soil-pipe in my house in Brooklyn burst, and after some days we accidentally discovered that water-closet filth had leaked down and saturated a large place in the cellar-bottom, which is simply the natural soil, not cemented, nor even floored over. Now that warm weather is coming on, I am afraid of consequences and think of moving out. I have taken dry, clean earth and spread over the saturated place, and that has seemed to purify the air. Is there anything else to be done? Are there any disinfecting substances which can be tried with success, or must the cellar be dug out? I may say that the landlord of this house will do nothing if not compelled to. It was only when the plumber whom he hired refused to patch up the pipe and insisted on putting in a new one that he would have it done.

A. We should remove the foul earth and replace with new.

HOW TO HEAT A BATHING-POOL.

Q. WILL you please inform me how I can heat a bathing-pool, 84 feet long, containing about 72,000 gallons of water, the size of pipe that would be necessary, and how long you think it would take to heat? Also the size of boiler necessary.

A. If you wish to warm 72,000 gallons of water, say from 30° to 70° Fah., it will take the heat of about 2,160 pounds of steam to do it.

If you wish to do it in an hour from the time steam is turned on, it will be necessary that the boiler should have a heating-surface of not less than 800 square feet.

If noise is no object when warming the water, a 4-inch steam-pipe leading to a 4-inch header at the bottom of the tank, from which about 30 lengths of 1-inch pipe are run, open at the free ends, but reduced to the size of about a $\frac{3}{4}$-inch pipe, may be used to good advantage.

A more expensive apparatus, which may be made noiseless, is a somewhat similar coil of $1\frac{1}{4}$-inch pipe, but closed, the condensed water being pumped back to the boiler instead of being allowed to mix with the water in the pool, as in the first method. The surface for this coil will have to be a matter of experiment.

At the New York Natatorium, Fifth Avenue and Forty-fifth Street, the water is warmed by being circulated directly through the boiler, as in a hot-water apparatus, and is the system we would recommend, a boiler of about 300 feet of surface being sufficient, on the assumption that the time for first heating the water is no object, say three to five hours, after which a slow fire can be made so as to maintain the temperature required.

Of course, where the water from the boiler is discharged into the pool, care must be taken that the hot current cannot scald any one, a crib or some arrangement being required.

OBJECTIONS TO GALVANIZED SHEET-IRON SOIL-PIPE.

Q. In a specification with plan, recently published in the *Bulletin*, for a cheap farm-house and barn, I notice that the architect provides for a 4-inch tile-drain from cesspool to sink, the sink to be connected with the drain by a 2-inch lead pipe ; also that a cast-iron slop-hopper is to be connected with the drain by a 3-inch No. 24 galvanized-iron pipe. Now, is not this bad practice? Will there not be considerable difficulty in connecting a 2-inch lead pipe with a 4-inch tile-drain, so that there will be no leaks? and should not the use of galvanized-iron for waste-pipe be condemned, on account of difficulty of making a tight seam?

A. You are quite right in your apprehension about the use of galvanized sheet-iron between hopper and drain. It is a little better, possibly, than canvas, because it might be tight a little longer, but we should expect it to be full of holes inside of a year. With care the lead pipe might be connected with the tile-drain, but a 4 x 2 Y should be used, and the connection should be below ground and carefully cemented, for, while it might be water-tight, we think it doubtful whether, if exposed, it would long remain gas-tight.

TO PREVENT RUST IN A SUCTION-PIPE.

Q. My pump is situated about sixty feet from the cistern, with a 1-inch iron pipe for suction, but every time the pump is used a large quantity of water has to be wasted, on account of the rust in the pipe. Would you have the kindness to let me know that if I use a tin pipe in place of the iron one if it would be perfectly safe to use the water which remains in the tin pipe overnight? Would there be any danger in using lead pipe?

A. Unless there was some peculiar character to the water of which we have no knowledge, a tin pipe could be used safely. We should not recommend the use of lead pipe in such a case. It would probably be necessary to waste as much water as with the iron pipe now in use.

AUTOMATIC SHUT-OFF FOR GAS PUMPING-ENGINES WHEN TANK IS FULL.

THE following inquiry has suggested a description of an automatic arrangement for turning off the gas-supply to a hot-air pumping-engine, recently arranged by Messrs. Pasco & Palmer, plumbers, of this city:

Q. Can you let us know whether there is any device whereby the gas-supply to the caloric pumping-engines can be shut down to a mere spark when the water-tank is full, and turned on again when the tank is empty, automatically?

A. The device represented in the drawing does not do what our correspondent asks for, which would seem to be a much more difficult thing to accomplish than to simply turn off the gas, since the hot-air pump in most common use is a single-crank engine, requiring the proper adjustment of the piston before starting.

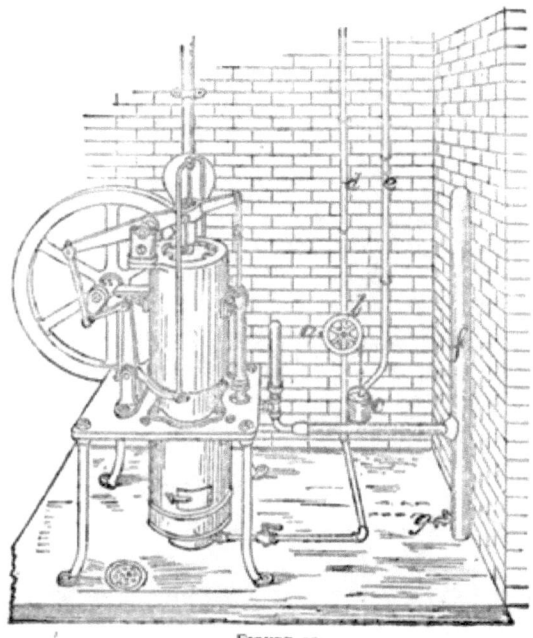

FIGURE 57.

The following is an explanation of the arrangement shown in the sketch: On the gas-pipe d supplying the engine is a stop-cock, on which a grooved iron wheel takes the place of a handle. A chain, attached to a pin at the point a in the circumference of the wheel, passes over the top and supports a small tin pail, c. The end of the tank tell-tale e is brought over the pail, so that the weight of the water discharged into it will cause the pail to fall, thus turning the wheel and closing the valve on the gas-pipe. Before starting the pump again the pail is emptied. The large pipe f, shown on the right hand, is an air-chamber on the suction-pipe to supplement the smaller one attached to the pump. The stop-cock g, at its foot, is for removing all the water from it.

There are other devices for the same purpose, such as a small tank under the tell-tale, containing a float connected with the valve on the gas-pipe, but the arrangement shown above is simpler than anything we have seen for the purpose.

PAINT TO PROTECT TANK-LININGS.

Q. Please inform me of the best mixture of paint to use on lead-lining of tanks. The lining is full of pin-holes, and has only been in use a year. It is lined with 6-pound sheet-lead. The tank is used for supplying water-closets.

A. We know of nothing better than what is sold as "black varnish." There are two different articles sold under this name. One has a basis of coal-tar, and when used may be diluted with naphtha; the other has a basis of natural asphalt, and may be diluted with spirits of turpentine. We do not know that one is more durable than the other. The tank should be perfectly dry when the paint is applied. We do not know how long, at the longest, such a coating will last, but it can be renewed at a trifling expense whenever the tank is cleaned.

VACUUM-VALVES NOT ALWAYS RELIABLE.

Q. My inquiry of October 13, to which you now very kindly reply, was prompted by the fact that in a new building fitted with a copper boiler of the best make, supplied with the safe and vacuum valve of your illustration, the boiler suffered a total collapse when the water company suddenly turned off the water, a few days before the date of my letter. The water company promptly replaced the boiler with a new one, because they neglected to give notice of their intention to turn off the water; but I now desire to learn whether or not such accidents are preventable. I always use the open-end relief-pipe where there is a tank to carry it above, but when you have city water at 45 pounds pressure what do you do?

A. It would seem that your experience justifies our opinion that it is not always safe to rely on safety and vacuum valves on range-boilers. Under the conditions named by you—viz., that you have a public water-service with an average pressure of 45 pounds to the square inch—we should advise you to take this supply to a tank, controlling it by a ball-cock. Then take your supply to the boiler from this tank, returning the hot-water pipe above and over the tank as a relief-pipe. You can then use copper boilers with safety.

The only other plan is to use galvanized-iron boilers. This is cheaper, but not so desirable, although generally done. How your water will be affected by contact with galvanized-iron you can ascertain by trial.

SIZE OF WATER-PIPES IN A HOUSE.

Q. Please inform me the size of lead pipes used for cold and for hot supply in an ordinary house with water on three stories. Also, what should be the size of the circulation-pipe as compared with the hot-water pipe?

A. The size is somewhat controlled by the ordinary street-pressure. A 1-inch main-supply from street-tap to rear of house, with ¾-inch branch to boiler and as far as the baths, ⅝-inch beyond that, and ½-inch branches to basin-cocks and water-closet cisterns, will give a good flow at all times. If pressure is very strong and cost is an important consideration, these may be reduced one size. The return hot-water circulation-pipe should be at least ½-inch.

HOW TO MAKE RUST-JOINTS.

Q. Please explain the best method of making rust-joints. Are they as good as lead joints?

A. They are sometimes used for joints in iron pipe, but are not so certain to be tight as well-calked lead. The best method of making such joints is to mix iron filings and a little sal-ammoniac, wet, and ram them into a joint over a gasket before it has been mixed long enough to rust the filings. The process of rusting expands the iron, and may, perhaps, make the joint tight if carefully mixed and filled—not otherwise.

COVERING FOR WATER-PIPES.

Q. A customer of mine would like your opinion as to what covering is the best for lead water-pipes, to prevent freezing. I suggested various things now in use, but he desires me to inquire of you as an authority, knowing you generally exhaust a subject when your views are solicited.

A. In answer to this question we would say that a plumber whom we consulted says that mineral-wool was altogether the best thing he knew of. Before that came into use he used asbestos, but of late he has used mineral-wool exclusively. Another had never used mineral-wool, and could say nothing about its efficacy or comparative cost. He generally used felting (which comes in sheets), but he always turned that over to his "felter"—never did it himself. Where the pipes were to be exposed to the weather, as above roofs, he had the canvas covering painted.

He also frequently used plaster of Paris, inclosed in a wooden box surrounding the pipe. This was cheaper and quite as effective, if properly done, though not so elegant. He also has used sawdust in boxes surrounding the pipe for the cheapest work. Not knowing the particular circumstances of the case, he could not say which he should use. And a well-known sanitary engineer, to whom the matter was referred, also adds: "The above is all sensible, and covers the subject."

SIZE OF SOIL-PIPE FOR AN ORDINARY CITY HOUSE.

Q. WHAT is the best size of soil-pipe for an ordinary city house, and should not traps be larger than the pipe to allow water to flow through them easily? I have been told they should be.

A. Four inches is large enough for such pipes. The traps should be no larger, for they would then become cesspools to a certain extent which is to be avoided. In fact, a 3-inch trap would be more cleanly than a 4-inch one, and preferable on this account for most water-closets, provided a good air-vent be provided.

HOW TO CONSTRUCT A SUNKEN RESERVOIR TO HOLD TWO THOUSAND GALLONS.

Q. GIVEN a spring on a high hill, in a country of severe winters, how is it best to form a 2,000-gallon reservoir at the spring (to accumulate and to be free from pollution of anything thrown in), and to conduct the same to a tank on top of a house at a lower point?

If the reservoir is sunk, what shall it be not to rot? Will it then gather all the water readily? If *above* ground, what will last best, etc.? Anybody who is experienced in this line, please post me, and as to winter effects.

A. Sink a cask well tarred on the outside for a small reservoir. If it must hold 2,000 gallons, make a brick well eight feet in diameter and six feet deep, and roof it over.

WHERE TO PLACE BURNERS TO VENTILATE FLUES BY GAS-JETS.

Q. I noticed a peculiar and very effective way of ventilating a hopper water-closet and urinal in a Boston store, and I think it would be of interest to your readers. I inclose a sketch of arrangement, and would like to ask a question.

The fixtures were located in a dark basement. It was necessary to provide a light. This light was utilized in the manner shown to produce the ventilation of closet and urinal. A brick flue was found, and from it was taken a 4-inch spiral sheet-iron pipe, D, and carried across the room, taking out the 2-inch pipe C to the water-closet and 2-inch pipe G to the urinal, connecting them as shown, with openings close to the water in the hopper and outlet and drip from the urinal.

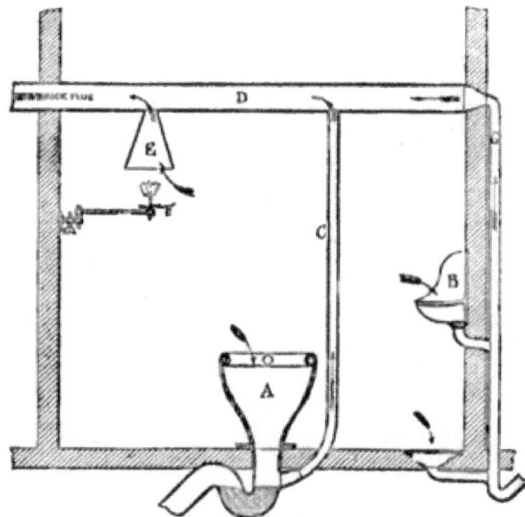

FIGURE 58.

An opening about an inch in diameter was made into the pipe D over the gas-flame, and an inverted funnel attached, with the large end about six inches above the flame. In practice the heat of this flame (an ordinary 4-foot burner) was found to cause a very strong current of air toward all the openings at the fixtures, as shown by the arrows, and, of course, thoroughly ventilate each one.

Should you not suppose a large quantity of air would enter the pipe at the open funnel from the room, as shown by the arrow at F, and would it not be better to close that opening and place the flame close enough to the outside of the pipe to give it the necessary heat, and then would it not produce a stronger current of air at the openings at the fixtures? Please give your valuable opinion on this little thing, if not too much trouble, and settle a dispute between the writer and another.

A. The change you suggest would be open to two objections. First, you would, as in the present instance, waste half the heat produced, if not more; and, second, the products of combustion of the gas would thus be left to defile the air of the house, and the flame of the burner would be likely to melt the solder of the pipe and would deposit soot upon the outside and make a dirty mess of it. The proper way to use a gas-burner to create draught is to inclose the burner in a small fixed glass box or lantern, with a hinged opening for access to the inside, so the burner can be cleaned, as well as the glass, when needed. Then connect the top of the lantern with the chimney-flue, and the bottom of the lantern with the closet-bowl and urinal, by about three inches diameter. By this arrangement all the heat evolved by the burner will be utilized to make the draught, and all the products of combustion will be carried off, while the air will be all drawn from the points desired—viz., the closet, bowl, and urinal.

Q. I wish to produce a draught in a ventilating-flue by using a gas-jet for that purpose. Two arrangements of the jet have been suggested. One is about as follows :

The gas-jet is set under a flat metallic hood, made double, as shown in the sketch, it being intended that the jet shall heat the metal of the lowest hood, which will in its turn heat the air which passes in between the two hoods, or parts of the hood, as indicated by the arrows. The other is to simply inclose the jet in a small

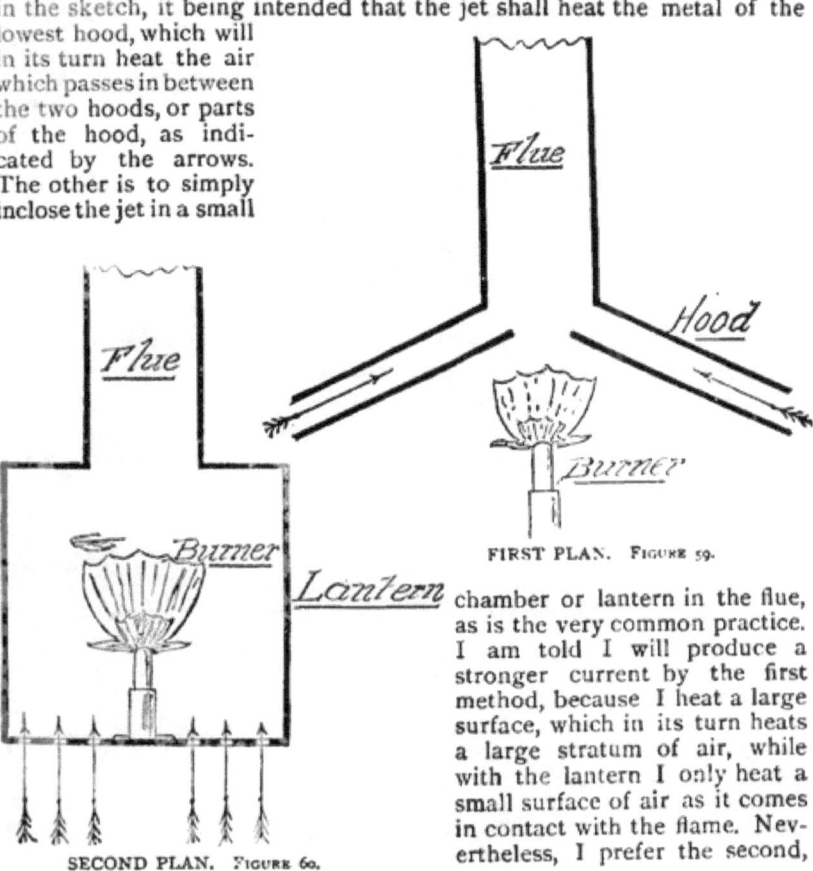

FIRST PLAN. FIGURE 59.

SECOND PLAN. FIGURE 60.

chamber or lantern in the flue, as is the very common practice. I am told I will produce a stronger current by the first method, because I heat a large surface, which in its turn heats a large stratum of air, while with the lantern I only heat a small surface of air as it comes in contact with the flame. Nevertheless, I prefer the second, because I think I can heat air better by *bringing it directly into contact with the flame* than if I used the flame to heat a metal surface first Indeed, the idea first suggested seems to me like inventing fictitious heat to make up for the loss which always occurs in heating the metal surfaces.

A. We believe the best results will be secured by the latter plan, since less of the heat is lost by radiation into the room.

HOW TO PREVENT WATER-HAMMER.

Q. We carry 80-pound pressure, and I have a piece of work of a bath-tub and water-closet. The pipe keeps bursting from water-hammer. I have an air-chamber a foot long connected on top at the bath-tub. The pipe is ⅝-inch strong. Please inform me what is best to do without putting up a tank, as the parties do not want one in the room. The closet is connected from the street.

A. There is no satisfactory way that we are acquainted with to entirely overcome the water-hammer you complain of, with such a pressure as you name, unless a tank is used from which fixtures are supplied. By enlarging your air-chamber and placing a pet-cock on it so that you can replenish the air occasionally, when it is absorbed by the water, you may reduce this hammer somewhat. This, however, will require more attention than people like to give it, and you will have to shut the water off the house every time you desire to admit air. In our opinion, no satisfactory work can be secured when there is a heavy pressure unless a tank is used. The placing of several air-tight rubber balls in an air-chamber has been known to give satisfactory results for a time.

WHY A HYDRAULIC-RAM DOES NOT WORK.

Q. Will you please give me reasons why a hydraulic-ram stops working? The spring is 106 feet from where the ram is set; the feed-pipe from spring to ram enters the spring about two feet below the top of the water in the spring. It has on it a perforated copper strainer. The feed-pipe from spring to ram is 1½-inch galvanized-iron pipe. The ram is one of Rumsey's No. 3. There is a fall of eight feet from strainer to ram, and ten feet from top of water in spring to ram. From ram to house is 450 feet of ½-inch galvanized pipe, and the ½-inch pipe runs over a hill. It will work at times for three or four days, and then again will stop, sometimes in half a day. I think it air-bound where it goes over the hill. Am I right or wrong, and how can I remedy it? The end of ½-inch pipe is open all the time.

A. It is very probable that the pipe does get "air-bound" at the summit. A small air-chamber at the summit, made by a branch with a vertical pipe on it at the summit, would relieve the pipe. There should be a cock on the upper end of the branch, to be opened occasionally while the ram is working. The force-pipe is too small to expect good service from the ram. The friction in 450 feet of ½-inch pipe is very great.

AIR IN WATER-PIPES.

Q. I would like to have the following question answered: A gentleman in the country has a well on a hill, and he runs a pipe from it to his barn. Now, he says he has to put a pump on every once in a while and pump out the air; they tell him the air gets in from the water, and I contend he has a leak in his pipe.

I would like to know if water can have air in it to stop a pipe from working, as he says.

From the top of pipe in well to top of spigot it has twelve feet of a fall.

A. There is always air in water. It is not uncommon for syphons to lose their charge in consequence of an accumulation of air in the bend. In the large 24-inch syphon-pipe at the Kansas City Water-Works, the pipe is only kept free of air by an air-pump attached to the pumping-engine. If there were a leak in the pipe mentioned by our correspondent the pump would have to be applied a good deal oftener than once in a while.

PROPER SIZE OF WATER-CLOSET OUTLETS.

Q. Will you please inform me what you consider the proper diameter (interior) for a water-closet trap? I find many of the closets of recent make contract the diameter of the trap to *three* inches, or even less. While a pipe of this diameter has the advantage of more thorough scouring at every flushing, and might prevent many things from entering the soil-pipe which have no business there, would it not be liable to be clogged when large or stiff paper is used, especially in public places? On the other hand, if the diameter of the trap is too large, the body of water to be moved is heavier, the scouring less, and, where 3-inch soil-pipes are used, as is now occasionally seen, danger of obstruction therein is greater. For hopper-closets should you consider $3\frac{1}{2}$-inch a good dimension?

A. As 4-inch seems to be the size of soil-pipe most used, it is desirable that the outlet of a hopper or water-closet should not exceed $3\frac{1}{2}$ inches. With good flushing, we do not apprehend any trouble from stoppage, even if the outlet is only three inches.

IS A CEMENT FLOOR IMPERVIOUS TO AIR?

Q. WILL a cement floor for a cellar allow ground-air to pass through it, bringing in contagion in case the soil is polluted, as it must be in Baltimore, judging from a recent letter in your paper?

A. Ordinary hydraulic cement, as commonly applied upon cellar-floors, has too much sand mixed with it to stop the passage of air. In fact, it is difficult to make a cellar-floor air-tight without an application of asphaltum, or other similar substance, applied hot.

TWO TRAPS TO A WATER-CLOSET OBJECTIONABLE.

Q. I DESIRE a little information in regard to a method (proposed to me by my plumber) of connecting the waste from wash-basin and bath-tub with that from water-closet *before* piercing the main 4-inch iron soil-pipe. He proposes to trap both basin and bath-tub separately (the traps being ventilated to the roof) and to unite these waste-pipes below the traps and carry the waste into the upper part (*above* the water-line) of a large trap situated just *below* the trap of a Jennings all-earthen closet. Both the earthen trap of the Jennings closet and this large lead trap are to be ventilated to the roof. In this case you will observe that all three wastes are separately trapped and ventilated, and that the united waste passes into another trap, also ventilated, before discharging into the main soil-pipe. Is this arrangement good from a sanitary point of view?

Another question: The ventilating-pipes from these different traps just referred to he proposes to *unite* at convenient points *above* the level of the traps, and to carry the whole in one into a 2-inch ventilating-pipe and thus to the roof. Is this arrangement as good as to pierce the 2-inch pipe in four different places for the separate ventilating-pipes, and thus ventilate to the roof?

A. In answer to the first query, we should say that, assuming that each fixture is separately trapped and properly ventilated, the advantage of the large trap just below the water-closet trap is not apparent. On the other hand, we consider such a trap as objectionable, for the reason that it retards somewhat the flow of waste matter without securing any adequate advantage as an offset for its being there. From the question as it stands, and in the absence of a sectional drawing, we should consider the several fixtures, trapped and ventilated as described, as amply protected, assuming, of course, that the house-drains are otherwise all right. A needless trap is an injury rather than a benefit.

Secondly—As we understand your last question, we should say that the choice of methods was simply a matter of convenience and economy in the use of pipe, provided that the 2-inch pipe was used solely for ventilation and received no drainage.

CONNECTING BATH-WASTES TO WATER-CLOSET TRAPS.

Q. We have a job of work which was done according to the inclosed plan. We would like you to inform us, if possible, why it is that there should be a smell of sewer-gas through the bath-tub pipe. A is the soil-pipe, which is extended through the roof; the sewer in the cellar is carried to the chimney, and run up next to a hot flue to the top of chimney. B is a 2-inch vent-pipe from closet-trap. C is a plunger-closet, with a trap. D is a lead trap under the trap of the water-closet. E, waste-pipe from bath-tub to water-closet trap, which is taken out above the water-line. F is the 1¼-inch vent-pipe from the bath-tub trap. G, overflow of bath-tub where the sewer-gas smell is the strongest.

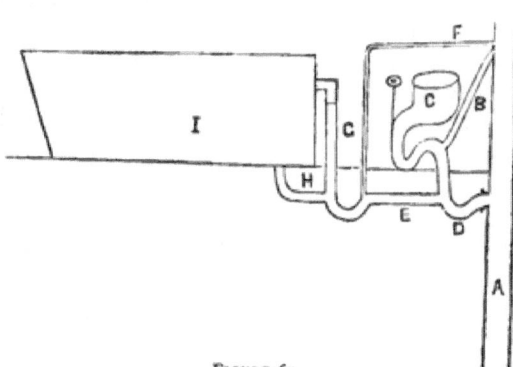

Figure 61.

H, waste from bath-tub, through which there is some smell. I, bath-tub. None of the traps syphon out, for we have tried them thoroughly. Almost instantly after pouring in water the smell comes up through the opening H and I. We would like very much to have you explain, if possible.

A. The overflow-pipe does not seem to enter the dip of the bath-tub trap, which permits a circulation of air down H and out at G, or *vice versa.* The smell, you will doubtless find, is caused by the fouling of the overflow-pipe. It is possible this smell is produced by servants rinsing out bedroom vessels in the bath-tub. Heat a flat-iron and place it against the overflow, and see if you can detect a smell of urine. It is, of course, presumed that no drainage enters the soil-pipe A above the vent-pipes B and F.

On the foregoing reply a correspondent writes:

"While you suggest a probable cause, I don't think you go far enough. In the first place, the person lifts the handle of the water-closet, which has a large body of water discharging instantly into the soil-pipe. This heavy plunge of water drives the air before it with such a pressure as to force the confined air (between the trap of water-closet and the trap D, shown on the plan) through the trap of the bath. As the air-pipe from the bath-trap, under the circumstances, is entirely too small to allow the compressed air, caused by discharge of water-closet in the confined space between the two traps, free vent, it therefore finds vent through trap of the bath, the waste of which appears on the sketch to be larger than the air-pipe from the same.

"The proper remedy is to take the lower trap D out entirely, and give the soil-pipe of the water-closet a free vent into the main sewer. What the plumber put the lower trap in for is beyond my comprehension, and the sooner it is removed the better. I presumed, as you did, that nothing empties into the soil-pipe above the vent-pipes F and B, for in that case the vents would be of no use whatever, as they would, in all probability, be stopped up by slime and filth."

We quite agree with our correspondent that the lower trap D should be removed, and his theory of the cause seems reasonable, although similar complaints are frequently made, and the cause has been traced to the source indicated. As this particular style of water-closet holds only $1\frac{5}{8}$ gallons of water, and that is discharged through a side-outlet $3\frac{1}{2}$ inches in diameter, consuming a little time in its delivery, it is a question whether with the vent-pipes F and B, $1\frac{1}{4}$ and 2 inches respectively, the compression of air could be so sudden as to greatly displace the water in the bath-tub trap. Moreover, the space between the two traps, ventilated as shown, and frequently flushed, could hardly be as foul as our correspondent intimates. The lower trap, however, should not be there, and it was a neglect on our part in not advising its removal.

OBJECTIONS TO LEACHING CESSPOOL AND NEED OF FRESH-AIR INLET.

Q. I HAVE a water-closet on the second floor of a country house, with the soil-pipe carried to the roof and ventilated. The waste runs into a closed cesspool some thirty feet distant, with a trap shutting it off from the house. I should like to ask, first, if it is necessary to have a vent on this trap which would be of necessity only a few feet from the water-closet vent, one just within and the other just without the wall. There is no chance for foot-ventilation, as there is only a grass-plot near by where children play. Second, is there any harm in a covered cesspool, which has never filled up in ten years, but which leaches through a gravelly, sloping soil into a small sewer, with no wells or neighbors to contaminate? There is a dispute about the vents being necessary, and it is hard to decide where doctors disagree. I wish you sanitarians would come to some agreement on certain points, and then we laymen would not so often be nonplussed, and, as it were, liable to fall between two stools.

A. Your waste or drain pipe should be extended to the "small sewer," and not be allowed to contaminate the soil near the house. There should be a vent just inside the outer trap, and there is no harm in having this open on the front lawn, for the draught is *inward* at this opening and up through roof of house by the soil-pipe. Since the water-closet trap is on the second floor, there must be twelve feet or more between the traps, and even if less, the lawn vent-hole is needed to establish a thorough draught. No sanitarian who is worthy of the name will question the propriety of establishing such a draught.

Secondly—With a cesspool in a gravelly soil only 30 feet from the house, there is great risk of foul gases making their way into the house. As regards differences of opinion, it is as well to remember that not every one is a sanitarian who calls himself such. Amateur counsel in such matters is plentiful, but in the end often terribly expensive.

THE THEORY OF THE ACTION OF FIELD'S SYPHON.

Q. WILL you explain the theory of Rogers Field's syphon? The obscure point is the pneumatic action involved, by which the sealing of the long leg of the syphon enables a very small stream to charge it, while, were it not so sealed, the liquid would merely dribble down the long leg, and the air would not be expelled. The books give no adequate explanation.

A. The dipping of the lower leg or outlet of the syphon in water facilitates the expulsion of the air in this way: the water, as it falls through the tube, carries with it by friction particles of air, just as a stream poured from a pitcher into a basin will carry bubbles down under the surface of the water into which it falls. The sealing of the end of the tube prevents any of the air from getting back after once being carried out, so that a continuation of the process for a few minutes generally takes out air enough to set the syphon in action: Any contrivance by which the water may be made to fall into the basin at the foot of the outlet-limb freely—*i. e.*, without dribbling down the sides of the tube—will hasten the expulsion of the air by mixing air and water together on the way down. For this reason pure water works better than sewage, for the impurities of the latter soon collect upon any points or edges from which the water may be made to pour clear of the side of the tube, and by forming a lip leads the water back to the side of the tube again. For this reason it is difficult to make the annular syphons work on a small scale with sewage. The free admission of the air to the syphon after the tank is emptied is essential to the success of the device. If not so admitted—*i. e.*, if both ends remain sealed, with the syphon full of water—the tank will not fill again, but the water will pass out through the syphon in driblets, as it comes in. In order to secure the emptying of the syphon, Mr. Field provides either a small syphon to discharge the lower basin after the tank is emptied, or a V-shaped notch in the edge of this basin to allow the water-seal to be broken by draining the water below the end of the outlet-limb. The seal is restored again as soon as the flow becomes enough to fill the notch. In this point, as we understand it, consists Mr. Field's invention, on which the patent for his curved pipe-syphon depends. The choking of this notch or lower syphon by the impurities of sewage forms the chief impediment to the general use of the invention, for it often ceases its automatic action when used for sewage, unless occasionally looked after to clear the rubbish from this point.

HOW TO DISINFECT A CESSPOOL.

Q. CAN you tell me any way to get rid of those bugs called Croton bugs, or cockroaches, as they are sometimes called? They seem to appear always where water-pipes are put in, and pay no attention to insect-powder. Also, what is the best means of disinfecting sinks, drains, cesspools, etc.?

A. We have, in several cases, known these "water-bugs" to be exterminated by a sprinkling of powdered borax distributed around the shelves, drawers, etc., where they most do congregate.

The best disinfectant for sinks is hot soapsuds, applied with elbow-grease and a scraper.

For drains, the best way is to see that no pockets or places of deposit occur by defective planning or construction, ventilate at both ends, and apply plenty of water. If obstructions occur, remove them at once.

For cesspools, copperas-water is good, but it acts only for the time being. It is a good plan to clean them out often, if you must have them, and apply copperas-water to the sides liberally after such cleanings.

DRAINAGE INTO CESSPOOLS.

Q. An architect of this city directs me to you for some information. I am putting two bath-tubs and three wash-basins in my house, and was about to empty them (the waste-water) into a well about 15 feet to the west of my house. Can you let me know a better course? Is there any objection to emptying into this well? If so, what is it?

This, and any information you can give me, will be very thankfully received.

A. If you have no sewer to drain into, a "well" (or cesspool, we presume you mean) must be accepted as a compromise. It should be perfectly water tight, and if it must be as near as 15 feet to your house, it should be tightly covered, with two pipes extending from it, with their open ends above your house, or far enough away to prevent the smell from being disagreeable. The contents should be frequently removed, and great care taken to prevent a nuisance. The proper construction of a cesspool is described in Philbrick's "American Sanitary Engineering," pages 90-93.

SLABS FOR PANTRY-SINKS—WOOD VERSUS MARBLE.

Q. Information on the below-mentioned points is very much desired and will be thankfully appreciated. A client wishes, in altering a butler's pantry, to have the marble slab removed and wood substituted, because, as she says, the servants break the china. Reasons *pro* and *con* are wished. The client also wishes to have the butler's sink removed. In refitting, no means for washing the soiled dishes in a *permanent* sink are wanted (a movable pan will be used), but simply the faucets for water and an opening into the waste for emptying the pan and also, say, a pail of water; the idea being to prevent servants from washing the utensils in a permanent sink, it being difficult to keep same grease-clean. Can you suggest some appliance covering the requirements as to waste?

In the kitchen, the odors of cooking permeate the house, regardless of several closed doors. A hood over the range, leading to the kitchen-flue above, was suggested, but it was thought the draught of fire below would be affected. Is there any means of quickly and effectively leading away cooking fumes in a city-house kitchen, having range as ordinarily arranged?

If the reasons for using *wood* around butler's sink are predominant, is anything else required, besides oiling and Wheeler's filler, to prevent water and grease soaking into the wood surface?

A. Marble slabs are often complained of as borders for butler's sinks, on the ground of breakage of china. Some people use wood for borders, though it is more difficult to keep clean. If only a slop-sink is wanted, in which the dish-tub can be emptied, it is best to make it of earthenware, which is easily kept clean. The ordinary white-glazed ware is made in several forms suitable for the purpose. Of course, a ventilated trap must be applied at the waste, not a bell-trap at the strainer.

Planished or tinned copper is often used for butler's sinks, with wooden border or shelf. The tin soon wears off, leaving the copper bare, and the wood border is subject to warping and cracking, from its frequent soaking in warm water spattered upon it, and is, therefore, objected to as difficult to keep clean. In Philadelphia, pantry-sinks made of wood and lined with sheet German silver are used; they, of course, retain their color when worn, as they are of one metal.

To remove smells from the kitchen, a hood is desirable, but it should connect with *an independent flue* in the kitchen-chimney, but not with the smoke-flue, as the draught would be affected, as you suggest.

TEST FOR WELL-POLLUTION.

Q. A WELL is so situated with regard to a privy and cesspool that I am persuaded its water is contaminated from those sources. How can I prove it? I think I have read somewhere of a color-test, applied by introducing some color into the cesspool, and having the same color shortly appear in the water. I don't care to apply the chemical test, as it would not convince the parties using the well-water.

A. Clean out the cesspool thoroughly, then empty a barrel of coarse salt into it, and put in some water. A saline taste in the well will then indicate contamination from the cesspool.

CESSPOOL FOR PRIVY-VAULT.

Q. Would there be any special objection to using a water-tight cesspool as a privy? This would insure its ventilation. Would it be likely to be offensive to those obliged to use it? It is 136 feet from any house.

A. We see no objection, except that it might be disagreeable while using it, as suggested; and in frosty weather the frost would collect on the underside of the covers in an annoying manner.

CORROSION OF LEAD LINING.

Q. I am at work on a lead-lined tank, which is used only in the summer season. In the fall the water is allowed to run out, and it remains empty over winter, but in running out there remains about half an inch of water over the bottom of the tank, and this is allowed to dry out. This spring when I examined the tank I found the bottom eaten full of holes varying in size from the point of a pin to an inch opening. I never saw anything like it before in sheet-lead, and would be much obliged if you would give me an explanation of it. The water used is very hard water and heavily impregnated with lime.

A. The fact that the water contains lime-salts would not account for the holes in the bottom of the tank. The presence of carbonate of lime in the water would tend to form an insoluble carbonate of lead on the surface covered by the water. It is possible that the holes were produced as the result of some galvanic action between the lead and some other metallic substance—either an impurity in the lead itself or another metal accidentally left in contact with the lead.

SIZE OF FLUSH-TANK TO DEAL WITH SEWAGE OF A SMALL HOSPITAL.

Q. What should be the dimensions of the flush-tank and settling-basin for disposing of the sewage of a hospital of twenty-five beds by subsurface irrigation?

A. We should make each about five feet diameter and five feet deep below the water-line, or of equivalent capacity; broader and less deep if more convenient. The storage would then amount to about 750 gallons. There would be needed from 2,000 to 2,500 feet of distributing tiles, depending on the porosity of the soil, the more porous soils needing less pipe than clayey soils. The above is based on the supposition of an abundant water-supply under constant pressure. If water is to be supplied by hand-pumping, half of the above capacity would be ample.

DETAILS OF THE CONSTRUCTION OF A HOUSE-TANK.

The tanks are on the top floors, and are built with a view to distribute the weight evenly over a great many joists, and for this

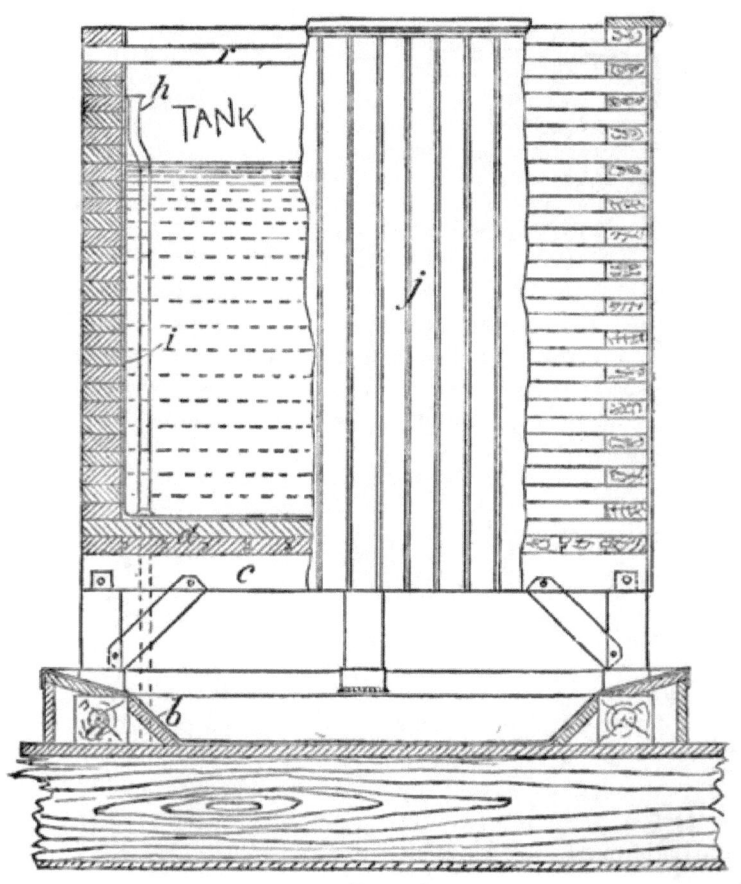

Figure 62.

reason they are but five feet wide by fourteen feet in length, the depth being five feet.

The particulars are: A sill, *a*, 6"x6", made of spruce, with its centre under the centre of the walls of a tank, is carried all the way around upon the floor. Into this sill are set the trusses *c*, the height from the floor to the top of the truss being two feet, and the distance between the centres of the trusses three feet. The trusses are braced as shown, and mortised into the sill, all mortises and tenons being draw-bored and treenailed. On these trusses a deck or bottom, *d*, is formed by two thicknesses of spruce plank 1⅞ inches thick by 4 inches wide when planed. They are laid in contrary directions, the first layer being across the trusses, and are nailed and clinched. The sides and ends of a tank are formed by spruce planks 4 inches wide by 1⅞ inches thick when planed, built on their flat from the bottom up, in the manner shown in Figure 63, which we believe is nearly the same as in the construction of grain-elevator bins. The courses are laid *one* at a time and spiked to the ones next below them; 6-inch spikes being used, so that the point will always enter the fourth plank. This, it will be seen, gives a solid thickness of *four* inches to the side of the tank, and it is claimed, on account of the manner of constructing the corners, that it gives greater strength and stability than if 4-inch thick plank were used on their edge, and requires no strapping.

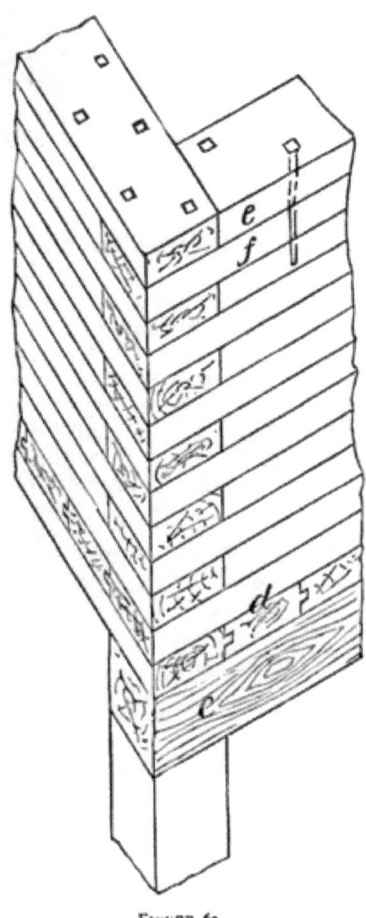

FIGURE 63.

In the long direction of the tank wooden stays, *r*, are introduced to prevent straining on the long sides when full of water. This wooden tank thus formed is lined with 18-ounce tinned copper, which is carried to the top of the wood-work. The outside of the tank is cased with yellow pine match-boarding (i).

The tank-safe is formed, as shown at b, by giving the space bounded by the sill an appropriate incline with wood, and extending it over and beyond the outer edge of the tank, and lining it with *four*-pound lead.

Between the *two* tanks (one being in each house) an arrangement of piping is made whereby the water from the tank in any one house may be used in the other should either the tanks or service-pipes be out of order or one of the pumps be inoperative. These tanks were constructed for plumbing-work done by Mr. John Renehan, under direction of Mr. James E. Ware, architect, described at length in Volume IX. of the *Sanitary Engineer*.

THE CONSTRUCTION OF A CISTERN UNDER A HOUSE.

Q. WILL you have the kindness to give me your opinion as to the best manner of remedying the following? A party has a cistern under his house. A brick floor and the foundation-walls cemented forms this cistern; the joist and floor of same forms the cover or top. The cistern not being arched with bricks, at times there is an offensive odor of decayed mud coming up through the manhole. Now, the owner wishes to abolish this cistern. It was suggested to fill it up with earth. Would it be prudent to do so, or would it be better to thoroughly dry this cistern and whitewash the walls, etc.? If you can suggest any better way you will greatly oblige.

A. It will be best to fill the cistern with clean, dry earth, since if it is left empty there will always be a certain element of danger connected with it, unless it is used for some purpose, and its presence thus kept constantly in mind. If it is left empty, means should be provided for its ventilation in the form of two tubes, one opening into it near the top, the other near the bottom, and both communicating with the external air.

Care must be taken that the earth used for filling does not contain organic matter; a mixture of equal parts of clean sand or gravel and clean clay is better than either alone would be. If the level of the subsoil water in the vicinity is below that of the bottom of the cistern, the cement bottom should be broken up before the cistern is filled, in order that the earth within and without may communicate freely.

Q. I AM building a cistern under my house to contain rain-water which will be used for drinking, etc. I wish to put in a terra-cotta pipe through the top to the bottom of the cistern in order to deposit the fresh water at the bottom. Would the terra-cotta pipe be in any way injurious to the water?

A. Terra-cotta pipe will not injure the water for drinking purposes, but it is highly unadvisable to place a cistern under a dwelling-house, since by doing so one runs a triple risk—viz., of injuring the house by dampness; of injuring the health of the inmates of the house, especially if any of them have a tendency, however slight, to lung disease; and lastly, of injuring the water by placing it where it can absorb the organic and ammoniacal exhalations connected with the presence of animal life.

TO PROTECT LEAD LINING OF A TANK, AND CAUSE OF SWEATING.

Q. What is considered the best receipt for coating a lead-lined tank to preserve the lead and prevent sweating?

A. Pure waters act upon lead more energetically than those containing carbonates. Water containing carbonates will form a carbonate of lead coating in the tank, and so prevent or retard the solution of the lead. We know of no instance where this has been practically applied. By the sweating in this case we presume you mean the condensation of water on the outside due to the lower temperature of the water as compared with that of the surrounding atmosphere. This cannot be helped, and in good work safes are provided under the tanks to catch this water of condensation.

STAINS ON MARBLE.

Q. I often hear plumbers speak of finding stains on marble washstands or toilet-stands which they cannot remove or give a suitable explanation for. I have been told the cause in some instances is from ladies using a certain kind of perfumed tooth-powder which contains quinine, but I am not chemist enough to say if such a compound would create a permanent stain. Please suggest a remedy.

A. Marble, especially that which is called statuary marble, is porous and absorbent, consequently it retains any moist foreign matter which comes in contact with it, and stains are easily seen. The best Italian marble is less likely to show stains than the white, and is much better for plumbing purposes.

LIGHTNING STRIKING SOIL-PIPES.

Q. I WOULD like to have your opinion regarding the extra danger from lightning where cast-iron or wrought-iron pipes are run through the roof of a building for vent-pipes. Is there not more danger of such a house being struck by lightning? Where an iron pipe is run to the roof from a lead trap, will the lead waste-pipe act as a conductor and carry the lightning to the ground?

A. If the house is provided with lightning-rods, as every house should be, the extra danger from vent-pipes run through the roof amounts to very little, if anything. Chimneys are sometimes struck by lightning, but no one thinks of abolishing those necessary structures on that account, and the same may be said of the vent-pipe. The electrical conductivity of lead is small, only about one-half that of iron, but under ordinary circumstances, and in the case supposed, it would serve as a conductor. Joints should always be of metal, however, to avoid the mechanical effects consequent upon the lightning jumping from one conductor to another. In several cases on record more damage has resulted in consequence of a lightning-rod not properly connected than would have resulted had the rod been connected with gas or water pipes even.

WILL THE CONTENTS OF A CESSPOOL FREEZE?

Q. IN this climate, what is the average temperature of sewage in cold weather? and would an intercepting cesspool be liable to freeze under the following conditions: Cesspool or grease-trap, to intercept the waste of house with eight inmates, to be of 300 gallons capacity, tight, with arch just under surface of ground, a cold, open winter, and the ground over cesspool to be covered with a foot and a half of straw, held down by boards?

A. The average temperature of sewage in winter in this climate (near New York City) is considerably above the freezing point. It could not freeze when in a tight cesspool, protected as above described. Even if the covering of straw were omitted, there would be no frost if the drain were constantly used by a continual flow of water, except a condensation of hoar-frost on the underside of the cover, and possibly a disturbance of the upper courses of the brick-work and plastering near the top of the ground. If, however, ample ventilation were provided by any means which would cause a circulation of cold, frosty air through the interior, the fluids would probably freeze over, and possibly obstruct the pipes by ice in a winter like the last one.

BAD-TASTING WATER FROM A COIL.

Q. I HAVE been asked to try to remove a cause of bad-tasting water from a cooler. My doctor got a plumber to put a ⅜-inch galvanized-pipe coil in his ice-box, to be used for drinking-water purposes. The plumber never made one before and was not particular with it, and it tastes badly from oil and lead used in connecting it. The coil is one foot wide, with galvanized elbows. The doctor has the water drawn from the spigot, then placed in a charcoal filterer, and then put in a stone jar, which connects with the coil for use. I have made them before, but was very particular not to use oil in cutting threads, and did not use lead to connect together. I have brought this coil which I am telling you about to my house and run concentrated lye-water through it, and then run lime-water also, and yet it tastes.

Please inform me, if you can, what to do with this coil. The doctor wants this one cleaned. The ice sits in the coil, which forms a box when connected together; the water, after it is filtered, stands in the coil and gets cold, and they draw from the spigot at the bottom for table use.

FIGURE 64.

A. If the water passing through the coil tastes "badly from oil," doubtless there is oil in it, which the treatment with lye-water has failed to remove. The treatment with the alkali should be very thorough, and every part of the inside of the pipe should come in contact with it. A gentle heat—say steam at low pressure—might destroy the oil without injury to the coil.

As the coils made by our correspondent give no trouble, there obviously is one remedy left in case the above fail—that is, to throw away the old coil and make a new one. These coils should be tin pipe.

HOW TO FIT SHEET-LEAD IN A LARGE TANK.

Q. To SETTLE a dispute, will you inform me, if it is not too much trouble, the proper way lead should be fitted in a tank for wiped seams in the corners?

A. Much depends on size of tank and weight of lead. A tank is say 8 feet long by 6 x 6 feet of 6-lb. lead. Order the lead to be rolled —one piece for bottom, 8 x 6 feet, two pieces each, 14 x 6 feet 1 inch, rolled up separately. Then countersink about two feet apart in sides and ends, for dots to secure the lead to, dots to be about half an inch deep and two and a half inches in diameter. Then nail into two of the opposite upright corners hollowed strips of wood, but previously unroll the bottom in place and dress it down. Then take one of the side and end rolls and turn half an inch of the edge; set the roll on end in the tank, placing the turned edge in one of the square corners; brace it from opposite side; unroll the sheet in place; then take a strip of board one quarter of an inch thick, tack it temporarily on top edge of tank; dress over the edge of the lead; then remove the wood strips, previously bringing slightly forward the lead at the bottom; remove the strips and tack the top edge securely, and dress all around; bottom corner to be beaten in with chase-wedge. This will leave one-quarter of an inch to close the seams. Back of ladle can be used to dress the lead into the dots.

After the other side and end are in place, prepare the dots for wiping, and drive in a few tacks to keep the lead in place; then drive in a stout iron screw in each dot, allowing the head to project slightly; then wipe the dots, and while the metal is being reheated prepare the upright seams, which will next be wiped, and proceed in like manner with the bottom corners.

Avoid tinned tacks, as zinc is more or less in the metal used in tinning them. Small tanks for water-closets and other purposes can have bottom and two sides in one piece, which will be put in first.

Q. I have read your reply to my inquiries regarding the proper way lead should be fitted in a tank for wiped seams in the corners, and I beg to differ with your ideas of lining tanks with sheet-lead in the manner you have here described. In the first place, your idea of first dressing the lead into place in the tank before preparing the edges of the lead for wiped seams in the corners seems to me to be rather a bungling way of going about it, as there cannot be as neat or as good a job made of preparing the seams in the corners after the lead is in place in the tank as can be made before the lead is put in place.

Now, my idea of lining a tank of the size you have here described, 8 feet by 6 x 6 feet, is: Cut the lead in the same manner as you have described, cutting one piece of lead for the bottom 8 x 6 feet, cutting the edges of the lead perfectly true. Then cut two pieces, each making a side and end; these two pieces should be cut the exact size, so as to fit snugly into the corners of the tank when in place; then proceed to prepare the seams by first rolling out the bottom piece on the floor and dressing around the edges. Next measure in four inches from the edge for width of soiling and mark line with straight-edge; then run chalk on 4-inch space to be soiled, so as to take off the greasy surface of the lead. Now, having a pot of good hot soil ready, proceed and soil to the line four inches wide all around. While the soil is drying mark off the dots in tank, two feet apart; countersink them half an inch deep and two and a half inches in diameter—just as you have described— and proceed to shave the seams by first marking off the width of seam, say three-quarters, seven-eighths, or one-half inch in width, according to whatever width one prefers having it. Then mark a line on each edge with a straight-edge, then placing the straight-edge under the lead a little in from the edge, shave the lead to the line on the four edges, and level off the edges of the lead with the shave-hook all around. Then roll up the lead, place it in the tank, and unroll in place. Nail into two of the opposite corners strips of wood so as to make rounding corners where no seams are wiped, then prepare the seams on the two pieces to make the sides and ends in the same manner as the bottom, shaving the bottom edge and ends and beveling off the edge of the lead with the shave-hook. Roll up the lead and place two thin boards in the bottom of the tank, one down the side and one across the end, close to side of tank. Set the roll on end in tank, placing the beveled edge of the lead snugly in the corner of the tank, brace it from opposite side and unroll in place, dress in bottom edge and slip the boards from under, letting the lead settle down snugly into place. Then dress over top edge on tank and tack down securely. Proceed in like manner with the other piece. When all in place forming close mitre-joints in the corners of the tank, drive in the tacks in the joints in the corners, catching on both edges of the lead and setting them in pretty well, giving a good opportunity to properly cover over the heads of the nails when wiping the seams. Dress the lead well to the sides of the tank, having the metal and irons good and hot; grease the seams and proceed to wipe. While the metal is being reheated dress the lead into the dots in the tank on sides and ends with back of ladle, striking a circle with the compass, then soil and shave to the edge of countersink to secure the lead to dots. Put in two or three good screws, being careful not to set them up too snug to the lead, and wipe them over flush. In this way a good, first-class, and neat job can be done; but after all, much the easiest way to line such tanks is to put in each piece separately, wipe down the four corners, and around the bottom. It takes a little more solder, but I never could see the use of turning the edge in the corner to close the joint, as the proper place for the tacks is in the corner, and you leave one-quarter of an inch to close the seams of bottom corners. It is in the way in wiping a nice seam, for you have to look out that it is properly covered over with the solder.

A. At Mr ——— request we gave our opinion on the proper way lead should be fitted in a tank for wiped seams. After having asked for and received our reply, Mr. ——— sends us his own views, as above.

We venture to say that if he has ever lined a tank 8 feet by 6 x 6 feet, or one-half that size, previously preparing the seams for wiping, without having afterward had to soil shave them when the lead is in place, it is the first one that has been done without making a "bungling" job—such as he has been pleased to call our method of doing it. Mitering the lead in the corners, as he describes, cannot be done without leaving openings for the solder to run under the lead, thereby causing its bulging, which would crack the seams as fast as wiped. The further the tacks are set in as decribed the more solder would run under the lead, and instead of fifty pounds, which should be a sufficient quantity to make a good job, twice that amount would be consumed, and but poor work obtained with the best hand at the cloth.

WHY WATER IS "MILKY" WHEN FIRST DRAWN.

Q. WHAT is the cause of water when it is first drawn being just as white and thick as milk, but if you let a tumblerful of it stand for about one minute it will become as clear as you could wish? It leaves no sediment at the bottom, and you cannot by stirring or shaking, make it white again.

A. The milky appearance is probably due to air confined in the water under the pressure in the pipes, which escapes when the water runs from the faucet.

MATERIAL FOR WATER SERVICE-PIPES.

Q. I SEND with this the engineer's report upon our water-works, not yet completed. All things considered, is there anything better than the lead pipes for tapping the mains? I understand that these only are allowed by the Water Board. Is experience against iron pipes?

A. Whether lead or iron service-pipes are better depends upon the chemical constituents of the water which is supplied. Wrought-iron pipes are liable to become corroded, particularly with soft waters. They are used for service-pipe in a great many towns, however, but lead-pipe is generally to be preferred for this purpose as less liable to leak from settlement.

CARVING-TABLES.

Q. I HAVE arranged several steam or carving tables, to heat the water by running a pipe through a range, as shown in the inclosed

FIGURE 65.

sketch, but in every case the carving-table has been on the floor above, but in this house the table and range are on the same floor, and I cannot get more than two feet rise from range to table-doors, and windows

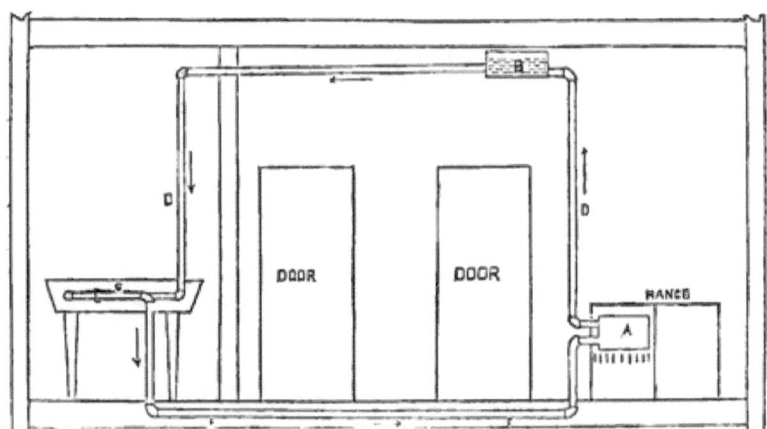

FIGURE 66.

prevent my running the pipe along the wall. Will it work as marked, or can you suggest a plan by which I could make it work?

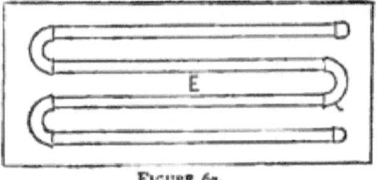

FIGURE 67.

A. There are several ways in which your object can be accomplished. The one we illustrate here is as simple as any. A is the water-back and B the expansion-tank, which may be either open or closed.

If an open tank is used, supply by ball-cock, and place overflow near the top of the tank. If a closed tank is used, have sufficient space in same to allow for the expansion of the water (not less than about $\frac{1}{20}$ of the quantity of water in the apparatus). C is the carving-table, D the flow-pipe, E the coil in the table, shown also in plan, and F the return-pipe.

IS GALVANIZED PIPE DANGEROUS FOR SOFT SPRING-WATER?

Q. Can you give me any opinion as to danger of water-poisoning from the use of galvanized pipes for soft spring-water?

A. We referred this question to Prof. William Ripley Nichols, whom we consider an authority. The following is his reply:

"It would be difficult to give an opinion of any value without more knowledge of the character of the water than is conveyed by the term 'soft.' If the water is what we should consider soft in this region, if a fair proportion of the dissolved salts consists of carbonates, and if there is no excess of carbonic-acid, the so-called galvanized pipe can, no doubt, be used with perfect safety; if the water is effervescent, or contains an excess of carbonic-acid without actually effervescing, especially if chlorides are present (or sulphates other than sulphate of lime), it would perhaps be better not to use the pipes. Even in the latter case, however, if in the morning or whenever the water has remained for any considerable length of time in the pipes, enough water is wasted to thoroughly flush the pipes before any is used for drinking or cooking, there will probably be no danger. In this case a filter of bone-coal would be an additional safeguard.

"As to the general question of the action of water on zinc, the matter was quite fully studied a few years after the manufacture of articles of the so-called 'galvanized' iron began, and the experiments of Mallet (British Association Reports, 1838 and 1840) are justly considered classic. All ordinary waters act more or less on galvanized-iron with the formation, as a rule, of oxide of zinc, which is subsequently changed to a hydrated carbonate. This coating may be to a certain extent protective, and, when once formed, it may check the corrosion of the underlying metal. It is not, however, very coherent, and where there is a flow of continually renewed water, as in the interior of a pipe, the coating is continually removed and reformed. Water drawn from such pipes, especially after standing for some hours, usually contains more or less oxide or carbonate of zinc in suspension, and, at the same time, some zinc in solution. It is stated—and it is the experience of the writer—that the corrosion from the first takes place irregularly in patches; at any rate, after a longer or shorter time, depending upon the quality of the pipe and the character of the water, the iron becomes exposed in spots; then the corrosion proceeds more rapidly, and after a time—in fact, from that time—the pipe has no superiority over a plain iron pipe.

"As to the danger to health: Although certain compounds of zinc are known to be poisonous if taken in sufficient quantity, it is generally held by those who have given particular attention to the subject, that ordinary water may be conveyed with perfect safety through zincked pipes. Some chemists have reported finding so much sulphate and so much chloride of zinc in a given water, but, as any one acquainted with chemistry knows, these compounds cannot be *identified* as such when they occur in small quantity, and the cases are exceptional where it is not erroneous to *regard* the zinc as thus existing. In most waters it is justifiable to regard the dissolved zinc as existing as carbonate, and the amount, at the most, is so small that the action on the system is not to be feared, at least from an allopathic point of view. It is said that 'there are on record a number of cases of zinc-poisoning from the use of galvanized-iron pipes.' This may be so, but in some of the cases, at any rate, the records are decidedly open to criticism. The question of the use of galvanized pipes, tanks, etc., was investigated quite thoroughly in 1873 for the Massachusetts State Board of Health by Dr. W. E. Boardman, who gives the *pros* and *cons* in the matter. No doubt the investigation was undertaken partly because of the then somewhat recent occurrence in the neighborhood of Boston of cases of sickness and death which were *ascribed* to the drinking of water which had passed through 'galvanized' pipe. Dr. Boardman and other competent physicians concluded that there was not in 'these cases adequate evidence to establish the correctness of the opinion given as to the nature of the illness in the way of cause and effect,' and other cases were investigated with a similar result.

"The writer would not wish to be understood as implying that there may not be cases of well-authenticated ill effects; he is familiar with waters in connection with which he certainly would not advise the use of zincked pipe, but these waters would not be recommended for domestic use. The largest amount of zinc *in solution* which the writer remembers at the moment to have met with was 0.85 grains to the gallon; this would correspond to nearly 1.1 grain of oxide of zinc. A much larger amount could exist in solution, even in the form of the difficultly soluble carbonate. As much as six grains has been reported in *solution and suspension* together, but in such cases probably the larger part was in suspension. For the particulars of the effects of the different compounds of zinc, the size of doses given medicinally or for experimental purposes, and for other similar data any persons interested are referred to the paper of Dr. Boardman alluded to above."

HOW TO ARRANGE HUSH-PIPES IN CISTERNS TO PREVENT SYPHONING WATER THROUGH BALL-COCK.

Q. In a recent number of your valuable paper, Mr. J. W. Hughes, of Montreal, objects to a hush-pipe in water-closet cisterns, as it forms a syphon when the supply-pipe is full. Will it? He recommends fitting the ball-cocks above the water and using a deafening-pipe, the construction of which I do not understand; what is it?

Would it not be desirable, if water-supply were abundant, to have a constant light flush for water-closets, thus tending to keep the soil-pipe freer from foul deposits, and would not such a flush offer an obstruction to ascending sewer-gas that might form in the house drain?

Will you briefly recapitulate the reasons why a rain-water conductor should not be entered into a soil-pipe?

Do you think it desirable to ventilate under the seat of a water-closet when the plumbing is well trapped and otherwise well ventilated? There would be very little odor, and that might be removed through the ventilating system provided for the room.

What is a bidet?

A. In some circumstances we think the danger of syphoning, to which Mr. Hughes' letter referred, might exist, and it is therefore desirable to fit up the ball-cocks, as he recommends, above the surface of the water. The "deafening" or "hush" pipe is a pipe fitted to the ball-cock and carried below the surface of the water in the cistern, so that the cistern will fill noiselessly, the discharge taking place under water, and open at its upper end so it can serve as the short leg of a syphon.

A "constant light flush," if we understand you aright, would be useless, for a driblet of water does not wash away anything in its course. Nothing can be useful for flushing short of a body of water that would completely fill the drain-pipes.

A rain-water leader should not enter a soil-pipe by a tight connection, because it is difficult to keep its trap supplied with water during a dry time, and, if not so trapped, the chamber-windows may receive the air from the drains or sewers through the upper end of the leader or through leaky joints. It is better to connect the rain-water leaders with the drain over the main house-drain trap, just outside the house, where the rain-water can pour into a tunnel in the manhole-chamber, by which access is had to this trap, and without a closed connection.

A good air-draught from under the seat of a water-closet is a desirable thing, but not so essential to health as many others. It is better to remove disagreeable odors directly at their source than to suffer a whole room to be tainted by them, and trust to any general ventilation of the room, the proper operation of which would require one hundred times as much air to be removed as is required for the special purpose referred to.

A bidet is a small bath-tub used in bathing parts of the body when a complete bath is not wanted.

DEPTH OF FOUNDATIONS TO PREVENT DAMPNESS OF SITE.

Q. How DEEP below foundations should drains be laid around a building to prevent dampness of site?

A. At least two feet below the foundation-walls.

WHERE TO PLACE A TANK TO GET GOOD DISCHARGE AT FAUCET.

Q. How LITTLE difference in elevation can exist between the top of cold-water tank and hot-water faucet and maintain a good delivery at said faucet, the two being in the same room and connected through a hot-water boiler in story below?

A. This depends altogether on what is meant by a "good delivery." The discharge depends entirely on the difference of level between the cold water in the tank and the faucet. If your pipe is twenty feet long, and you want to draw two gallons a minute, your faucet must be about twenty-seven inches lower than the water, but if you want four gallons a minute it must be about seven feet lower.

SELF-ACTING WATER-CLOSETS.

Q. WILL you be kind enough to help a young man who is puzzled? I would like to find out how to rig up a self-acting water-closet, one that will flush when the door is opened. I do not understand how the cranks and valves are arranged.

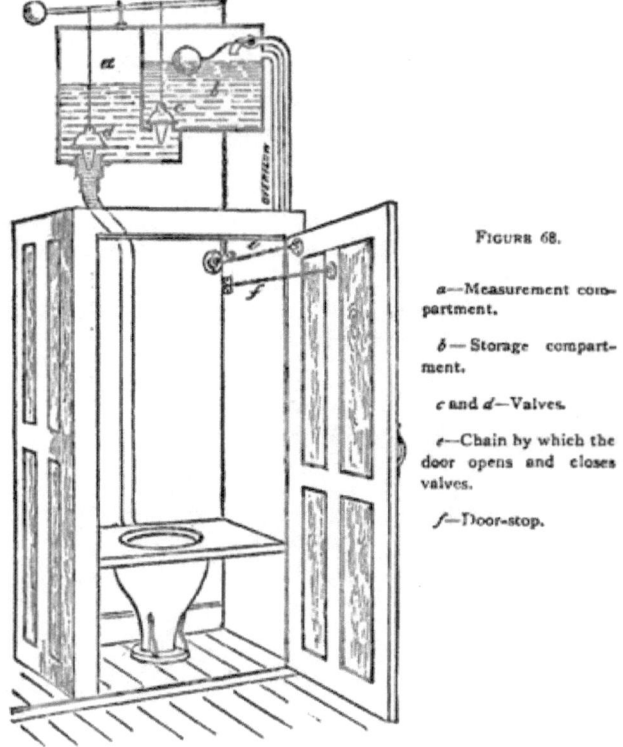

FIGURE 68.

a—Measurement compartment.

b—Storage compartment.

c and *d*—Valves.

e—Chain by which the door opens and closes valves.

f—Door-stop.

A. The above sketch will give you an idea of how to arrange a chain to work the valves in a cistern to flush a water-closet. This shows a cistern directly over a water-closet, but when it must be located elsewhere, it can be made to work by using more pulleys. The chain *f* is to act as a door-stop, in order to prevent opening the door so wide as to break the chain *e*. It will be noticed that we have, for the purpose of illustration, selected the kind of waste-preventing cistern approved by the New York Board of Public Works. The door should have a spring on it to keep it closed.

In such situations a waste-preventing cistern is desirable, so that if the door is held open, only a limited amount can be drawn off.

WIND DISTURBING SEAL OF TRAP.

Q. Some time ago I had the soil-pipe of my house ventilated through the roof, capped with an ordinary cowl, and the old filthy pan-closet removed.

I put in place of it an improved form of hopper-closet of all-earthenware, and had the bath and bowl wastes enter soil-pipe below closet. It is now free from smell and works perfectly, except that during heavy winds I notice that the water in closet is violently agitated and almost emptied, so as to almost break the seal of trap.

Thinking the air from sewer or soil-pipe was being forced into the house, I sponged out enough water to almost unseal the trap, and was surprised to find a strong suction into soil-pipe from the apartment.

I should like to know the cause of it, and have sketched the position of my fixtures, which are all in the rear of house and discharge into a sewer in front street about 80 feet from vertical soil-pipe, with trap outside of house, as my plumber says, but without any inlet for fresh air.

If there is a trap in drain without an air-vent, I presume the wind blowing across the cowl produces a vacuum in soil-pipe, and consequently trap of the closet is partially syphoned out ; but if there is no trap in the drain, how could the wind blowing into the sewer produce similar result when the soil-pipe is open on roof, 12 or 15 feet above closet, as I am told by one party must be the cause ? Could a downward draught through soil-pipe and into sewer produce such action on water-closet, and if such was the case would it not prove that there was no trap in drain? My house is located on a hill, where the wind has full sweep in one direction, and the sewer is some 15 feet deep in street. There are perforated manholes on the sewer every few hundred feet.

A. The most simple way to account for the disturbance of the water in the closet-trap is by supposing the plumber's statement to be correct—viz., that there is a trap on the main drain with no fresh-air inlet, and that the wind blowing across the cowl on the top of the house creates a partial vacuum in the soil-pipe. This is probably the state of the case.

HOW TO DRAW WATER FROM A DEEP WELL.

Q. Can a pump be got that is workable by one man to draw water from a well 100 feet deep ; and, if not, what is the greatest depth such a pump will draw, and where obtained ?

A. The pump-bucket must not be more than 20 to 25 feet above the water, in order that the pump may draw. A pump can be made with the foot-valve and bucket 80 feet below the surface, but it would take a pretty powerful man to work it, for at every stroke he would have to lift a column of water 80 feet high of the diameter of the pump-bore.

CAUSE OF SMELL OF WELL-WATER.

Q. PLEASE explain to me the cause of water smelling bad for two or three months at a time, which is pumped from a cistern through galvanized-iron gas-pipe previous to showing the bad odor? The water seemed perfectly pure, and it then became good again—that is, no smell was noticed. It bothers some of the oldest pump men that have worked for me. Please explain also how I can stop the noise caused when the waste-water is running from my bath-tub. I send a sketch, showing their location and down-stairs connections with my pipe. My stand is in the corner, and tub-waste connects with it on a line of the floor; down stairs a stand-waste connects with same, which empties in front gutter.

A. If water smells badly it is contaminated. An analysis might reveal in what manner. The sketch sent by our correspondent is rather indefinite. The size of the waste-pipes is not given. The noise referred to in all probability is caused by the waste-pipe being of smaller diameter than the outlet of the bath, or there may be traps in the waste-pipe which retard the flow and produce a gurgling noise. If the waste-pipe is of sufficient size so that it cannot be charged, and there are no traps or depressions in it, there will be no noise to cause annoyance.

ABSORPTION OF LIGHT BY GAS-GLOBES.

Q. I WAS reading the other day of the different globes for gas-fixtures and their loss of diffusion, and it stated as follows: A plain glass globe they say loses 12 per cent., a ground glass globe 40 per cent., and an opal porcelain glass globe 60 per cent. Please tell me if you think this is correct. The reason I ask for this explanation is, that I took four ground globes out of a parlor; the cause of so doing was, they did not give enough light, and I substituted four opal globes, and two of these lighted gives more light than the three of the ground globes, and the workings of the opal globes does not conform with opaque rules. Please tell me your opinion of the matter.

A. The amount of light absorbed by glass globes varies somewhat according to the nature of the glass. A plain glass globe absorbs from 10 to 15 per cent.; ground glass from 25 to 40 per cent., and opal, from 35 to 60 per cent. Determinations recently made with the globes now in common use, having large openings at the bottom and top, show that 26 per cent. of the light is absorbed by ground glass, and 55 per cent. by opal glass. One advantage of globes with large openings at the bottom is that some of the light escapes into the room through the opening, and if these globes were substituted for the old-fashioned ones

MISCELLANEOUS. 119

with small openings, considerable would be gained. Aside from this, globes having small openings cause a flickering and smoky flame, by producing strong currents of air through the globe.

DEFECTIVE DRAINAGE.

Q. ENCLOSED please find diagram of our office, with drainage arrangements, which are defective to the extent that at times we are almost driven from the building on account of foul gases. Any suggestion you can make will be thankfully received and acted upon. I may say we have a bountiful supply of water for the water-closet.

A. From the sketch sent it looks as though your water-closet trap syphoned itself out whenever used, the vent to protect it being placed

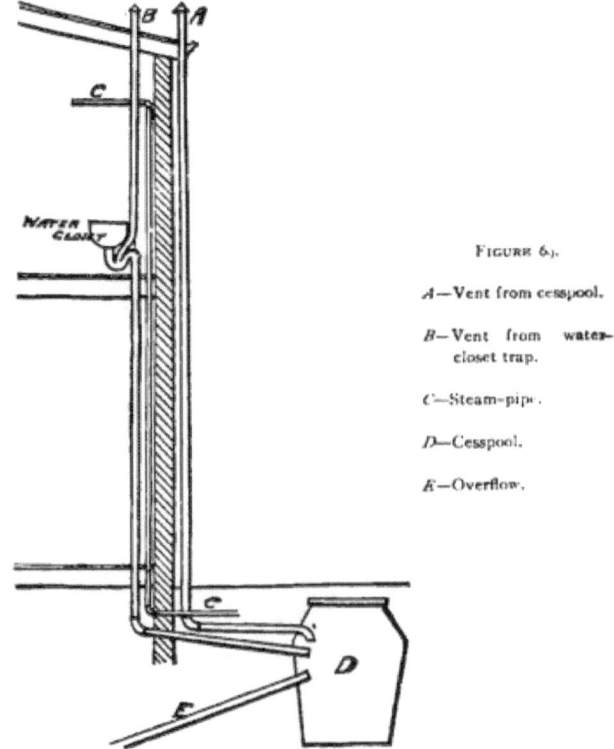

FIGURE 6).

A—Vent from cesspool.

B—Vent from water-closet trap.

C—Steam-pipe.

D—Cesspool.

E—Overflow.

inside the seal instead of outside. If this is so, the gases from your cesspool would naturally be drawn into the warm interior of your house, rather than up the vent-pipe on the outside, especially at this time of the year.

FITTING BASINS TO MARBLE SLABS.

Q. WILL you explain the usual method adopted in New York to fit a basin to marble slabs?

A. The following, from the articles by "Sanitas" on "Plumbing Practice," in Volume IV. of the *Sanitary Engineer*, gives the information:

"The practice in this city (New York), and I believe in many parts of this country, is to fasten the bowl to the slab by what are called basin-clamps. (See Figure 70.)

Figure 71 shows the underside of the slab, which contains three holes, into which the heads of the screws are inserted and molten lead poured in, which, on cooling, holds the bolt firmly, as will be seen by noticing the shape of the hole in Figure 72.

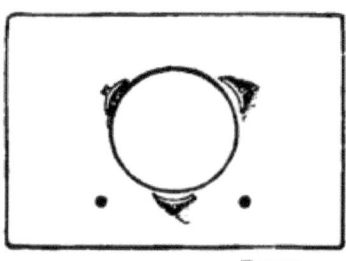

FIGURE 71.

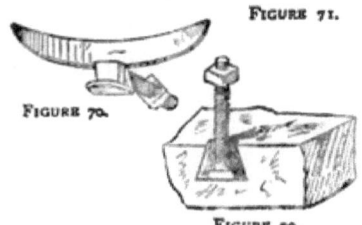

FIGURE 70.

FIGURE 72.

"The edges of the bowl are held tightly to the slab by screwing up the nut, so that the clamp is held securely in its place. I should mention here that the edges of the earthenware basins are not perfectly true and level, and in all properly-executed work these edges should be rubbed down smooth and even. The bowls are then set in plaster of Paris, which is mixed to about the consistency of molasses, and poured around the underside of the slab, adhering about the portion against which the edges of the basin are to rest. When properly done this makes a neat and water-tight joint.

"In some parts of the country the old practice of setting basins on a wooden shelf or top is still observed, notably in and around Boston.

"The carpenter is required to construct a frame-work, into which a hole is cut for the bowl to set in. The edges of this wood-work are countersunk to receive the flange of the basin, plaster is spread over the flange of the bowl, and the marble slab is set in place. When the frames are well made and perfectly plumb, this arrangement does very well, until the wood begins to decay, when the basin will be apt to settle, and seams will be opened between the edges of the bowl and the slab, through which the spatterings of water will run and hasten the decay of the wood-work."

INTERMEDIATE TANKS FOR THE WATER-SUPPLY OF HIGH BUILDINGS.

THE extraordinary height of many of our office buildings and apartment-houses is such that water forced to a tank at or near the roof and distributed downward has a pressure altogether too great for many of our ordinary plumbing fixtures and for lead pipe of usual thickness.

In the case of the Tribune Building in this city, the height water is pumped is about 170 feet, which to distribute backward again would bring on a fixture in the basement or cellar a pressure of from 70 to 75 pounds per square inch—in itself too much for fixtures, but that, when taken in connection with the "water-hammer," which will be likely to occur, would be almost sure to destroy the strongest made valves, etc.

To obviate this, in the above-mentioned building, Edward E. Raht, the architect, provided an intermediate tank *t* and placed it midway between the floors on which water-closet and bowl fixtures are used. The plumber who did the work was Alexander Orr, of New York. The cisterns for the water-closets on the fifth floor and all fixtures above them take water from the upper house-tanks (H T), while the wash-bowls on the same floor and all fixtures below them take their supply from the intermediate tank.

The diagram shows the arrangement of the tank-pipes and system generally. The pipe from the Croton main connects with the meter M,

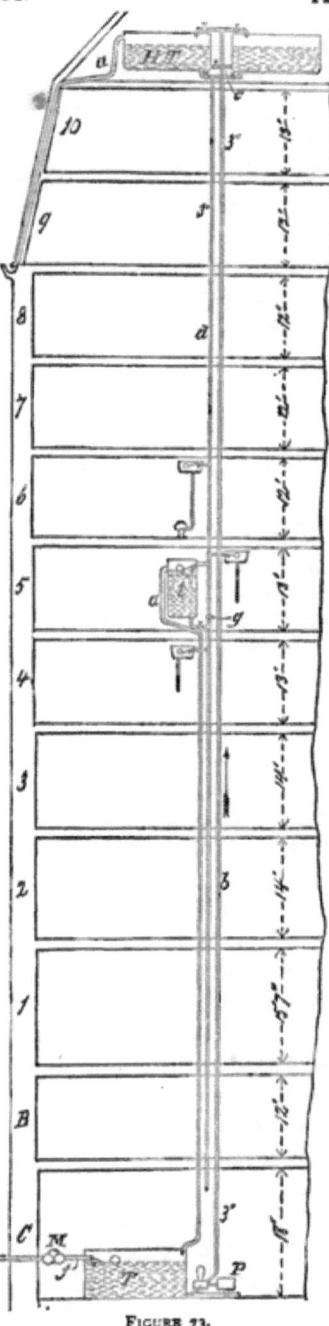

FIGURE 73.

and the water is regulated into the lower tank (T) by a ball-cock; this tank is below the sewer-level and has no overflow. From the receiving-tank the steam-pump (P) elevates the water to the upper house-tanks. These tanks overflow to the eaves-troughs and have no direct communication with the sewers. Tank t takes its supply from the upper tanks and is regulated by a ball-cock; it is also furnished with an overflow-pipe a, whose lower end is carried to the receiving-tank. This is to prevent loss of water should the ball-cock fail. It also acts as a tell-tale. Two house-tanks are used, with a system of change-off valves and an equalizing-pipe. All the tanks are of wrought-iron.

HOW TO CONSTRUCT A FILTERING-CISTERN.

Q. WILL you please favor me with the most approved plan for constructing a filtering-cistern, and dimensions therefor, for a family of five or six persons? The owner of the dwelling desires to use rain collected from the roof of the house for drinking purposes, in preference to that supplied by the city.

A. This was answered in a former issue by Mr. S. F. Copley, of Stapleton, S. I., as follows:

"AUTOMATIC CISTERN-FILTERS.

"Wherever rain-water is the main-supply for family use, some means of cutting off decaying dirt from the roof, so as not to foul the cistern, should be the first consideration, that we may have water for use as pure as the rainfall, uncontaminated by rotting leaves, shingles, road-dust, etc., the amount of which is only known to those who have cleaned out a cistern or a filter after one or more years' use.

"There are many ways of doing this. The most simple and inexpensive I saw in use in Norfolk, Va. It consisted of a loose elbow-joint at the end of the leader, made to turn in or out of the cistern connecting-pipe (at ground line). The rule was to keep the cistern cut off from the roof, until the rain had washed it, and the gutters cleaned before letting the water in. At first thought this would seem all that could be desired; but, like all the rest of the cut-off systems, it is not only wasteful of water, but unpleasant to attend to, as it must always be done in the wet; and when water is scarce, few people would be willing to give so large a share out of every shower for washing their roof, etc., or go out in the rain, especially on a stormy night, to turn the pipe in.

"So the question was, How to have good water without loss or trouble? This was the problem I had to solve for myself two years ago, when I built the present filter, which has worked well ever since without the least loss or trouble; and, believing it a step in advance of anything of the kind, I send you the plan and section, in answer to one of your correspondents (I think Dr. J. S. Billings), who called attention to the great need of some '*automatic cut-off for a cistern.*' Its simple construction and working will be best understood by referring to the sketches. Figure 74 shows the plan and Figure 75 the section. The plan is like a long, square box (sunk in the ground), with a sloping bottom and a centre partition or trap, F, dividing it in two parts —the cut-off and a filterer.

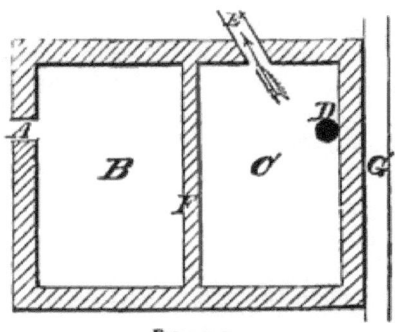

FIGURE 74.

The part C next the house in Figure 74 is the cut-off, and receives the water direct from the roof through the inlet-pipe D, while the other part, B, is filled with *clean-washed sand*, with a layer of gravel and stones at the bottom, as shown at I, Figure 75, which is the top of the sand, J being the gravel and K the stone. By referring to the section, Figure 75, it will be seen that the partition, or trap, F, is raised one inch from the flagstone bottom L, while the top is above the top of the overflow-pipe E, which is also shown on the plan, M (Figure 75) being the ground line, H the water line, and A the outlet to the cistern, so that *all the water that enters the cistern must pass under and up through the sand;* while any dirt that would sink is *kept away from trap and filter by the steep slope of the bottom* and collected at N. Also, anything that would float can be seen and removed, if not carried away by the overflow. While the water remaining in this part is not only of value for the garden, being tempered and at hand, but every

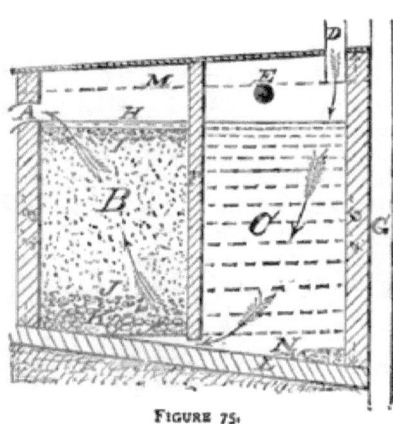

FIGURE 75.

pailful taken out is, in fact, washing the filter by just that amount of clean water being drawn downward through the sand, washing any settlement back into the cut-off, which, if emptied and cleaned out, by throwing clean water in the filter, a thorough inspection can be had without removing or renewing the sand. This inspection and cleaning costs but little labor, as there is nothing to decay, and so foul the water, in its construction.

"For convenience and economy of construction, materials were chosen that are the most easily obtained in any village, and that would only require rough labor to build up. The bottom is formed of one flagstone, four inches thick, five feet long by four feet broad, set with a slope to the house of six inches. On this the four walls are built, four inches thick, and up to just above the ground, all laid in cement, and well coated with Portland cement on both sides (the inside floated smooth). The trap (partition) is also formed of a flagstone (in one piece), two and one-half inches thick by four feet broad and four feet high, built in the side walls and raised up one inch from the bottom. The overflow and cistern outlet-pipes are of vitrified and glazed stoneware, built in the walls, with their openings protected with wire cages against insects, while the lid is formed of matched floor-boards, made light, to be easily removed for inspection, etc.

"The filter holds five and one-half barrels of sand, etc., which is washed clean before putting in, placing the stones on bottom, then the gravel—about half a barrel of each. It costs complete about $16."

Q. The cistern-filter represented in you issue of April 1, 1881, is just what I have been looking for, and I think will meet the requirements of those living in the country who depend upon cistern-water. Would it not be better to make the pipes of cast-iron, rather than of vitrified stoneware—as the former would be less likely to crack or break if they should happen to freeze? How would it do to put a faucet or valve near the bottom of reservoir C, and connect it with a pipe so that the filter could be emptied by allowing water to soak away into the ground?

A. We referred the above to Mr. F. S. Copley, who designed the filter in question, and he sends this reply:

"I do not think iron would be as good as stoneware, as the pipes are empty. The iron would rust and discolor the water, and spoil it for laundry use; and last winter's frosts have not broken or cracked mine, although in wet ground. As to putting a valve or faucet in the bottom of cut-off, I think the dirt (road-dust alone) would choke and fill the pipe up in a season, to say nothing of the loss of so much *tempered water*, which every florist too well knows the value of to waste, especially when enriched with road-dust, etc."

OBJECTIONS TO RUNNING VENTILATING-PIPE INTO CHIMNEY-FLUE.

Q. AGAIN I will trouble you in regard to a question. I am about to fit a water-closet up in a bath-room, and I want to run the 4-inch pipe to the roof and put a cap on it, but the owner wants it run into the chimney, which is alongside of the closet. I tell him it will not be as good a job as if taken through the roof, but he differs with me. Now, from what I have read, the chimney-flues are condemned in general. Please tell me who is right.

P. S.—The container will be ventilated.

A. We repeat an opinion often given. The soil-pipe should be taken through the roof, not run into the chimney-flue. You cannot depend on having an up-draught in the flue all the time. It is difficult to make a joint where you run a soil-pipe into the chimney which will keep tight, and the soot is liable to choke up the end of your ventilating-pipe.

SIZE OF WATER-SUPPLY PIPE FOR DWELLING-HOUSE.

Q. How LARGE water-pipes ought I to have in a house where there are six wash-basins, two water-closets and baths, with kitchen-sinks, laundry-tubs, etc.? Will the size of hot and cold water pipes be the same?

A. That depends somewhat on the pressure in your street-mains. Assuming it to be forty pounds per square inch, we should say one inch from street to near the boiler, three-quarters of an inch from that to each bath-tub, with ½-inch branches to each water-closet cistern, basin-cock, and ⅝-inch branches to sinks and wash-tubs. All these dimensions might be reduced one size if the money saved thereby was of more consideration than the extra time required for drawing the water through smaller pipes.

FAULTY PLAN OF A CESSPOOL.

Q. WHAT do you think of the following arrangement, to be used as a cesspool where there is a city water-supply but no sewer?

The outer walls to be laid in hydraulic-cement; the central partition to be of brick laid in common mortar, so as to act as a filter; the outlet on the other side of this partition to run the liquid to a pile of loose stones, where it will soak into the soil. Of course, the organic germs will still remain in the liquid after it leaves the cesspool, but will there be enough to do any harm in a place where the water-supply is obtained from the city and the soil is a light sand? The object in this is to save the expense of a cesspool large enough to hold both the solid and liquid waste of the house for any length of time. The lot will be about 140 feet deep in the rear of the house. A is the inlet from house, B vent, C outlet, and D D apartments separated by a brick wall.

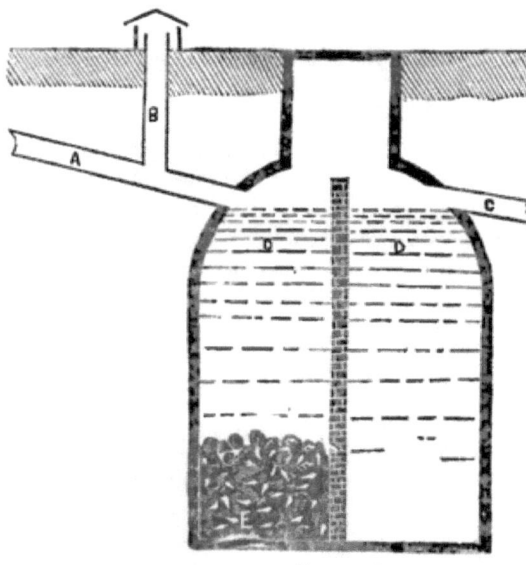

FIGURE 76.

A. This arrangement will not act as intended. First, the partition—which is meant to act as a filter—will have its pores filled tight with solid matter in a few days, and cease to soak water. The contents of the inlet side will then rise and pour over the top of the partition.

If kitchen-sink drainage is discharged into this receptacle, the grease from dish-washing would soon collect as a scum on the surface and choke the outlet-pipe. The apparatus would act very well as a grease-interceptor if it is close to the house (not otherwise), by making one or more holes in the partition about half way down, by taking out a brick, and attaching a T-branch to the outlet-pipe, so it may take water from a point a foot below the surface, and avoid taking in the floating grease.

As to allowing the tank to overflow into a pile of stones, that will make a nuisance at this point and pollute the soil. The proper method is to distribute the contents of the tank on to the surface of the soil, by dipping it out when filled, or by irrigation-pipes under the surface. It is a mistake to suppose that the fluids of house-drainage are less harmful than the solids so-called. The latter all become fluid or gaseous in a very short time, and do not *settle* to the bottom, as supposed. The only sediment found in such places is composed of the sand used in scouring floors, and such particles of dirt as may adhere to it.

CONNECTING REFRIGERATOR-WASTES WITH DRAINS.

Q. I HAVE frequently read your warnings about connecting refrigerator-wastes to the drain, so I had mine arranged as shown by the accompanying sketch, which may interest some of your readers and call out suggestions as to how it can be improved.

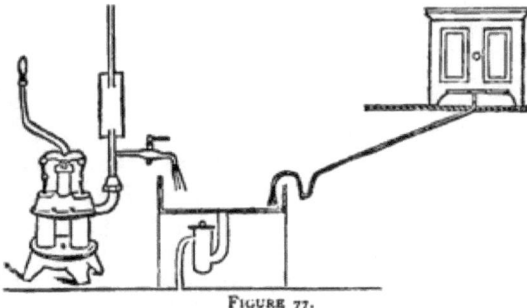

A. The arrangement seems a very good one. If the trap was placed close to the refrigerator it might prevent the ice melting so rapidly.

FIGURE 77.

DISPOSING OF REFRIGERATOR-WASTES.

Q. IN your issue of January 12, 1882, we notice an article from "Architect," regarding the draining of refrigerators, and your offer to print methods adopted by others of your readers. We herewith hand you a sketch of the method we use in draining our refrigerators where a connection is made with the drain of the house. In this manner we trap the pipe at A, when the water comes from the refrigerator, by using a syphon. From this the water drops into drippan B, which is again trapped (by a syphon, C); thence the water drips into another drip-

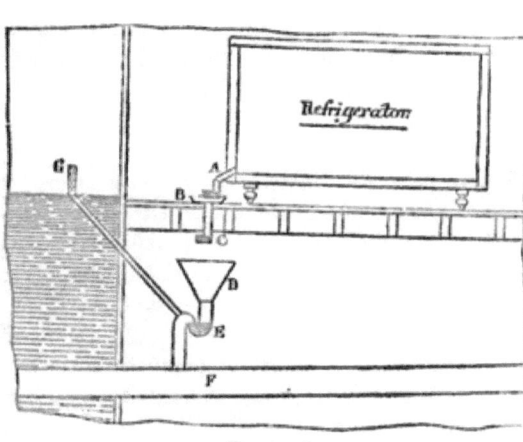

FIGURE 78.

pan D, which is also trapped at E. This being a confined trap, we ventilate the trap through pipe with opening out of doors at G. This method we consider perfectly safe, but would be exceedingly obliged for your valuable opinion of it.

A. This method of disconnecting the refrigerator-waste from the drain, and at the same time preventing the ascent of cellar-air into the floor above and into the refrigerator, is a good one, provided some certain means are taken to maintain the seal in the trap E, when ice is not melting, as in winter. We fear the average servant cannot be depended on to always attend to this. If, therefore, the drip from the lower so-called syphon C were into a sink having some other source of supply than the melting ice, the plan would be improved.

PUMPING AIR FROM WATER-CLOSET INTO TEA-KETTLE AS RESULT OF DIRECT SUPPLY TO WATER-CLOSETS.

Q. I NOW live in a house in which the plumbing was finished last July and passed by the Board of Health Inspector. On the second floor is a valve pan-closet. This valve is supplied direct from the rising main to the pump that is intended to pump water into the tanks and over sinks on each floor above. I have seen the pump upstairs discharge water over the sink when the water-closet below was in use, that smelled like the contents of the water-closet. Of course, the closet happened to be in use at the moment, and the valve being open the suction from the pump above drew the foul air from the closet-bowl so that the water was impregnated with it. I thought it was against the law to connect any more closets to drinking-water mains. How is this?

A. The editorial comment on this was as follows: "It is probable that the work in this house was begun before the plumbing law went into operation, which was about October, 1881. We have taken the trouble, however, to have a sketch prepared, so that all our readers can fully realize the character of the risks incurred when valves on water-closets are supplied by branches from the main water-supply from which water for drinking and cooking is drawn. Figure 79 fully illustrates the nasty practice, and its very probable consequences, yet water-closets are fitted up in this way in great numbers of houses in this city, and aside from the wastefulness of water attendant on this method, the risks to health which have been demonstrated over and over again are such as should compel our health authorities to institute a systematic inspection of all the houses in this city, and they should, as rapidly as possible, require the disconnection of all direct supply to water-closets, and the abandonment of the filthy practice that ignorance and cupidity has made so prevalent."

MISCELLANEOUS.

FIGURE 79.

DANGER IN CONNECTING TANK-OVERFLOWS WITH SOIL-PIPES.

Q. I find it is very common to connect overflows from tanks with soil-pipes and leaders, putting a trap at some point, which, however, has no means of being kept supplied with water, as the overflow is usually above the tell-tale and hence this trap dries out. Will it suffice to arrange a small pipe from the supply-pipe from pump to connect with the trap and keep it fed at all times, or how would you arrange it?

A. Disconnect the overflow-pipe from the soil-pipe entirely. Under no circumstances should they be so connected.

ARRANGEMENT OF SAFE-WASTES.

The arrangement shown in Figure 80 was carried out by Mr. Alexander Orr, plumber, in the residence of Mr. Henry G. Marquand, New York City.

Figure 80.

It is a view in the cellar where the "safe-wastes" are brought together over a sink. The pipes *f* are the safe-waste pipes from the principal divisions of the house. At their ends over the sink they are furnished with "swing" check-valves to prevent a current of air from the cellar passing up them. The sink is galvanized, and is let into the wall at the end and back, and leaded so as to dispense with a leg at the outer corner. The arrangement of the trap and vent (*b*) are shown, as well as the main water-pipe (C), with its branch (*d*), and part of the house-drain, *a*.

Figure 81 is the method employed in the residence of Mr. W. H. Vanderbilt, in New York City, by Mr. Robert Ennever, the plumber.

The safe-waste box is illustrated in the engraving. These are placed on the partition-walls of the basement — generally in the hall, but sometimes in storage closets — near the ceiling. At *a* is a ground coupling-valve to prevent odors from the basement rising to the rooms from which the pipes come when there is no water in the trap. There is a separate pipe from every safe, though several pipes sometimes come to one box, and the origin of each is marked on a plate on the box below

FIGURE 81.

it. From the box the waste, should there ever be more than enough to fill the trap, would escape through *b*, a pipe running down through the floor to the broken stone underlying the concrete foundation, and is provided in connection with the underdrainage.

THE KIND OF MEN WHO DO NOT LIKE THE "SANITARY ENGINEER."

I HAVE read your paper since its first issue and take a great deal of interest in its contents. I have endeavored to get you some subscribers from among the plumbers here in Bridgeport, but find they don't readily take hold, there being but two or three who are really to be trusted with a piece of work.

In your issue of November 1, 1879, the article on plumbers doing crooked work takes the right view of the matter, and all should be punished who deserve it ; and if a plumber is not, who does a piece of work that deals a death-blow to many an innocent person, then we should like to know what *is* criminal, and who *should be* punished ?

It is only a few months ago that a plumber did some work with water-closets, sink, and wash-basin, without so much as a trap under any of them, and all wastes were carried to drain through 4-inch galvanized sheet-iron, soldered together, although the specifications called for traps and cast-iron soil-pipe and ventilation, but the owner was the superintendent, and he allowed the work to be done in this crooked manner ; but he had to get another plumber in a month, and rip it out and have it done over again. It would have paid him to have employed his architect to do the superintending.

This same plumber only last week repeated nearly the same thing in two tenement-houses, using for wastes sheet galvanized-iron, and not carrying up to attic and connecting with flue for ventilation. The latter he thought entirely unnecessary, although it was specified, and he had agreed to do it so ; but as there was an architect superintending it, it was pulled out immediately, though some of it was covered in the walls. The plumber was politely requested to make it right just as quick as he could—and he did it. The sooner all such "skin" plumbers as this are out of the business, I should think, it would be better for the community at large ; but perhaps the employment of such is due to the sub-contract system, which is a very great evil where good mechanics and good work could be had by owners of buildings if they would but employ them direct, and not leave their work to a general contractor.

Diphtheria and scarlet fever have had their day. Only last summer a gentleman bought a house, went to reside in it, and before he had been there long he lost his children, and nearly his wife, by scarlet fever, and on examination of the plumbing it was found to be without traps and emptying into a drain running under five or six other houses, all dropping down into the same drain. This was a speculative builder's work, and, of course, what could be expected from one without principle, who does it merely for gain?

What should be the penalty that should be inflicted on parties who do such scamping, and thereby commit murder, or worse ? And is there not some legislation necessary on this point ?"

It is not surprising that the so-called "plumbers" described by our correspondent don't take readily to our paper. When the community at large are more familiar with its columns, it will not be so easy for such fellows to get a chance to poison some family. There are good men in the business in Bridgeport, and architects should insist that no others should be allowed to work under them, for no architect, however vigilant, can secure good work from a botch or safe work from a knave. If sickness or death follow from "scamped" plumbing, the man who did the work is largely to blame, and should be made to suffer the consequences.

WHAT IS REASONABLE PLUMBERS' PROFIT.

Q. I was told that in some of the earlier issues of the *Sanitary Engineer* there was an article explaining the percentage a plumber should get on the cost of materials in order to make a fair profit, and that in one case it was of use in satisfying a customer that the bill was a fair one that he considered exorbitant. Will you refer me to it?

A. It appeared in the *Sanitary Engineer* of February 18, 1878, as follows: "In our last issue we stated under this title that the merchant or banker whose annual transactions are by the million naturally looks upon a gross profit of 30 or 40 per cent. on the part of a plumber as something monstrous, yet on a moment's reflection any fair-minded man will admit that the margin of profit should be governed entirely by the nature of the business, the amount possible to do safely in a year, and the proportion of expense in doing the business to the amount done. To illustrate: In this city there are about nine hundred so-called plumbers, besides a large number of idle journeymen ready to take any job that offers. The average amount of business done by each firm is not over $10,000 annually, including contract work for builders, jobbing, and days' work. As a rule, contract work pays little or no profit to men who do the work properly and pay for the labor and materials, and it is only taken by good parties to keep extra journeymen employed. Allowing a man to do an annual business of even $20,000, what gross profit should he require to pay his business expenses and have left a living and something to lay by for a rainy day? for every man hopes to make something besides shelter, food, and clothing.

EXPENSES AND LOSSES.

Rent of store, which must be in location accessible to customers who live in best parts of the city	$1,000
Book-keeper and clerk to attend store while proprietor is giving personal attention to work	800
Interest on capital, and sundry expenses doing business, collector, etc.	500
Keep of horse, wagon, and boy for driver	500
Bad debts in jobbing business, not counting possible losses through working for speculating builders	500
	$3,300

"If these figures are correct, and we believe they are, we contend that 30 per cent. average gross profit is not exorbitant, but entirely legitimate. Merchants know that different articles pay varying degrees of profit, and as certain materials used by the plumber are limited to 5 and 10 per cent. margins, others must pay more to make up the average. For instance, the proportion between the different rates of profit may be thus represented in tabular form :

```
$5,000 @ 10%..................................... $500
 6,000 @ 25%.....................................  1,500
 5,000 @ 40%.....................................  2,000
 4,000 @ 50%.....................................  2,000
                                                  ------
        Yielding gross profit....................$6,000
        Deduct expenses..........................  3,300
                                                  ------
        Net profit...............................$2,700
```

"Few plumbers in this city make $2,700 net annually, notwithstanding the hue and cry made about exorbitant profits, and where it has been made we contend it is not too much, considering the hazards of business, for a man to make, who has the intelligence and capability that would render it safe to employ him to attend to such important matters as house-plumbing. It is, however, too much to pay ignorant men to do imperfect work, and the public should not employ the latter class and thus curtail the business of the former, making it necessary to obtain an even greater margin on a smaller business.

"In this article it is not proposed to insist that any one should pay these profits, but only to show that what in some branches of trade might be exorbitant is in this business only reasonable, legitimate, and necessary, even considering the matter simply from a mercantile standpoint."

HOT WATER CIRCULATION IN BUILDINGS.

BATH BOILERS.

THE following chapter on "Bath Boilers" is taken from the series of articles entitled "Plumbing Practice," by "Sanitas," that appeared in the fourth and fifth volumes of the *Sanitary Engineer*.

WITH the average working plumber there is no feature of his trade of such interest as the fitting up of a hot-water boiler, under the varying conditions of water-supply in the United States and the demands for domestic consumption of hot water, the latter being much greater in this country than elsewhere.

So little is understood of the theory of hot-water circulation by many who essay to arrange the apparatus for it, that we must attribute to that fact the greater portion of the defects complained of by householders generally.

It is not my purpose to dwell on the physics of the subject, as that has been extensively referred to in the pages of the *Sanitary Engineer* during the past three years, but I shall briefly allude to some of the various means employed abroad to secure hot water for domestic purposes, and compare them with the practice adopted in the leading cities in this country. I am of the opinion that, for our needs and conditions, our best practice is cheaper, more effective, and quite as free from danger as any other that I am acquainted with. Before illustrating the various hot-water apparatus, it may be of interest to some readers of the *Sanitary Engineer* to have briefly pointed out the cause of the most common sources of complaint and the course to be pursued in dealing with the difficulty.

I shall confine these remarks mainly to the cases of hot-water boilers supplied directly from the street-mains, which is the custom in most cities in this country, and which is liable to more mishaps and casualties than when supplied from tanks, as is the practice in Boston, the reasons for which will appear in the course of these articles.

The principal complaint the householder has to make is that of a rumbling or pounding noise in the boiler. The most common mishaps are the collapsing of a boiler or the bursting of a water-back in the winter time after the range fire has been rebuilt, and when the water in the water-back or connecting-pipes is frozen.

The rumbling or pounding noise, most heard on ironing days, when a hot fire is kept in the range and not much hot water is used, is occasioned by steam being generated in the water-back, which, when it meets with water cold enough to condense it, produces a vacuum. The water coming together again to fill this void space causes the concussion, which makes this noise. The generation of steam is also often due to the fact that the water-back has too much heating-surface for the capacity of the boiler and the domestic requirements for hot water.

To stop this noise and get rid of the steam, it is the custom to open the hot-water faucet. This will accomplish it; but if the hot-water faucet is opened suddenly there is danger of the boiler collapsing if it be a copper one, for the reason that the cold water, suddenly returning to fill the space occupied by the steam, condenses the steam instantly and produces the vacuum, which results in the collapse of the boiler. It is safer to open the hot-water faucet very slowly and thus prevent the sudden condensation of the steam. The risk of collapse is also greater in a city where the water-pressure is very light, as in New York, for the steam meets with so little resistance, by reason of want of pressure, that it more readily forms and more easily forces the water out of the boiler and through the pipes back to the street-main.

The other danger alluded to, and one that this winter has several times been experienced, is the bursting of the water-back, and the consequent demolition of the range. This is solely due to ignorance or carelessness. If a range fire is let down on a cold night, and the water in the water-back or in the connecting-pipes between it and the boiler becomes frozen, so that circulation is impeded, the building of a fire in the range under such circumstances is almost certain to cause an explosion, which might prove fatal to life as well as disastrous to property, for it is manifest that as soon as the water-back becomes heated steam is generated, and if it is confined, and not permitted to circulate, something has to give way, and an explosion is the result. The same thing might occur if both the hot and cold water pipes become frozen. Householders should therefore see to it that during cold weather a fire is kept in the range, so that the freezing up might not occur. If for any reason it is necessary to let the fire out for any period, care should be taken to empty the boiler, to uncouple it from the water-back, and to *blow out all the water that may be in the water-back*, using a plumber's force-pump for the purpose.

Explosions have been known to occur because so-called plumbers have disconnected the boiler for repairs and forgotten to blow the water out of the water-back, which afterward became frozen, and then, when connecting it again, neglected to ascertain whether the means of circulation were impeded or not.

In considering the various styles of hot-water bath-boilers in use, I will illustrate first a form frequently seen on the Continent of Europe. It is shown in Figure 82.

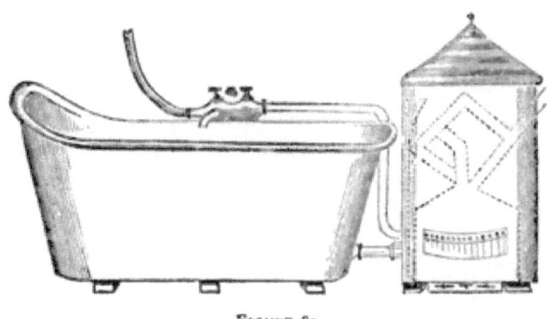

FIGURE 82.

This consists of a cylinder set over a gas-stove. This reservoir holds about enough hot water for one bath. The cold-water supply from the cistern is connected to it, while another pipe conveys the heated water from it to the faucet over the bath-tub. The gas is lit under this reservoir when a person desires to bathe, and in a few minutes the water is sufficiently heated to satisfy the wants of people who have no conception of a more expeditious method.

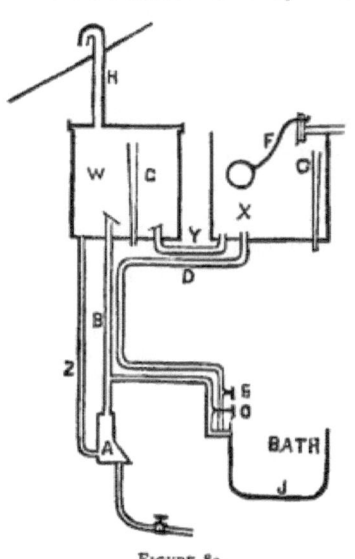

FIGURE 83.

Figure 83 (which is reproduced from Buchan's "Plumbing") shows a plan formerly in vogue in Great Britain, which, as will be seen, consists of two tanks communicating with each other. X is the cold-water cistern and W is the hot-water cistern. The water reaches the latter through the pipe Y, on which is a light copper flap, which can be lifted by the pressure of the incoming cold water, but which prevents the return of the hot water. Z is the cold-water pipe to the boiler A, while B is the pipe that takes the heated water from A to the hot cistern W. In the sketch this cistern has a cover, with the pipe H, to permit the escape of steam. When they are not covered the steam is an annoyance in the room in which they are placed, and the tanks soon collect dirt, and require frequent cleaning out. It will be noticed that what is here called a boiler (A) is substantially like what we call a water-back.

Of late years the fitting up of hot-water apparatus in England has been gone into more elaborately, and in some respects is carried out essentially the same as it is done in Boston, at least so far as to have tanks or cold-water cisterns to supply their boilers. The latter seems to be a compromise between our water-back and the back-log boilers used in Philadelphia. Figures 84 and 84A show two forms of boilers. The latter is termed a "saddle-boiler," and is made the shape of the arch of a stove front, and is fixed in the stove as shown in Figure 85. The dome-top bath-boiler shown in Figure 84 is set in brick-work, as shown in Figure 86. It will be seen that this requires a separate fire, which with us is avoided, as the ordinary kitchen-range performs the duty of heating a limited amount of water for domestic purposes, in addition to its other functions.

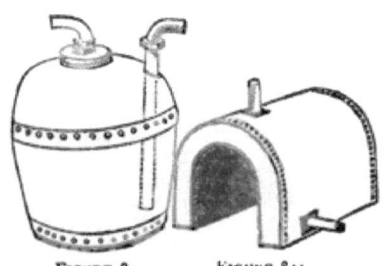

FIGURE 84.   FIGURE 84A.

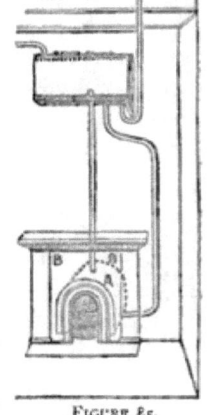

FIGURE 85.

By extracts taken from the English papers, I notice that the bursting of hot-water boilers, as they are there called, has been very frequent this winter, and in several cases has been attended with very serious results. This has doubtless called out the circular issued by the Manchester Steam-Users' Association, in which some good suggestions are made to householders.

In the newspaper accounts of these casualties I notice they always speak of the "boiler bursting," but I apprehend it is what we in America call a water-back. The unusual number of these occurrences this winter is doubtless due to the very cold weather and the want of proper provision to prevent the freezing of the hot and cold water pipes, which might be expected in a country where such extreme cold was an uncommon thing. To this fact and to the ignorance of servants in building a fire in a range before it was certain that there was no impediment to the circulation of water in the pipes, must be attributed these disasters, and in reading of them it is plain to be seen that the ignorant plumbers and householders are not all on this side of the Atlantic.

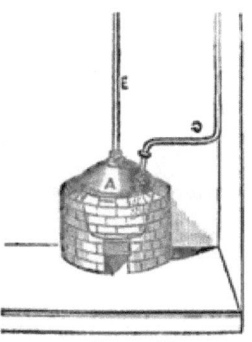

FIGURE 86.

Figure 87, which is copied from an English catalogue, shows a more complete arrangement than those illustrated before. In this there is a range to do the duty of heating the water. B is the boiler or water-back; C the hot cistern, which in this case is tightly closed. It is made usually of galvanized wrought-iron, and really answers the same purpose that our boilers do which we place alongside our ranges. D is the cold-water pipe from the hot cistern to the boiler or water-back; E, the return or hot-water pipe to the hot cistern, and F is the cold-water tank. G is the pipe to convey cold water from the tank to the hot cistern; I is the pipe to convey hot water to the bath-tub; K is a relief-pipe from the hot cistern to above and over the cold-water tank.

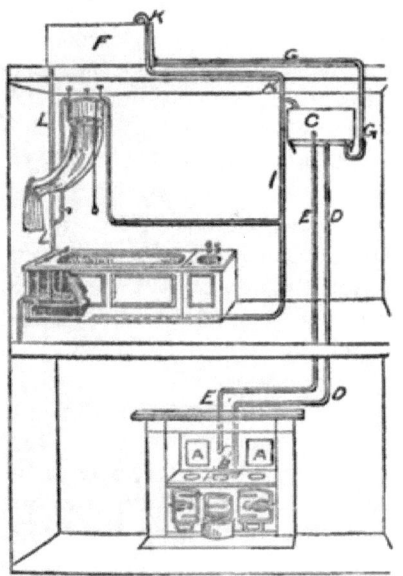

FIGURE 87.

The place selected for locating the hot cisterns depends on circumstances; it is usually placed above the points where it is proposed to draw hot water, but it is sometimes put in the bath-room at the end of the bath-tub, with a warming-closet or linen-warmer placed just above it, so that it can secure some of its waste heat for the purpose of warming towels, etc.

The editor of the *Sanitary Engineer* has received a description of the usual manner of fitting up hot-water boilers in Montreal, from Mr. J. W. Hughes, of that city, and I am pleased to give it herewith. Mr. Hughes says: "Having read the articles by "Sanitas" on the different styles of setting hot-water boilers, it occurred to me a short sketch on the prevailing method of fitting hot-water attachments for bath and other purposes here might be of interest to my American colaborers at the plumbing trade. Boilers, or, as you call them, copper reservoirs, are the exception; and the cistern plan is the rule, although I have fitted up several houses on the American plan.

"The greatest objection to the cistern plan is, that they are usually set immediately over the closet (pan water-closets generally used here), and as they are fed from the cistern supplying the water-closet, said cistern being uncovered, they are not at all right in a sanitary point of view, especially when, as is frequently the case, careless servants take hot water from the taps for cooking purposes.

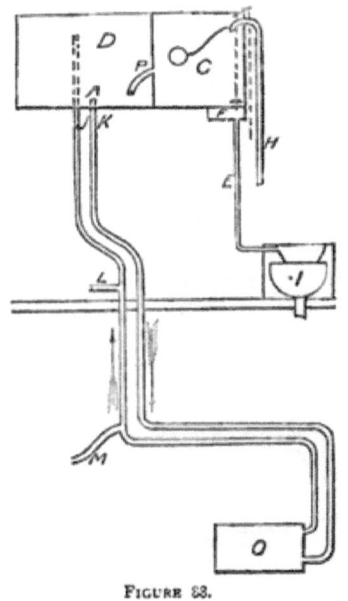

FIGURE 88.

"In the plan, Figure 88, A is the hot-water compartment, usually lined with 5-pound lead or light copper; B, the division between hot and cold cisterns; C, the cold cistern supplying the water-closet, and also hot-water cistern through pipe P, which is joined about the centre of division, the end in hot-water cistern being turned down to within one inch of bottom. A galvanized-iron cover is fitted tight on the hot-water cistern; E is the ball-cock on city service for cold water; F, service-box; G, service-pipe; H, cold-water supply-pipe; I, water-closet; J, hot-water circulating-pipe, standing up about eight inches from bottom of cistern and carried direct to ceiling over range or stove, to which it is connected from top outlet of heater by an iron pipe. From this pipe, J, are taken branches L M N, to supply hot water to bath, basin-sink, etc. K is the cold-water circulation taken direct from bottom of the cistern and joined to the heater, as shown. O is the heater in the range; the arrows show the direction of circulation-pipes J K, generally ⅝" 6-pound to the yard lead pipe. A good supply of hot water is obtained by this method.

"The sketch shows front of cistern removed; if the water boils or steam is made in large quantities, a 2-inch galvanized ventilator is run from the cover D."

Having described the various methods of fitting up hot-water boilers in England, and have also given a description of a plan in vogue in Canada, I shall now refer to the various methods adopted in the United States, and I will allude first to the "back-log boiler," which has been extensively used in Philadelphia and in other portions of Pennsylvania. It takes its name because, like the large log in the old-fashioned fire-place, it lies across the chimney-breast, behind the ovens, and across the flues.

The flame passes under and back of the boiler, and so up the flues. They are generally bricked in; they last about eight or ten years before burning out. One difficulty experienced is that when any repairs are required, the brick-work must be removed and the range taken out. They do not heat water as rapidly as the ordinary circulating-boiler, but, being cheaper, have been largely used in the city referred to. It will be borne in mind that the tenement-house, as we know it in New York, is there but little known, so that every mechanic can have his house; and even in these humble dwellings they have their bath-tub, and bath-boiler to make hot water, as I have here described.

These back-log boilers are made of wrought-iron, the same shape as our circulating-boilers, with cast-iron heads and bottoms. They are usually not galvanized. They have two couplings on one end, one for the cold water to enter and the other for the hot water to pass out.

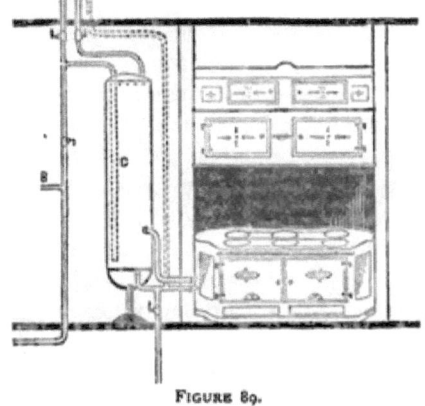

Figure 89.

he ordinary wrought-iron circulating-boilers were, I believe, first made and brought into general use also in Philadelphia within the last fifteen years. They have very largely superseded the copper boilers, mainly because in most cities the boiler is supplied from the main direct, and not from a tank. This, as will be seen, subjects them to whatever pressure the water exerts, which in many cases is quite heavy. Take, for instance, a city where the water is distributed by what is known as the "Holly system"—namely, by pumping through the mains. This, under ordinary circumstances, keeps the pressure at about 50 pounds per square inch; but when a fire occurs it is suddenly increased by speeding up the pumps to 150 pounds per square inch. It will be manifest that under such a pressure boilers and all pipes are subjected to a very severe strain; in fact, one which the ordinary copper boilers, as sold in the market, are unable to withstand.

Copper boilers could, no doubt, be made to stand more than the present so-called "Brooklyn" and 'Croton" pressure ones will; but competition during the last twelve years has resulted in bringing these standards down, so that boilers made in conformity thereto will not long remain tight under more than 30 pounds cold-water pressure.

There is no doubt that the water passing through the galvanized-iron boilers will, after a time, be more or less affected by rust, and that the copper boilers, with their interior surfaces well tinned, are more desirable, provided they can be so fitted up as to be durable. This can unquestionably be done, but in doing it the plan of fitting up boilers will have to be materially changed in most of the cities of the United States; in other words, we must adopt the plan in vogue in Boston, which I decidedly prefer, and which I will illustrate further on.

In Figure 89 is shown the usual way of fitting up galvanized-iron or copper circulating-boilers, when supplied direct from the main. A is the cold-water pipe, with a branch to the coupling on top of the boiler, the dotted line C indicating the circulating-tube, which in a copper boiler is made of tinned copper, and has a small hole in it about four inches from the top to admit air, to prevent, under certain conditions, this tube acting as the short leg of a syphon. In galvanized-iron boilers wrought-iron tubes are used; this hole should also be drilled into these tubes for the same reason, but as a rule it is not done by dealers, and many plumbers never think of doing it. The dotted line E indicates the method of running a circulation-pipe, if it is proposed to have one, and D is the hot-water pipe.

The advantages and disadvantages of this system will again be referred to.

It frequently happens that householders complain of an insufficient supply of hot water where the heating-apparatus is arranged as shown at Figure 89. There are numerous reasons why this contingency occurs, many of which have been repeatedly stated in answers to queries in the columns of the *Sanitary Engineer*, but when the cause is due to the fact that the heating surface of the water-back is not large enough, an arrangement made in this city, which is shown in Figure 90, can be and has been used with advantage.

This, as will be seen, is an auxiliary water-heater, which is placed under the boiler, and also serves the purpose of a stand. It can be used with a range, or separately. The cut shows the arrangement of the pipes to connect the heater with the boiler, and also the method of connecting with the water-back of the range.

FIGURE 90.

Figure 86 illustrated an English form of boiler that requires a separate fire. In Figures 91 and 92 a boiler is shown for use under simlar circumstances. The figures give the elevation and section of a conical hot-water boiler made by the same firm that makes the one shown in Figure 90. These are intended for heating water for baptisteries, barber-shops, bathing establishments, laundries, conservatories, and places where a large quantity of hot water is required, and where a range is not needed, or other means for heating water are not provided. As will be seen by the sectional view, the boiler consists of two conical cylinders, one within the other, with a space for water between the two; the inside one forms the fire-chamber, and reaches nearly to the top of the boiler, with an outlet to the smoke-pipe or chimney. There is also a flattened cone connected with the crown of the chamber and extending to within a few inches of the fire, and there connecting at the side of the chamber with a pipe for the passage of the water. The water enters through the lower pipe at the back part of the boiler, and is distributed through the space surrounding the fire-chamber and through the flattened cone, and, as it becomes heated, rises and flows out of the pipe at the top.

FIGURE 91.

They are made, I believe, of various sizes, heating from 50 to 400 gallons of water per hour. It will be understood that a tank or reservoir is required. The water in the tank is heated by circulating through the boiler, the two being connected by pipes on the same principal as with a water-back, the boiler, with its independent fire, doing essentially the same duty as the range and water-back, only on a larger scale.

Figure 93 shows the ordinary method of fitting up a hot-water boiler in Boston. A represents the range with its water-back. B is a copper circulating-boiler. They seldom have less than three couplings on the top, and from that to six. In the sketch four are shown. It is said that the object of the fourth or additional coupling is to obviate the frequent breaking of the lead pipes, which is caused by changes in the temperature of the water. It is also claimed that a coupling for each branch near the boiler is often cheaper. C is the tank from which the cold water is taken. The tank is filled through a ball-cock, which is on a pipe taken direct from the street-main. By this plan it will be seen that the pressure on the boiler is not excessive, and is a uniform one; the consequence is that the copper boilers prove durable. D is the cold-water supply to the boiler, from which branches should be taken to the cold-water faucets (except where drinking-water is drawn) and water-closet cisterns upstairs. E is the hot-water pipe, while F is the return or circulation pipe, taken from the highest point of E. It will be seen that an expansion-pipe is carried up over and above the tank, with its end left open to permit the escape of steam. H is a cistern-valve, with an air-tube that extends above the water-line. It may be necessary to explain

FIGURE 92.

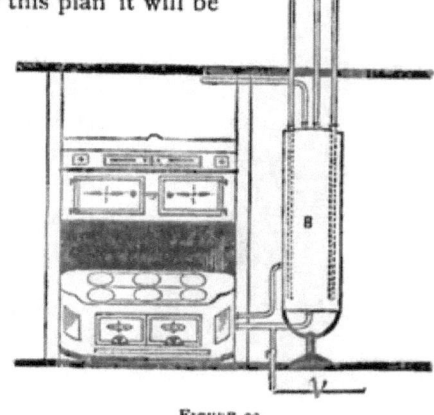

FIGURE 93.

to some of my readers that without this the water would not flow down the pipe D when the valve is closed, and it serves the same purpose that the air-vent in a cask of liquor does. I is a valve-slide by which the valve H in the tank can be opened or shut. This is often placed on the outside of the tank, and sometimes in the bath-room or other accessible place down-stairs, so that it can be readily reached in case of an accident.

These boilers are set on iron stands, just as in New York, but in old houses I have seen them placed on a soapstone slab with a brick foundation, on one side of which is an iron door. Inside of this latter is the sediment-cock to empty the boiler. It will be noticed that I have stated that fixtures upstairs should take the cold-water supply from the down pipe D, and not from the cold-water main to the tank K. In good work I believe this rule is observed, but in cheap work, or where plumbers desire to save every foot of pipe possible, they often take the branch from the rising main when that pipe is a little nearer to the fixtures to be served. Much of the complaint about ball-cocks jumping or making a noise, faucets leaking, and water-hammer, are due to this fact, and architects in writing specifications should be careful to specify from which pipe the branches should be taken, and then see that the specifications in that particular are carried out. Of course, I wish to be understood that the cold-water faucet over the kitchen-sink and the pantry-sink, or wherever it is desired to draw water for cooking or drinking, should not be supplied from a tank, but by a branch from the main in the cellar, *independent of the pipe to the ball-cock at the tank*, unless the disturbance of this ball-cock, whenever a faucet is suddenly shut, is no objection or annoyance.

In the issue of January 15, 1880, of the *Sanitary Engineer* an illustration of a double boiler was given. From correspondence concerning it at the time, it occurred to me that the explanations did not make entirely clear to all the readers of the paper the peculiar circumstances under which this form of boiler was used or required. For the information, therefore, of persons not residing in New York City, who may not fully understand it, I will explain that the class of dwellings in which double boilers are used are generally four stories high, besides the basement. The city water has not sufficient force to ascend above the second floor, and recently not always to that height. It is, of course, desirable to be able to draw hot water on every floor. This, however, would, under such conditions, be impossible, as the hot water cannot go above the cold water that supplies the boiler.

To place a tank in the attic or fourth floor from which the boiler is to be supplied, as shown in Figure 94, would involve pumping in that tank all the water that is afterward heated and used as hot water, as it would not flow there, as provided for in the sketch referred to. In the double-boiler system, therefore, the intention is to pump only the water required above where it will flow from the street-main, and this water is supplied to the inside boiler which furnishes the hot water for the upper stories.

It will be noticed that a double boiler, as shown in the annexed plan, consists of two copper cylinders, the space between the inner shell and the outer one being of the same capacity as the inside of the inner boiler—that is to say, an 80-gallon double-boiler means that the inside and outside boiler will hold forty gallons each. By reference to the drawing it will be seen that the cold-water supply passes under the sink, with a stop-cock at B, up alongside of the boiler, with a check-valve H, which is placed there to prevent drawing water from the outer boiler when the pump is working or the water is shut off in the street. Just above this check-valve a branch from this cold-water supply-pipe is taken and connected to the cold-water supply to the inside boiler which comes from the tank. On this is also placed a check-valve that will prevent the cold water from the tank from running to the main, while, on the other hand, it will permit the water from the street-main to fill the inside boiler at any time that the tank should become empty. It will be noticed that the hot-water pipes from both inside and outside boilers extend over and above the tank, with their ends open to permit the escape of steam. The hot water required at points above where the cold water will rise is taken from branches out of the hot-water pipe from the inside boiler, while the hot water required below that point is taken from the pipe that comes from the outside boiler. The tank is filled by a pump, which is usually placed in the cellar, instead of alongside the kitchen-sink, as shown in the sketch. A circulating-pipe is run from the outside boiler hot-water pipe, but not from the inside one.

It sometimes happens that these boilers are so fitted up that when the water from the inside boiler is drawn off it has collapsed from the pressure of the water surrounding it, by reason of some one ignorantly or carelessly emptying the inside one before the outside.

The arrangement of the sediment-cocks as shown in the drawing would prevent such an occurrence, because if the stop-cock G was opened, the water could not be drawn from the inside boiler until A was also opened, which would simultaneously empty the outer boiler. The outside boiler can be emptied without affecting the inner one, but not the reverse.

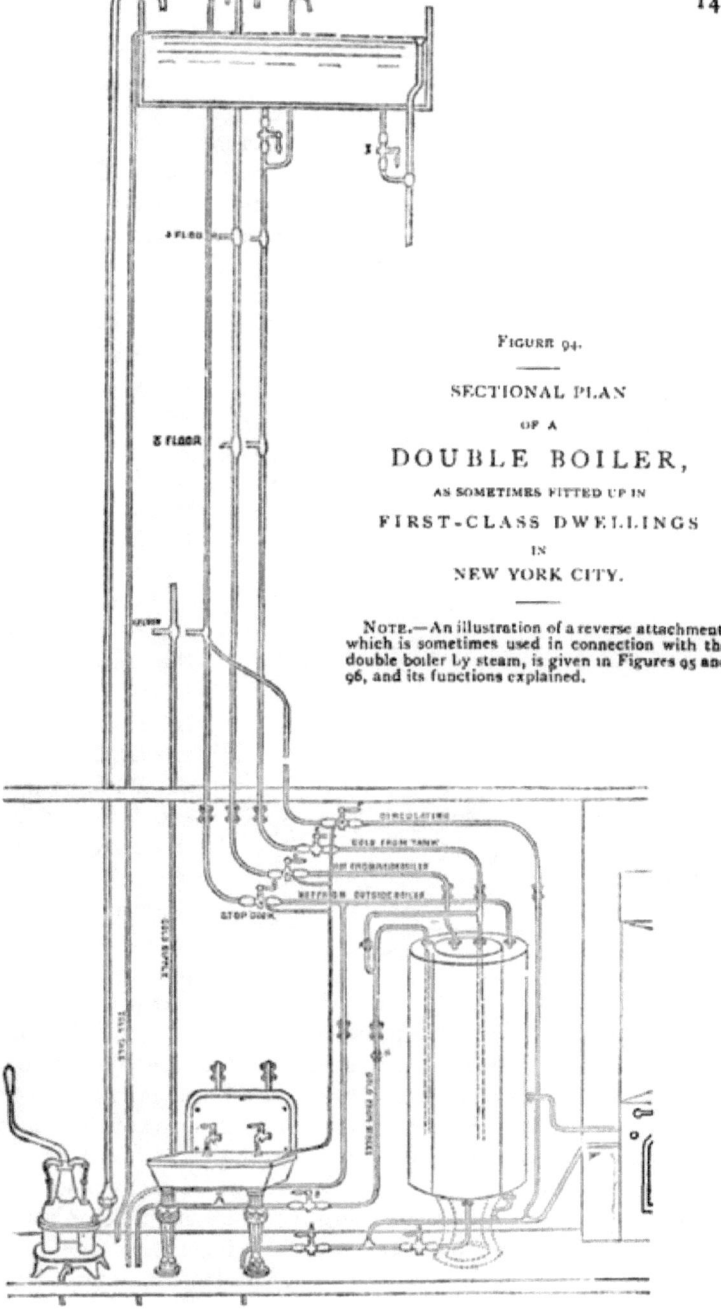

FIGURE 94.

SECTIONAL PLAN

OF A

DOUBLE BOILER,

AS SOMETIMES FITTED UP IN

FIRST-CLASS DWELLINGS

IN

NEW YORK CITY.

NOTE.—An illustration of a reverse attachment, which is sometimes used in connection with the double boiler by steam, is given in Figures 95 and 96, and its functions explained.

The reverse attachment alluded to in the note on the preceding page is illustrated in Figure 95. In order that the following explanation may be more readily understood, it will be well to refer to the illustration of the double-boiler system on page 147. In most houses where this system is adopted, it is found that on the second floor the flow of water from the street-main is intermittent—*i. e.*, at times water is not obtainable, by reason of an insufficient pressure in the street-mains; at other times the pressure is ample to supply that floor.

In such situations, therefore, the reverse cock is placed on the branch-pipes from both the tank and street-main hot and cold water pipes. This is put under a wash-basin or in some accessible place, so that when the supply from the main fails, a supply from the tank can be obtained by a turn of the lever, which, when closing the two stop-cocks on the supply-pipe from the street, opens the stop-cocks on the hot and cold supply-pipes from the tank. Of course, when these are open the water used is that which has to be pumped; consequently they are only kept open when the street-pressure fails to reach that floor. By reference to the sketch, it will be noticed that the pipes all come through the lead safe, which indicates its location under a wash-basin; of course a plumber will understand the various ways that the branches can be run so that they may come up through the safe as shown. It will also be noticed that I refer to this reverse attachment as being placed on the branches. I have no positive knowledge of the fact, but it is asserted that in some instances plumbers have connected one or more of the cocks in this attachment to the main pipes, either to save

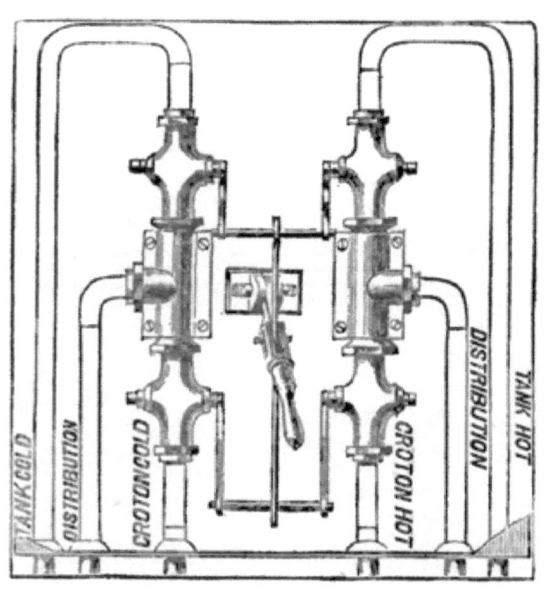

FIGURE 95.

pipe or because it was a little more convenient. By an examination of the double-boiler cut it will be made evident that this would be a dangerous proceeding, because the closing of one of these cocks would close the expansion-pipe that extends from the boiler over the tank, with its end open to permit the escape of steam, and would result in straining the boiler, if not the more serious casualty of an explosion.

Figure 96 shows the usual arrangement before the reverse attachment was made, which, as will be seen, consists in placing separate stopcocks on each branch from street and tank supply. This is also shown located under a wash-basin. It is customary to put a label on each stopcock to indicate its particular use.

Occasionally two independent boilers are used in place of a double boiler, to secure the same results; but in most kitchens a convenient space to locate them cannot be found, although when such an arrangement is practicable, each boiler can be larger—that is to say, from 50 to 80 gallons each, which would be equivalent to an 120 to 160 gallon double boiler, whereas the sizes most frequently used are from 80 to 100 gallons

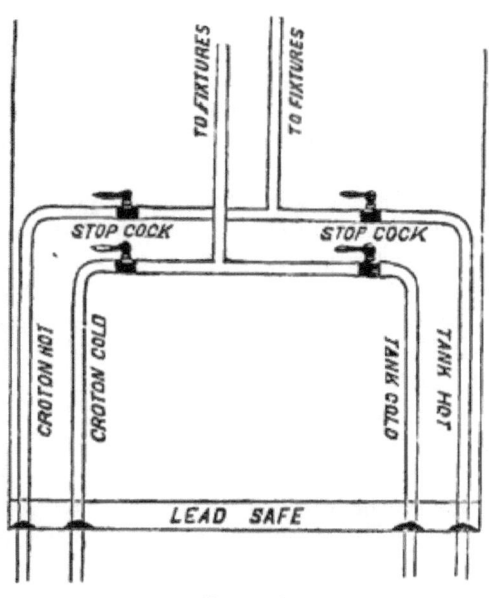

FIGURE 96.

capacity. As a general thing where double boilers are used, an independent single boiler of from 40 to 50 gallons capacity is provided for the laundry, and placed alongside the laundry range, and connected with its water-back. This is intended to supply hot water only for laundry purposes.

In the reference to hot-water boilers placed in the laundry of a private dwelling, mentioned above, I simply described the custom in New York City. It may be well to explain that in the New England States, or in the vicinity of Boston, water for laundry purposes is often heated in an open-top copper boiler, which is set in brick-work alongside of a set of soapstone wash-trays. The fire is built under this boiler, a draw-off cock is placed on it, and the hot water is drawn off and poured into the tubs as required.

I have, in the preceding pages, referred to the various methods of fitting up bath-boilers in this country and in Europe with which I am acquainted, and I shall now conclude the chapter on boilers by a few suggestions that occur in considering the conditions of their use.

In this city, where the building of flats has become so general, the question is frequently raised whether it is better to have a bath-boiler for each flat in each kitchen, connected with the water-back in the range, or whether the hot water should be supplied to each flat from some central source—as, for instance, a large boiler in the basement. In intelligently deciding this point various things must be considered. In the smaller flats, where steam is not required to run elevators, and is only needed to heat the halls in the winter time, it is the practice, and is, no doubt, more economical for the owner of the building to provide a boiler for each flat, as the fuel required by the family for cooking will also heat what water is needed, and this, of course, involves no expense to the landlord. As usually fitted up in flats, copper boilers are apt to collapse, because of the liability of the water being syphoned out of those on the upper floors when it is drawn off at a lower point. This could be guarded against, but specifications do not require the precautions to be taken, and the cost would deter any plumber from doing it in contract work, consequently galvanized-iron boilers are now almost universally used in such situations, as they are sufficiently strong to withstand the atmospheric pressure in the event of there being a vacuum formed inside of them by the withdrawal of their contents. One other objection is the fact that the boiler in the small kitchen of a flat adds to the heat of this, as well as of the adjoining rooms, and in hot weather this is sometimes an inconvenience.

In hotels and first-class flats water is heated for use throughout the building by placing a coil of brass or iron pipe inside a large wrought-iron tank, and heating the water by passing steam through this coil. Brass pipe is considered for this purpose to make the best job; but iron is most frequently used, although copper mains—such as are used in stills—are sometimes adopted.

Exhaust steam is sometimes availed of for this purpose, and is the most economical, although I think, as a general thing, live steam is taken from the boiler required to furnish the power to run elevators, etc. These hot-water tanks are supplied with water from the tank on the top floor; connections are also made to supply them from the street-main, with a check-valve on this pipe to prevent the tank-water from running back to the main, but to permit the street-pressure to supply the boiler when there is no water in the upper tank.

In these articles on hot-water boilers it seems proper to refer to the wearing out of hot-water pipes, which occurs with the most frequency near the range or between the boiler and the range. This is generally due, in the case of lead pipe, to impeded circulation or too much heating capacity in the water-back, there being considerable difference in this respect with the various makers of ranges. In some cases, where the water-back was large, I have known of a piece of wrought-iron pipe, this shape (⊃), to be substituted for a large cast-iron water-back. This will burn out in time, but is capable of making a great deal of hot water. Where lead is used for the hot-water pipe, it has been the practice, in first-class work, to have a copper pipe brazed on to the coupling of the boiler and of the water-back, and in order that the coppersmith could get the exact dimensions and the proper direction for this connecting piece, a lead-pipe connection was made to serve as a model; and to insure an absolutely tight and strong joint where the pipe was brazed to the couplings, a good soldered joint was wiped over it. Connections made as here described have been found much more durable than with the ordinary lead pipe.

Vacuum-valves have been largely sold for use on the hot-water pipes of copper boilers, to supply air and prevent a collapse. Some are made to screw into a spud attached to the boiler for this especial purpose. I have never considered them reliable, and I think the experience of plumbers has been that the valve, not being in constant use, is liable to stick to its seat and become inoperative when most needed. An expansion-pipe, as before explained, with its open end above the source of the supply to the boiler, which should be a tank in the upper part of the house, is, in my judgment, the only safe plan.

SETTING HORIZONTAL BOILERS.

MUCH information has been given from time to time of the best way to run the circulating-pipes between a water-back and boiler; but the proper position *in the boiler* for the pipe-connections does not seem to be understood, if I may judge from a boiler recently received from a large manufacturer, in which the couplings were so placed that only about one-half the capacity of the boiler would be available for use. The boiler was to rest horizontally—a position in which many boilers are now set, and the diagrams, Figures 97, 98, 99, show the pipe-connections.

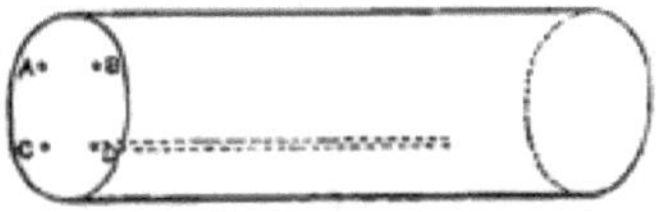

FIGURE 97.

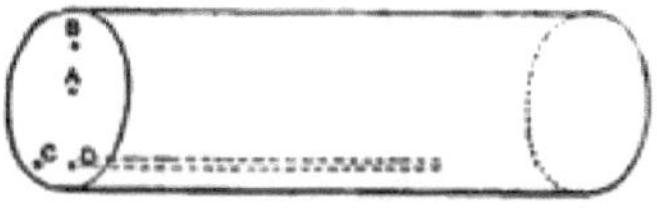

FIGURE 98.

FIGURE 99.

D, inlet for cold water, with tube running into boiler; B, for hot water to pass out; A and C, upper and lower circulating connections.

A moment's thought will show that water below C *will not heat*, and that the water above B *cannot be drawn off*. The capacity of the boiler is therefore only that portion between the horizontal planes passing through C and B, Figure 97, or very little over one-half the whole boiler. The proper position for couplings to horizontal boilers are shown in Figures 98 and 99, in which D represents the cold in pipe; B the hot out pipe; A, upper circulation; C, lower circulation.

Now, a moment's thought will show that the water below C *will not heat*, and that the hot water above B *cannot be drawn off*. The capacity of the boiler is therefore only the part between horizontal planes passing through C and B, in the case we allude to, just about one-half the whole boiler. Or, where the pipes can be conveniently connected at the top side of boiler.

In a vertical boiler we have never seen the couplings improperly placed. Care, of course, must be taken to have the inside tube upon the *cold*-water supply to boiler, but in horizontal boilers care is not always taken to observe the following rules, applicable alike to vertical and horizontal boilers:

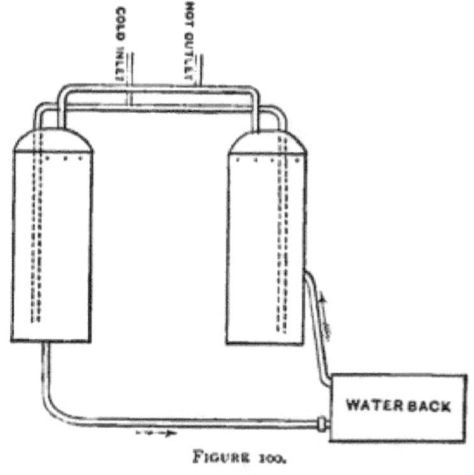

FIGURE 100.

First—Cold water should be delivered into the boiler at a point *near its bottom.* To prevent the boiler being emptied through this cold supply-pipe it is best to have the coupling near the top of boiler, and carry a pipe from it inside the boiler to near the bottom.

Second—The lower circulating-pipe should connect at or very near the bottom of the boiler, so that all the water in the boiler may be heated. The position of the upper circulating coupling is not material.

Third—The outlet-pipe for hot water should be at the top of the boiler, so that *all* the hot water may be drawn off.

Fourth—The inlet and outlet pipes should not be too near together, lest the rapid flow, when hot water is drawn, establish a current between them, and so fail to draw the hot water from the boiler.

Where a boiler is too small and it is desired to add another boiler, instead of throwing out the old one and replacing it with a single large one, I have coupled them as shown in Figure 100. Both boilers heat alike, and are drawn off together.

HOW TO SECURE CIRCULATION BETWEEN BOILERS IN DIFFERENT HOUSES.

Q. I HAVE a customer that occupies two separate houses adjoining, as shown in sketch. House No. 1, kitchen is only used to do laundry-work in; the range is heated up about three days in a week. House

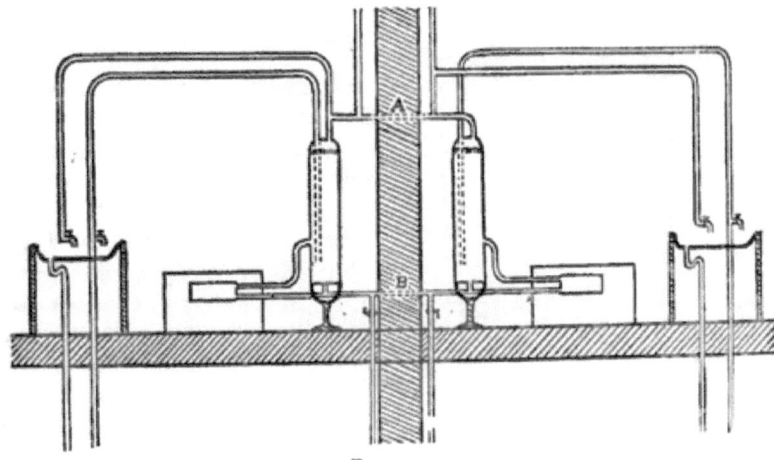

FIGURE 101.

No. 2, kitchen is in constant use, as the cooking is all done for both houses in No. 2 kitchen. Now, what is wanted is to connect these two houses together so No. 2 will assist No. 1 in having hot water there three or four days when No. 1 range is not in use, and so they will both work in harmony with each other at all times.

I would be very much pleased to have your views on this subject.

A. Connect the hot-water pipes from both boilers, as shown by dotted line A, and cold-water pipes to ranges, as shown by dotted line B.

CONNECTING ONE BOILER WITH TWO RANGES.

Q. I noticed in your paper of December 8, 1881, a method of fitting up a boiler with two ranges, so as to be heated from either or both at once, and herewith send you a drawing of another and better manner of doing the same, thereby securing a more perfect circulation, as I question if the water-backs would have a sufficient supply through the ordinary coupling when both ranges were in use at the same time. They would likely be unpleasant on account of noise, if not dangerous.

When only one range is used the cold-water pipe is brought into the water-back through the end nearest the boiler, and the hot-water pipe is carried out from the opposite end, and around behind the range between it and the brick-work, keeping at about the same level till near the boiler, where it rises and enters the side-connection.

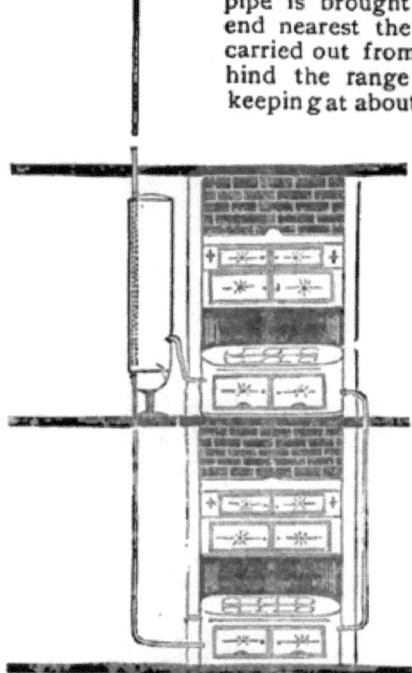

Figure 102.

A. The objection to this method is, as much water cannot be warmed by passing it first through one back and then through the other as would be the case if each back circulated separately to the boiler. This will be plain when we consider the water cannot take as much heat from the upper back as from the lower one, as the difference of temperature will be less between the water in the upper back and the fire than it will be in the lower one.

HOT WATER CIRCULATION IN BUILDINGS. 155

TAKING RETURN BELOW BOILER.

Q. I THINK the plumber is right and you are wrong about your advice to Mr. ———, when you say you can carry the return below the floor and then rise to the boiler and have circulation. If he does as

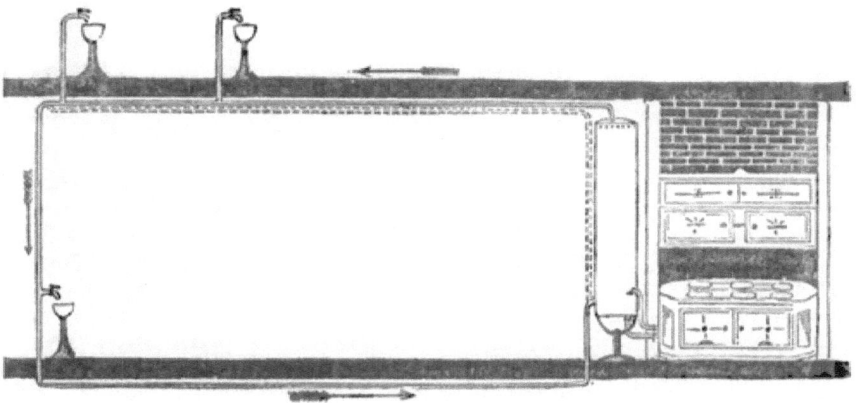

FIGURE 103.

you say he will get a trap where he rises, and the cold water will stay there and he can't get any circulation. I don't think it makes much difference how high the circulation is, either. I would say to Mr. ——— it is a waste of time and money to run the circulation-pipe as he wants to do it.

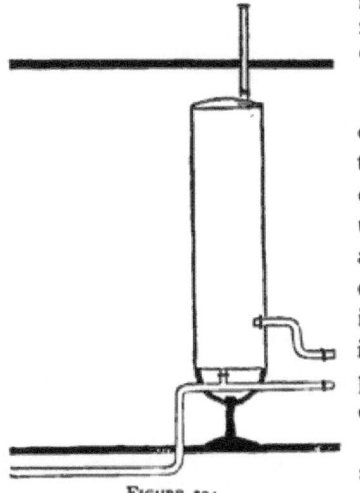

FIGURE 104.

A. We must still maintain that a circulation will take place in the pipe below the floor. It depends, as stated in the original article, on the cooling of the upper or flow-pipe. Then the density and the weight of the colder air in the descending pipe, at the left of the original diagram, indicated by the descending arrow, are greater than in the rising pipe, and it is this greater weight which causes the circulation.

We, of course, are not to be understood as maintaining that a circulation will take place at every distance below the water-back, and under all circumstances. How far below the water-back the return can be carried will depend on the height of the rising column. In the case submitted to us it is assumed that the upper pipe is at least six feet above the water-back, and the lower pipe not more three feet below it.

Figure 103 represents the plan we first proposed. Figure 104 is the method suggested by a firm in New York City which has had extensive experience in the fitting up of hot-water apparatus. It will be seen tha the lower return is here connected with the water-back return-pipe.

TROUBLE WITH BOILER.

Q. I HAVE recently had a job of plumbing completed here. Have in kitchen a 40-gallon galvanized-iron boiler; the cold supply comes to within twelve inches of bottom of boiler. The connections to water-back have proper slope; the circulation-pipe from second story connects into cold supply from boiler to water-back; the connections from boiler to water-back and entire system of hot water and circulation-pipes are ¾-inch pipe.

The range first put in was a portable one, with a small water-*front* made for ⅝-inch connections. With this we could get water barely warm. This range was then taken out and a larger one substituted, having a large water-*front* made for ¾-inch connections. This gives us plenty of warm water, but no *hot* water. In several houses here the same trouble is complained of. Is there any way to get hot water from a portable range with a portable water-*front* unless a pipe-coil is put in in addition?

A. The water-back may be too small, or it may be located too low in the range to get the heat from the fire, or it may be covered with ashes and clinkers. There are portable ranges made with water-backs of ample heating capacity to heat the water in a 40-gallon boiler, unless the family use an unusual amount.

AN IGNORANT WAY OF DEALING WITH A KITCHEN-BOILER.

Q. I PUT in a square boiler, holding about 25 to 30 gallons, in a country place, where it has to be filled with water from the top by the pailful. Now, the cold water passes through pipe No. 2 and through the water-back, and is heated and passes through pipe No. 3 to the sink. What is the reason that when the cock is open steam comes out for a minute or two and then the water comes out half-stream, and the water-hammer commences and acts on the boiler? What is the reason of this water-hammer, and how can it be stopped? and can the pressure be made greater?

This is the way the pipe runs. There is ½-inch 2 A A lead pipe. Don't you think there is water enough in the boiler to make it come out full stream into the sink?

A. The ignorance of the first principles of what is necessary to secure a hot-water supply for plumbing fixtures expressed in this letter and sketch is astonishing. Water is run from a tank into a water-back, and no provision is made for a return-pipe for the water to find its way back again to the tank when it becomes hot. The result is, you make steam in the water-back when there is sufficient heat in the range. This pressure, presumably, finds vent (backward) through the pipe No. 2 periodically and spasmodically, and with all the other symptoms of internal convulsions. When you open the cock at the sink the steam finds vent in that direction, the water following from the tank into the water-back. This condenses what little steam there is left, and a vacuum is formed, drawing water, air, or anything present in the pipes into the water-back, with all the phenomena of water-hammer or shock following.

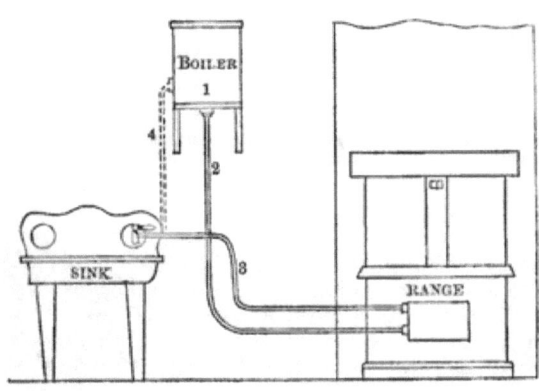

FIGURE 105.

It is a good thing the tank (or boiler) had to be filled through an open cover, for had it been a closed boiler it is more than likely we would have to chronicle the death of a servant girl or two, or may be a plumber.

Make a connection as shown by our dotted lines at No. 4, and see if it improves the condition of your apparatus. The water in the boiler must not be allowed to fall below the upper end of this opening.

It will be understood that the dotted lines are added by us. The original drawing and description makes no provision even for the ordinary circulation to and from water-back and boilers.

RETURNING INTO HOT-WATER SUPPLY-PIPE.

Q. I propose to put in my house a circulation-pipe, attached to the range as follows:

A, cold-water supply from street; B, hot water from boiler supplying several fixtures in basement; C, hot-water supply for upper

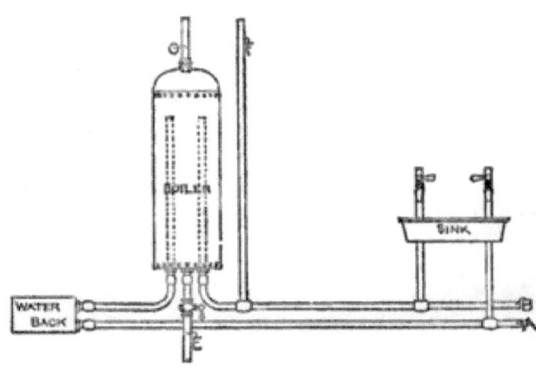

FIGURE 106.

floors; D, hot-water pipe from range to boiler; E, waste-pipe from boiler; F, circulation-pipe united to the pipe B and extending upward and uniting with the pipe C above the highest hot-water fixture.

The point on which I have doubt is whether the fixtures in the basement will injuriously affect the circulation through the pipe F. If you will kindly enlighten me, you will oblige.

A. There will be no interruption of the circulation in the pipes C and F, which will be apparent. Of course, water drawn at the sink, if drawn slowly, will have its temperature perceptibly affected by the return water from F, as it will mingle with it, but with ordinary use, with a good water-back, it should not be noticeable.

WHERE SHOULD SEDIMENT-PIPE FROM BOILER BE CONNECTED WITH WASTE-PIPE?

Q. Do you think it proper to connect the sediment-pipe of a kitchen-boiler directly to a soil or waste pipe?

A. If the sink-trap is below the floor it is better to run the pipe in above it. If not, we see no serious objection to connecting with the waste-pipe. Of course, the sediment-cock should not be left open if the boiler were emptied of water at any time.

HOT WATER CIRCULATION IN BUILDINGS. 159

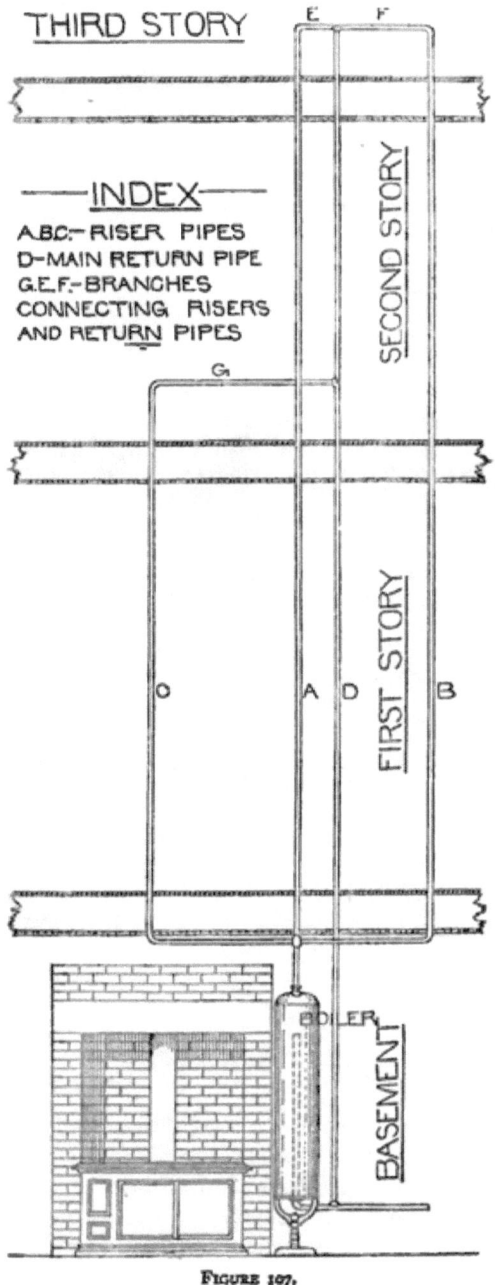

INDEX
A.B.C.—RISER PIPES
D—MAIN RETURN PIPE
G.E.F.—BRANCHES CONNECTING RISERS AND RETURN PIPES

FIGURE 107.

SEVERAL FLOW-PIPES AND ONE CIRCULATION-PIPE.

Q. I find it necessary to run three distinct riser-pipes from kitchen-boiler to the second and third floors. Can I secure a circulation by running a single return-pipe having branches connecting with each riser above the highest fixture? Would more return-pipes be any better?

A. Bring the branches E and F into the return D at slightly different levels to prevent the circulation in one meeting and checking that in the other, as they would do to some extent, certainly, if connected as shown. At the junction of G and D let G turn downward, so that the circulation in D may not be, in part, diverted into G, to prevent a circulation in the latter pipe. Then with a return-pipe large enough to carry the circulation in the three hot-water pipes you should get a circulation. We would advise that you make the pipes from boiler to junction a size larger than the pipe A, otherwise there is risk that the greater part of the circulation will take the easiest course through A, as that is in direct line, giving you little or no movement in B and C. If you intend to use iron pipe, Y-branches or "division-tees" (Figure 37, Hunter, Keller & Co.'s Catalogue) will give better results than plain tees.

If the work is to be lead pipe, the good judgment of the plumber must be exercised in making easily-flowing joints, which direct the water in the proper direction.

HOW TO RUN PIPES FROM WATER-BACK TO BOILER.

Q. INCLOSED I send you the plan of a house I have just fitted up with a circulating-boiler. The boiler is set about four feet above the range in a closet. Now, the landlord has built a summer kitchen, and wants a water-back put in to heat water in boiler from outside range, and I tell him he cannot do it unless he cuts out the back of the range in the main kitchen and runs the pipes back of the range in the main kitchen. But the range man says we can run down from the water-back under the beams to inside boiler, which will cause about two feet of a trap in the circulating-pipe. I say it will not work. Please tell me who is right. I was always taught that the circulating-pipe should have a fall from boiler to water-back. Please tell me which would be the best way to fix it to make a job of it. By answering this as soon as possible you will confer a great favor.

FIGURE 108.

A. You are right, and the range man is obviously wrong. There should be a gradual ascent from the water-back of the pipe that conveys the water heated by it to the side-coupling of the boiler. If the ranges and boiler are located as shown in the sketch, we see no proper way of connecting with the summer range except to run the pipes behind the large range.

HOT-WATER CIRCULATION WHEN PIPES FROM BOILER PASS UNDER THE FLOOR.

Q. I inclose drawing of boiler, pipes, and tank. I saw in the *Sanitary Engineer* of April 19, 1883, a plan for circulating, which I mark Figure 109. I have tried the plan, but it will not work. I then cut off the return hot-water pipe or circulating pipe, marked *c*, which ran to the bottom of boiler, and connected it to the circulating-pipe of stove and boiler, as by dotted lines, and it still will not work. The pipe can't be run on kitchen-ceiling nor over ceiling on floor. Evidently we must run through floor to cellar-ceiling, and up in partition to tank and bathroom. Can you inform me how to make a circulation work without changing the whole line of pipe? If you can give me any information concerning the circulation it will oblige me very much.

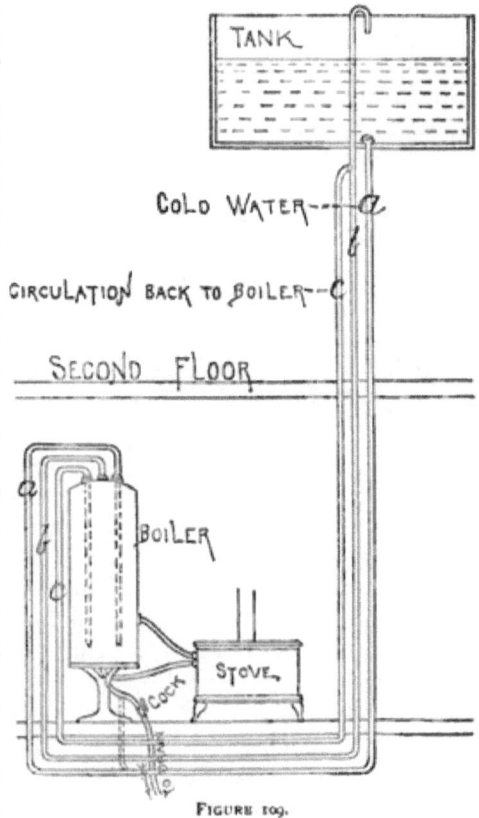

FIGURE 109.

A. Any circulation which has to drop after leaving the boiler is a thing of doubt, as there are so many circumstances which may affect the flow besides the actual direction of the pipe. When the pipe which has to convey the water away from the boiler has to take a downward course, or the pipe returning to it again takes an upward one, they separately and collectively preponderate against the force which naturally tends to assist the circulation. In your case, in *b*, from the boiler to the under side of the floor, the water is the hottest in the circulation, and would naturally rise, whereas it must go down to accomplish what you want. But in *c*, for the same perpendicular height, it is the coldest, as it is the end of the circulation, and would naturally fall where it is forced to ascend to accomplish what you desire. Thus, in these two pipes, from the boiler to the under side of the floor, you have a preponderance against you. In the pipe b, where it rises in the house again, you have a hot pipe, but not as hot as where it runs in the wrong direction at the boiler, and in juxtaposition to it you have the return-pipe c colder than it, though not very much so, and warmer than the pipe c where it rises. These pipes at this point tend in the right direction, but the difference of weight of water between them is not sufficient to overcome the difference which works against them in their course in the vertical position near the boiler.

If you clothe a flow or hot pipe where it ascends, and a return or cold pipe where *it also ascends*, and all level pipes, it will assist a circulation, as by that means you prevent a great loss of heat at these parts, and keep the column of water nearly the same temperature and density throughout its length, allowing it to cool only where cooling will tend to quicken the circulation by increasing the density — namely, where flow-pipe or return-pipes fall, but notably the latter. In your case, if b and c, where they run upward, could be extended indefinitely, you presumably would reach a point where the circulation would go on, and which Mr. Armstrong must have exceeded in his case, or his job in the Young Ladies' Seminary at Northfield, Mass., would not have worked. There may be influences at work, also, in his case, assisting him, such as a large quantity of cooling surface in his return-pipe compared to the bulk of water it will hold, or its being run in a position where the influence of cold draughts or cold pipes affects it. The method of entering the boiler at the bottom with the return-pipe is better than carrying it down inside in a tube.

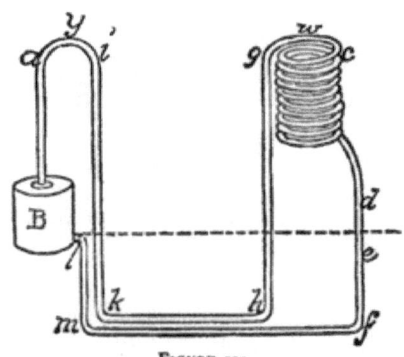

FIGURE 110.

We do not recommend this method of getting circulation, and no one should attempt it unless it was an impossibility to run the pipes any other way. Hood, in his treatise on warming, etc., says: "In Figure 110, B represents the boiler; and the effective or direct motion is in this case caused by the water in the coil and pipe $c\ d$ being so much heavier than in the boiler and the pipe B a that it overcomes the retrograde motion which is produced by all the other parts of the apparatus. Thus the water in $g\ h$ being *heavier* than that in $i\ k$, and that in $e\ f$

(below the dotted line) being lighter than that in *l m*, has in both cases a tendency to retrogression. * * * The motive power, therefore, entirely depends upon the quantity of heat given off by the coil ; for the water must be cooled down many degrees in order to give it sufficient preponderance over the water in B *a* to cause a circulation."

HEATING A ROOM FROM WATER-BACK.

Q. WOULD it be practicable to use a circulation system from a kitchen-boiler to heat a small adjoining dining-room ? If so, would it be necessary to increase the size of boiler and range, which are, if anything, more than ample to supply all the hot water a small family needs for washing, bathing, etc.?

A. We have seen a pantry or closet warmed in this way. The circulation-pipe from the water-back to the boiler was branched, and some of the hot water diverted into a coil in the pantry, the return going into the pipe leading to the water-back again. As to the question of requiring a larger water-back, it will all depend on the quantity of warm water required elsewhere than in the coil, and can be best found by experiment

THE OPERATION OF VACUUM AND SAFETY VALVES.

Q. WHAT is the principle on which the "safety and vacuum valve" on top of a boiler acts, and how should it be set ?

A. A vacuum-valve on a kitchen-boiler is intended to prevent the collapse of the boiler by the pressure of the atmosphere on its outside, should it become empty or partly empty through the shutting off of the water-supply ; at the same time, should there be a heavy fire in the range, steam may be generated within the boiler, in which case a safety-valve is intended to let the over-pressure escape. It also provides for the expansion of the water should a fire be started with a full boiler and

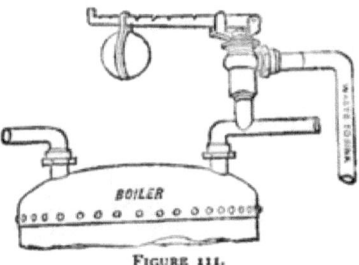

FIGURE 111.

pipes, with the street-cock accidentally shut. The annexed cut shows how a combined "vacuum and safety valve" may be set.

For hot-water boilers in houses we much prefer to have an open-end relief-pipe, to prevent vacuum and explosions, to trusting to vacuum or safety valves, because, unlike the valves on steam-boilers, they are not often tested, and when wanted they do not always work.

PREVENTING COLLAPSE OF BOILERS.

Q. WHAT precautions can be taken against the collapse of kitchen-boilers, when water is drawn off in the street-mains?

A. Put out the fire in the range and close the stop-cock in the service-pipes, so as to prevent the water running backward into the empty mains, and draw no water in the house until the street-mains are full again. It is better to supply the boiler from a tank or supply-cistern instead of from the mains direct, and have an open pipe carried from the top of the boiler to above the level to which the water can possibly rise.

COLLAPSE OF A BOILER.

Q. IN drawing the water from plumbing fixtures, arranged as follows, or similar to Figure 112, the boiler collapsed. Was the syphon enough to do it, or could there have been another cause?

The circumstances were as follows: The main pipe from street to tank was shut off; then a hot fire was removed from the range; all the water was then drawn from the tank through the faucets in the sink; a ½-inch hose was attached to the sediment-cock, and the cock opened; then the drip D in the hot-water pipe in the cellar was opened, from which some water flowed. Hearing a peculiar noise, on going to the kitchen, the boiler was found to have collapsed.

Could there have been any pressure in the boiler to have forced the water out of the drip and hose also? Or was not the boiler strong enough to resist the power of the syphon, which would have existed until the water lying in the hot-water pipe was drawn into the boiler?

The fall is as given in the diagram. Shall have an air-cock placed in top of boiler when it is replaced.

A. The syphon action was sufficient to collapse the boiler, and probably did so in this case.

When you drew the water from the boiler and pipe through the sink connections you still left the pipes and boiler nearly half-full, as indicated by the dotted line *a*, but when you attached the hose you made the long leg of a syphon, which for the height of six feet, as you show, and say three feet added for the height of water in the boiler and connections, gave you, we will say, a pull of four pounds per square inch. Against this you had a column of water raised in your hot and cold pipes alongside of the boiler by, we will say again, the "pull of the long leg of the syphon." Assuming the latter distance to be nearly equal to the other, which, it appears from your diagram, you may safely assume, you had an atmospheric pressure of three pounds per square inch, or what would produce it. You opened your hose, or the long leg of the syphon, *first*, and air did not enter through your sink-cocks, as they must have been closed. Had you opened the cock D first (the short leg of the syphon), you probably would not have had the collapse, as the small quantity of water it contained would have run out. When you did open it air entered by it, and made the noise you mention. Had the sink-cock been left open the whole trouble would have been avoided.

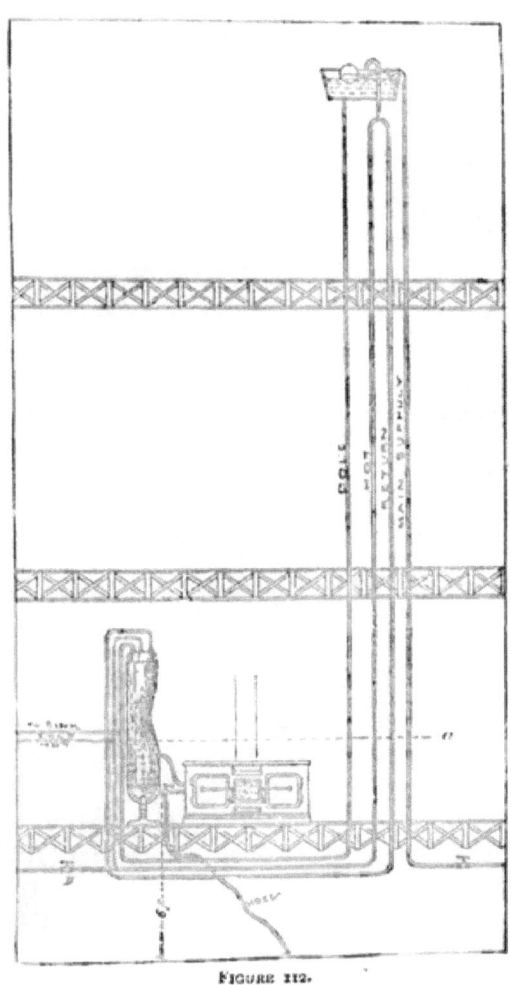

FIGURE 112.

EXPLOSION OF WATER-BACKS.

Q. The excessively cold weather of this winter is giving the usual trouble in regard to the freezing of pipes from boilers to water-backs. Lately in Chicago the explosion of a water-back was attended with loss of life.

I have had to disconnect my boiler and stop its use altogether, owing to the impossibility of preventing the freezing of the connecting pipes.

On two occasions, recently, the pipes were found frozen, and only by the personal precaution of thawing out the pipes previous to lighting the fire was an explosion avoided. I write this to ask you if it is not possible to devise some contrivance, such as a plug of fusible metal, or a cock to open at a high pressure, which, placed in the water-back, would obviate the danger of explosions when the connecting pipes are frozen, thus putting our cooking-stoves and their hot-water attachments within the intellectual range and ordinary care of our usual hired help.

A. We know of no contrivance that can be depended on in emergencies such as you suggest. The only plan is to keep up a good fire and not let the pipes freeze. If by accident the fire goes out, follow the directions contained in an article on page 286, issue of the *Sanitary Engineer* of March 2, 1882.

A PROPOSED PRECAUTION AGAINST WATER-BACK EXPLOSIONS.

Q. The usual catalogue of accidents from exploding water-backs, caused by freezing, has begun to appear in the papers. This suggests to me whether there is not a simple expedient by which the servants may ascertain whether the water-back connections are frozen or not. I would suggest the following for your consideration:

As close to the range as possible put a cock, A—Figure 113—not in the line of the connection, but opening from it, so that by no accident can it shut off the connection. Let this pipe terminate, say, over a pan, and let the servant every morning try the cock before starting the fire. If water will not run from this cock it will be clear proof something is wrong, and then the process of thawing out the connections, together with a very slow fire in the range to gently heat the back, can be proceeded with until water runs from the cock A. Would it not be worth while for range-makers to provide such a cock in connection with the spuds for the water-back connections?

A. In the hands of an expert, or with very cautious persons who had been specially instructed in its use, the plan suggested might prove of service. It is reasonable to suppose that the water in the pipes leading to a water-back will freeze before the water in the back can; and that if the cock mentioned ran water when opened the pipes would be clear, and that, consequently, the back would be also unfrozen. But its practical value, we think, would be very little, for the simple reason that people who blow up water-backs have generally very little knowledge about such matters, and would not know what to do if they were informed a water-back was frozen. In fact, they would be apt to reason that the heat of the fire would thaw all out.

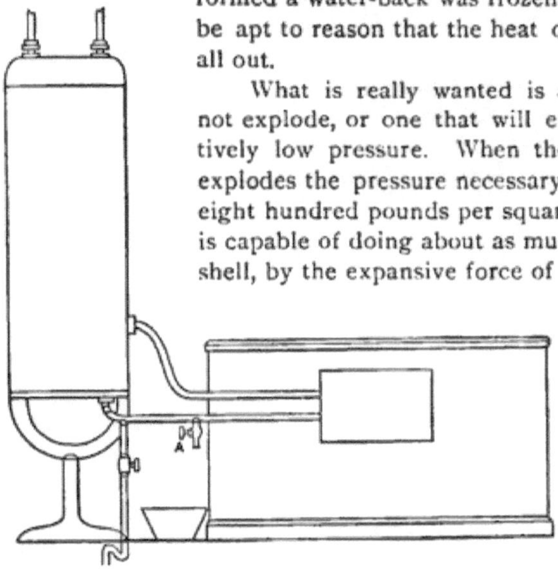

What is really wanted is a water-back that will not explode, or one that will explode at a comparatively low pressure. When the ordinary *box-casting* explodes the pressure necessary to burst it is seven to eight hundred pounds per square inch, or higher, and is capable of doing about as much damage as a bombshell, by the expansive force of the heat contained in the water necessary to exert such a pressure, the water flying into steam upon being liberated.

To lessen the extent and force of explosions in water-backs, pipe-coils might be used instead of box-castings, if it were not for the fact of their filling with lime-deposit, etc. With the pipe a bend may split or the pipe burst, but the whole thing will not go to pieces, and the discharge will be more gradual, resulting, it may be, in blowing the covers off the stove only.

FIGURE 113.

THE BURSTING OF KITCHEN-BOILERS AND CONNECTING-PIPES.

Q. I HAVE a boiler connected with a stove which causes a terrible rumbling whenever they draw water from the cold faucet, and it is bound to burst the pipe or boiler somewhere. Connections are all heavy lead pipe. I send you sketch of work (Figure 114). Please advise me, and oblige.

I have marked where it bursts; it is street-pressure, and these are all the connections in the house which you can see; 1¼-inch iron pipe is used for water-heater. Do you suppose the trap in stove causes it?

A. We think there are several good reasons why the pipes or the boiler, especially the first, when made of lead, should burst in an apparatus designed as that shown in your sketch.

The bursts in the pipe are due to the changes the lead pipe is subjected to, by frequent and extreme changes of temperature under pressure, due to your boiler being too small for the water-back; or the state of your fire or the efficiency of your water-back is too great for the intermittent use that is made of the warm water.

When a kettle of water boils on the top of a stove and blows the cover off, or ejects steam and water from the spout, the cook removes the kettle or adds cold water. When she removes the kettle she places the water already in the kettle, which has received all the heat it should, beyond the influence of the fire. When she adds more cold water she still leaves the

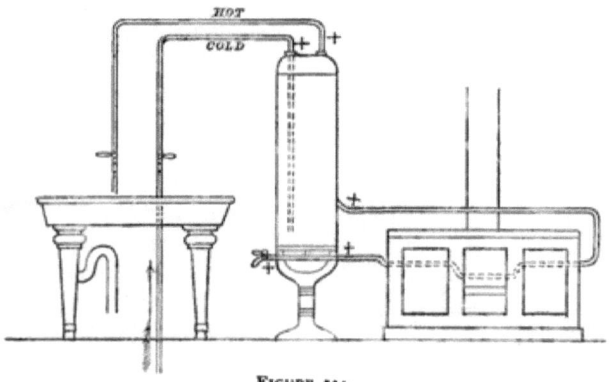

FIGURE 114.

kettle-bottom in a position to receive more heat, but as she has added water that is capable of absorbing considerable heat before the kettle again boils, she gains time by the operation, and has a larger supply of hot water on hand. Or, in the case of adding water, she may, when she finds the kettle boiling, should it be full, draw half of it off, and fill it up with cold water, in either of which cases she gains time and warms more water.

In many respects the range-boiler is similar to the water-kettle, and in others it differs from it. One point of similarity is that both are reservoirs; another is, the kettle receives heat through its bottom by the freest of circulations, while the boiler receives its heat through the "water-back" by a circulation which is more or less good, according to the skill and knowledge with which the connections are made.

The most striking point of difference is that when the kettle boils the cook can take it off the fire, but with the range-boiler it is beyond her power to prevent its receiving more heat short of putting out the fire, and there is nothing left for her to do but to run hot water in the sink until enough cold water passes into the boiler to reduce the temperatures all around, and which may perhaps carry her to a time—after dinner, for instance—when the fire will be poor, and she will not have to attend to it. But it will be said that such a state of affairs is not the rule with kitchen-boilers, which is very true; but the reason it is not the rule is, that most kitchen or range boilers have surface enough on their outside to counteract the warming and heating effect of the water-back long before the water reaches a point to make steam. Or if they have not cooling surface enough on the outside of the boiler, they have long circulating-pipes which carry warm water to distant parts of the house and return it again, every square inch of which is efficient heat-dissipating or giving-off surface, which is continually counteracting the efforts of a smaller but more intense heat-absorbing surface in the water-back. Rarely do we hear of overheating and rumbling except where there is a defective cooling circulation, or no circulation at all. The *Sanitary Engineer* pointed out some years ago that properly there were *three* circulations in connection with a domestic boiler. The first and principal one, which must always exist, is *the circulation through the water-back*; the second, a *local circulation* in the boiler itself, due to receiving the primary circulation from the back into the boiler well down, instead of at the top; and a third circulation, which takes place in the distributing-pipes. The first circulation is a heating one only; the second is a mixing and cooling circulation, because as the water moves around within the boiler, fresh particles of it are brought against the outside, where it loses its heat; and the third one, when it exists, is always a cooling circulation.

The influence of the second circulation in a cool kitchen with an ordinary-sized back is generally sufficient to keep the temperatures under control, but in restaurants and other warm places, with strong fires and no third circulation, nothing but a very large reservoir (boiler) will do, as by that means a greater quantity of water has to be warmed in the first place, and larger cooling surface is maintained for the secondary circulation to act on.

In your case, in addition to having too much back for the boiler, or too little boiler for the back, whereby you get the water up to the point of making steam, you have nothing like an air-chamber to receive the force of the shocks caused by the concussions which follow drawing water when steam is evolved When you draw hot water, cold water passes into the boiler, and a succession of short quick blows evidently follows. The act of drawing water lessens the pressure, and the water in the boiler, which is already at the boiling point, gives off steam suddenly. It is this steam which makes the water-hammering when being condensed as it meets the colder water.

The violent and sudden changes of temperature also assist in the disintegration and stretching of the lead pipes. The trap in the water-back is something we do not like, as its tendency is to retard this circulation, but in your case you evidently do not want to increase the primary circulation, and unless it is necessary to alter the coil for some other purposes it will do.

Hard-metal pipes (brass or iron) will resist the stretching from difference of temperature and pressure better than the lead, and a larger boiler may overcome the other troubles, such as noise, etc.

The rumbling caused when cold water is drawn is also due to the lessening of pressure whereby the steam passes into the cold-water pipe at the head of the boiler through the small hole in the inner pipe. Condensation follows, and a succession of small shocks are felt.

GIVING-OUT OF LEAD VENT-PIPES FROM BOILERS IN AN APARTMENT-HOUSE.

Q. THE accompanying sketch, Figure 115, shows the arrangement of six bath-boiler systems in a building in New York, constructed to rent in separate stories or flats. We would like the views of other plumbers as to the cause of bursting of the lead vent-pipes B, B, B, B, B, B, and suggestions as to methods of remedying the difficulty. The fractures do not present the appearance of frost burst, but where the break occurs the lead looks like burned or dried sole-leather. The lead looks puckered or crumpled near the break. We know it is caused by the action of steam. The ranges are Mott's "G" ranges, of small size, and the boilers thirty-five gallons. We suggested to put a fire-brick or soapstone in front of the water-back, but the boiler being so small there is already complaint of a deficient supply of hot water, and this method of limiting the heat in the pipes is not approved, although when all the hot water is not used the boilers get very hot. The pipes do not burst in any particular place or at any given distance from the boiler, nor does the season of the year seem to have anything to do with the bursting, as might have been supposed, for at times the vapor freezes on the roof. Might not a circulating-pipe at about the level of the tank (so that the system of pipe would always be full of water) down to the bottom of the water-back remedy the trouble? We would be pleased to have this question discussed by experts in the plumbing business.

HOT WATER CIRCULATION IN BUILDINGS. 171

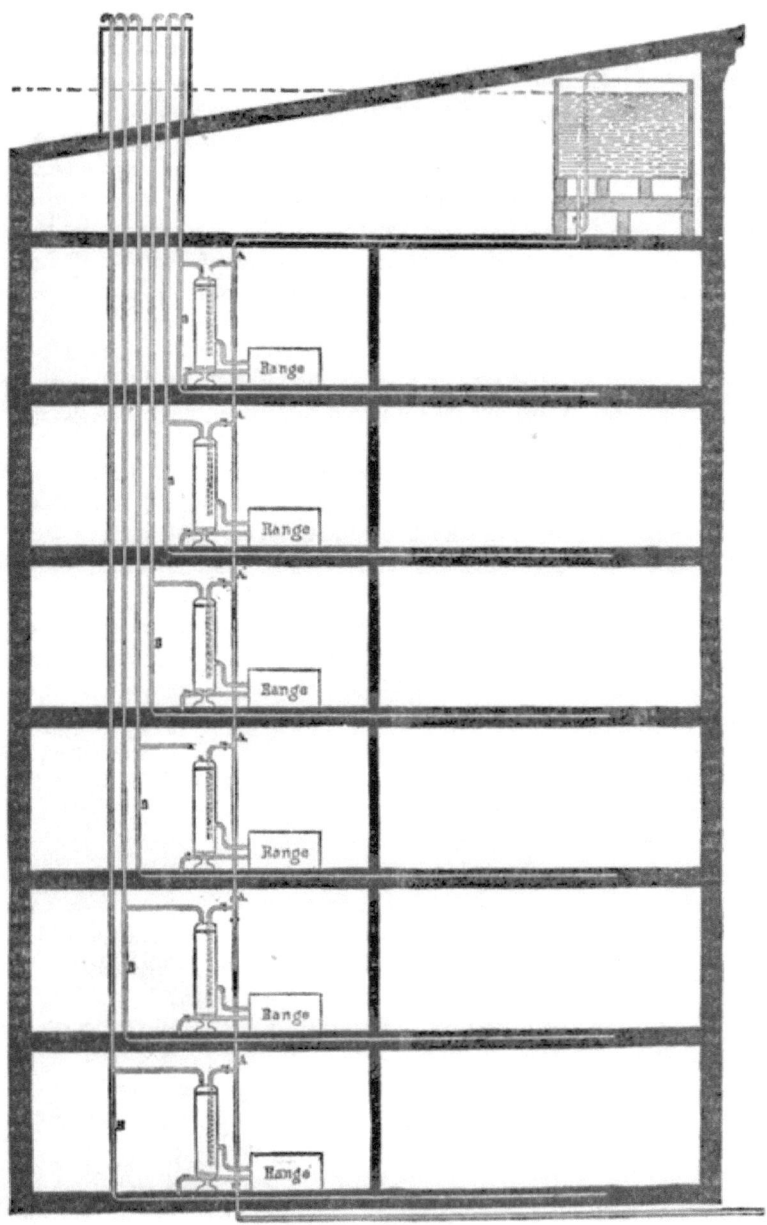

Figure 115.

A. An experienced plumber of New York City, to whom this was referred, says that, judging from the samples of pipe shown him, it probably came from a bend where the weight of lead above had caused it to bend out of the vertical at a place where it was not securely fastened to the wall or other support. The particles on the inner side of the bend tend to crowd each other out, and the tendency was yielded to at the ruptured place on account of imperfect lead. The strain on these pipes from contraction and expansion, and also from the shock given by the closing of supply-cocks, is very great, from their great length and heavy weight, and they break at the weakest points, where the metal is poor.

Another experienced plumber says: "From the description given with the cut, and inferring from the additional notes, we suppose the pipes to be of lead, in which case it is not always necessary to generate steam to cause them to burst, though from your description of looks of the material where burst, it is very likely that steam has been at times generated. We have on several occasions heretofore advised against the use of lead pipe for water-back connections, and the same is true in regard to hot-water pipes, especially so in small boilers, where the hot water is entirely drawn off and is replaced by cold water."

The inferences which we draw from the sketch and description are: (1) That the bath-boilers are too small for the service of hot water, as well as too small for the water-backs, so that in the common usage of the ranges the water in the boiler becomes overheated to the point where steam is generated under the small pressure which these low vent-pipes will produce. It would seem that the water and steam commingled in all of the vent-pipes ought to be lifting frequently, and especially in the vent-pipes in the uppermost stories. (2) It is inferred that the lead vent-pipes are confined or held without adequate freedom to expand and contract, or to *crawl*. As is suggested, lead is a poor material for pipes likely to be hot and cold; it is nearly worthless for a steam-pipe at any pressure, failing sooner or later, much as is described. Galvanized-iron pipes suspended from the top, or securely held at the bottom and free to rise at the top, are certainly preferable to lead pipes in this place.

The proposition for a circulating-pipe will not meet approval unless the upper bend be made in a small tank or vessel, where the steam can *separate*, which tank should be a closed one, with a safety-valve headed to a little less than the supply-tank head. Thus arranged the circulation would become solid, and not a "geyser-like" ebullition

CONNECTING A KITCHEN-BOILER WITH ONE OR MORE WATER-BACKS.

It frequently happens that the kitchen-boiler must be connected with two or more ranges. Sometimes the reason is that the water-back in a laundry-range must be connected with it for the purpose of getting more hot water on washing days, and again it frequently happens that a winter kitchen is on the first floor of a house, and that the summer kitchen is in an extension or in a basement. This sometimes happens and admits of several combinations. Sometimes they are a matter of choice, but more often of necessity.

When one range is in an upper room above another range in a room below, the diagrams *a, b, c*, and *d* illustrate the principles involved in the forms usually met with.

Diagram *a* is used when a boiler is provided with *two* side couplings and *two* bottom couplings, one set for each range. This requires just a little forethought and the knowledge that two water-backs are to be used. The increase in cost is inconsiderable, and it permits of entirely separate connections, which can in no way interfere with each other by influencing the flow of the water in either. From the lower water-back the flow of water will be more rapid than from the upper one, assuming they are alike in size and construction. The reason for this is that the up-take or flow-pipe and its return-pipe is so much longer, perpendic-

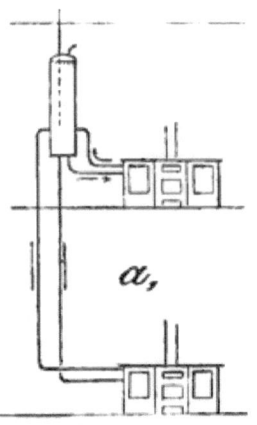

Figure 116.

ularly, than the same pipes from the upper water-back, that there is a greater relative difference of weight between the up-take and its corresponding *return*, that this difference increases with the increased lengths of the pipes, but in a very much inversed ratio, but still considerable and very marked to an observing plumber.

This (*a*) presumably is the most suitable connection for double ranges, but under one condition, at least, an objection has been made to it. It is claimed that should the lower range be in a cold or exposed place, and no fire in it, the water in the water-back and in the pipes leading to and from it will be inert—that is, have no circulation— and that they may freeze. This presumption is reasonable, and a method of securing a circulation from the boiler through them sufficient to prevent freezing is something for thoughtful plumbers to take into consideration.

In the case of the upper water-back and pipes freezing when the lower one is in use, the danger is not so great. The heat of the boiler is generally sufficient to warm the room beyond the danger of frost, and should the dampers of the stove be closed, so as to prevent a strong draught over the water-back, the danger is reduced to a minimum.

Diagram *b* shows the method generally followed when there is but one set of couplings on the lower part of the boiler. It is claimed by some that with this arrangement of pipes the water in neither back can freeze so long as one of the ranges is in use. It is claimed, for instance, that should the upper range be in use, the hot water flowing from the back into the boiler will draw the water from the lower back by induction, as it passes over it, thus keeping up a circulation through it from the return-pipe. However, this may be questioned. Of course, one can imagine how the stream of warm water from the upper range flowing over the end of the up-take pipe from the lower one may draw water out of it; but if we look a little further we will also see how the return-current to the water-back in the upper range will also be trying to draw water from the return-pipe to the lower water-back by the very same inductive principle which is applied to the other pipe, and that they may be assumed to balance each other and make abortive any claim that can be put forth for the principle. However, it may be that some accident of construction—some peculiarity of the making of a joint in lead pipe, for instance—may make one of the joints at their junctions a more favorable *injector*, if we may use the word, than the other, and that by this means the water will move in some one direction, which is just as likely to be drawn up through the return-pipe and into the water-back as passing up through the flow-pipe and into the boiler. As said, in lead pipe this can be assumed as likely to happen, but with brass or iron pipe the conditions of the junctions will be always the same, and positive circulation in the lower water-back without fire cannot be assured.

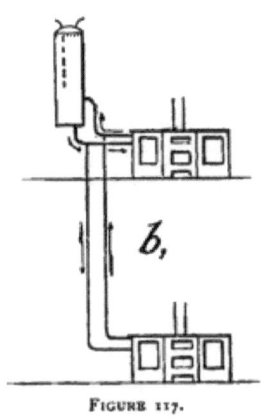

FIGURE 117.

Diagram *d* shows a method with which there is some hope of getting a positive circulation of the water through the lower back when the fire is out. It will be noticed that the flow-pipe from the upper back enters the flow-pipe from the lower one some distance below the side coupling of the boiler, and that there are two bottom couplings. The fact of there being *two* separate return-connections produces the result that there can be no inductive influence from one to the other on the return-flow in either. But, again, the fact of the upper flow-pipe joining the lower one at the level of the upper back makes it reasonable to assume that here an inductive influence may be at work. If instead, as in the diagram (*d*), the flow-pipe from the lower back entered the flow-pipe from the upper one, as in diagram *b*, there would appear to be no doubt of an induced circulation through the lower back. As *d* is now drawn, it is the most favorable for the inducing of a current through the upper back, if the lower range be in operation and the upper one cold.

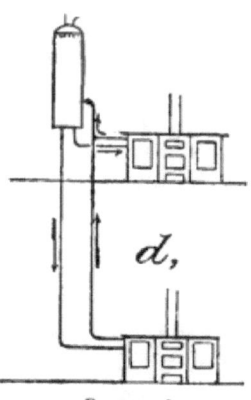

FIGURE 118.

Diagram *c* is a method which is claimed to be positive. The water is passed through the lower back first, then through the upper one, and into the boiler. When the lower range is in use this cannot be other than a positive method. On the other hand, when the upper range only is in use, there is reason to believe this method will not circulate freely under all conditions, and that at its best it will not do as well as separate or branched connections.

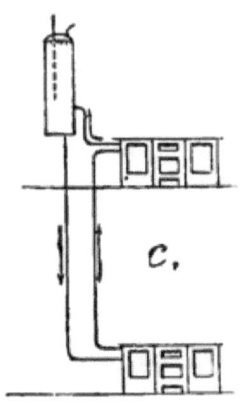

FIGURE 119.

The effect of this is to make a great *dip* or *trap* in the return-pipe. To have it circulate at all, the sum of the weight of water for a given height in the *two* flow-pipes—that is, the pipe from the lower back to the upper one and thence to the boiler—must be less than in the return-pipe, the perpendicular length of the return-pipe to be considered as just equal to the length of the combined flow-pipes; that part of the boiler below the side coupling being considered as part thereof. In this diagram (*c*), therefore, we have the water in the return-pipe of unknown density, but which we know to be less than in the flow-pipe between the water-backs, and greater than in the flow-pipe from the upper back to the boiler, having a power to produce the circulation, which we may illustrate this way: Assume the value or density of the water in the pipe between the two water-backs to be 100, as it is the coldest; assume the value of the down pipe to be 90, as it has not traveled so far nor through the water-back, and then assume the value of the water in the pipe from the warm back to the boiler to be 80. If we do so it will have $100-90=10+80=90$, or just a balance, and no circulation. If, on the other hand, we can give the pipe from the hot back to the boiler a value of 70 only, it will give a combined weight to this column only of 80, and as the corresponding cold column has a value of 90, the circulation will go on. But again, if we give it a value of 85 we will have a heavier column in the up-take side than on the return side, and an irregular, spasmodic effort of the water and steam to pass into the boiler will be the result every time the water in the back gets hot enough to make steam and force itself into the boiler during the momentary change of value in the weights of the columns due to the steam. An objection to this method, should it be used for the purpose of an increased quantity of hot water, and if both the water-backs would be constantly in use, is that the water, after passing through the first back, has been warmed so much that it cannot extract an equal quantity of heat in passing through the second back, and that, consequently, *two* backs separately connected to a boiler will warm more water in a given time than *two* backs connected in continuous order, as shown in diagram *c*.

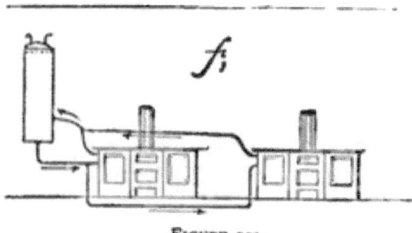

FIGURE 120.

Diagram *f* shows two ranges on the same floor connected with a single boiler. It is the usual method when there is only one side and one bottom coupling to the boiler, and when there are no doorways to pass. If the outer water-back is in a cold place there is almost always the chance of it freezing, as with *b*, because the inductive influence of the flow through the hot pipe from the near water-back is neutralized by the influence of the return flow in the return-pipe. A double coupling in the bottom, as shown in *d*, will prevent this.

Diagram *e* shows a method of connecting two ranges with the same boiler when a doorway has to be passed. It is not absolutely necessary that the flow-pipe from the first water-back should be connected as shown, as it may enter the usual side-coupling which is on all boilers, but it is necessary that the flow-pipe from the range beyond the doorway should enter the boiler as high as where it passes the doorway. Should this pipe be carried down to the side coupling, the chances are the circulation will be spoiled by an accumulation of air in the top of the syphon, or very much checked in its speed by the too nearly equal weights of the rising and falling columns.

The higher the flow-pipe from a water-back can rise before it enters the boiler—provided it is not exposed to the influence of cold air—the more rapid the circulation will be and the more water that can be warmed in a given time, the water-backs being equal in every other respect.

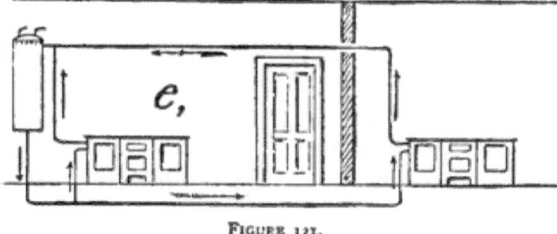

FIGURE 121.

The same laws that are true of circulation in a hot-water house-heating apparatus are also true of boiler circulations.

With diagram e it would be better to have one side-coupling at the top of the boiler, and two bottom-couplings, with a separate return. This would insure an inductive movement of the water in the range not in use and give the maximum effect in warming water. But this not only applies here, but to all boilers. The side-coupling of the ordinary boiler is too low down, if one desires to secure the best results with a given size of water-back. The rapidity of circulation depends on the difference in weight in the two columns. The longer these columns are the greater the difference will be. Again, the power of a water-back to absorb heat increases in a proportion nearly equal to the increase of velocity of the water up to a point which can never be obtainable with any but mechanical or forced circulations.

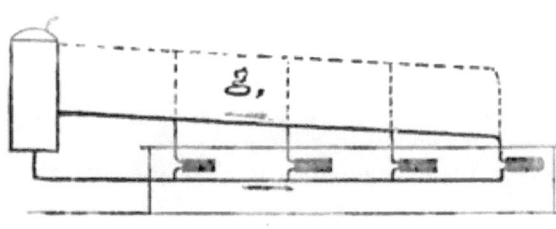

FIGURE 122.

Diagram g shows a method used to connect a large kitchen-boiler with more than one water-back in a long range, such as is sometimes used in a large institution or hotel kitchen, where much hot water is required, but there is no means of making it with steam. This shows the ordinary coupling arrangement, and it is probably the best connection that can be made with two couplings with the minimum of pipes. But the dotted lines show a method which will warm water much more rapidly.

It now and then happens that a plumber has to connect two boilers with one water-back. This, on general principles, he is opposed to doing, but it frequently happens that the maker of a range objects to putting an extra back into it, especially if he has to remove any of the fire-brick lining to do so, usually claiming that it will spoil the baking properties of his ovens, and he will allow the use of a coil or extra back only under protest.

To take out the single back and replace it with two small ones is no better than to connect the two boilers to the single back, because, as

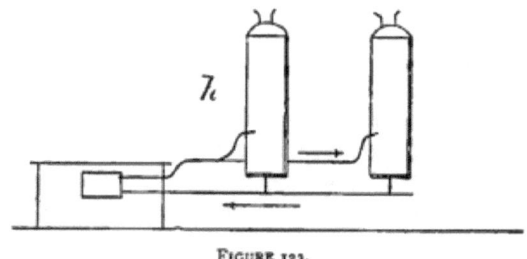

FIGURE 123.

a general thing, the surface of the backs cannot be increased. Therefore the plumber is compelled by circumstances to do the best he can with the range and back as he finds them. He might, of course, tap extra holes in the back—*two* flow-holes at the top and *two* return-holes at the bottom—but then it entails extra expense and trouble and alterations in the stove to get both sets of pipes through to the boilers, and thus he is forced to connect two boilers to a single water-back.

Diagram h is the way it usually suggests itself for the first time. It is the simplest, and all the flow-pipes have an upward tendency toward the boiler, with a level return-pipe, or it may be that the plumber can secure a little pitch toward the water-back.

This will work tolerably well if the two boilers are very near together—that is, the first boiler will heat fairly well, and the second one not so well, but as it is furthest from the range it is hardly to be expected of it, either in the opinion of the man who puts it up or the user; and hence the differences of temperature and the time of "warming up" are looked on as a natural result, and past correcting, at least with the majority of people. But the limit of improvement in this direction has not been reached, and it has been found that a simple change, such as that shown by diagram *i*, insures equal temperatures to both boilers. The flow-pipe must be carried across some short distance above the "side couplings" on the boilers, and the side couplings should be set so as to be on the same level. The flow-pipe should be made large after it leaves the range—say twice the diameter of the side-coupling connection. It should also be perfectly level beyond the point where it reaches its greatest height, just close to the range, and the branches which connect with the side couplings should be taken out in the same manner from the flow-pipe, and dropped a few inches before entering the boiler. By this method the flow-pipe has considerable capacity, and becomes a reservoir of hot water of

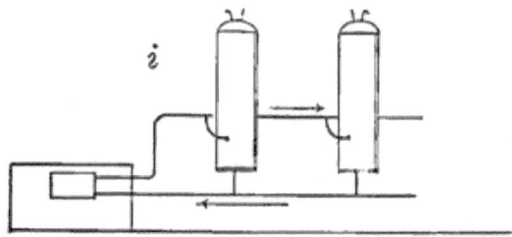

FIGURE 124.

practically the same temperature throughout. From this pipe the water to the side connections will descend by gravity, due to cooling, and the whole distance between the level of the flow and return-pipe, in a line through the boilers, forms the "down" legs of the circulation, while the "up" leg is the rising pipe from the water-back and the back itself. This method balances the conditions for both boilers, and each receives the same amount of the flow.

By using a large flow-pipe, a very considerable distance may be maintained between the boilers, giving results so nearly equal that the difference cannot be detected by the hand. This method forms a syphon, in the head of which air or steam might lodge when they are present, and for this reason an air-cock or branch to a sink should be run from the end of the flow-pipe. Generally this will not give trouble when the air is once drawn out, and with two boilers steam can scarcely be formed with an ordinary-sized back.

Should one of these boilers be beyond a doorway, as it is very likely to be should it be in a laundry or other room, the fitter will find it necessary to run the flow-pipe above the doorway to reach the further boiler, returning under the floor. If he attempts this at all, he is very likely to run his pipes as shown in diagram *j*. He is likely, as he brings his pipe from the water-back, to run upward about as shown, taking a branch to the side coupling of the nearest boiler as he passes it, then run up and along the wall over the doorway, dropping as soon as possible to the side coupling of the further boiler. The return of the nearer boiler he is apt to run in the usual manner—taking it back above the floor. The return of the other boiler he is forced to carry below the floor, to prevent a stumbling-block at the doorway, and to enter the water-back with it he is most likely to connect it about as shown into the return from the near boiler.

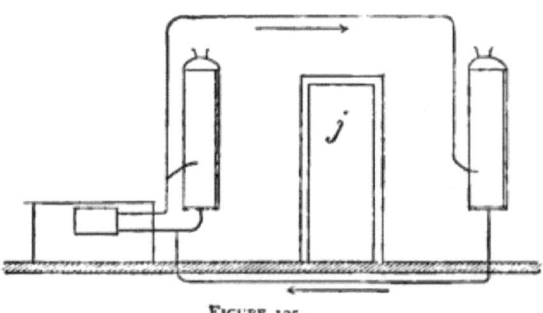

FIGURE 125.

The result of this is to produce a fairly rapid circulation through the first boiler, with a poor circulation in the boiler beyond the doorway. As in the first case, it is likely to be looked on as something that cannot be avoided—in fact, a natural consequence. Let us consider why it is. The distance between the boilers is a factor against the further one, but, after all, not a factor of as great consequence as is generally considered. What are the other factors for or against the circulation? Let us dismiss the idea of a "push" from the water-back, and consider only the difference of weights of the descending and ascending columns of water. The circulation to the first boiler (diagram *j*) is up through the flow-pipe and down to the level of the back again through the return-pipe. This makes a *hot* "up-leg" and a *cooler* "down-leg," insuring a circulation of unknown volocity, but, nevertheless, a positive circulation in the right direction, and about equal to that in an ordinarily set single boiler. The circulation to the second boiler (same diagram) is also up, making a long *hot* "up-leg," thence across the doorway to a "down-leg," which can be very little cooler than the "up-leg," *if the circulation is to be rapid enough to maintain warm water in the boiler.* If the latter is the fact, then the up and down legs of the flow-pipe to this boiler nearly balance themselves, the preponderance being slightly in favor of the down-leg. But the return-pipe of this boiler has not yet been considered. Taking it from the bottom of the boiler, it again forms a down-leg (which, in its fullest sense, is a part of the down-leg of the circulation), and has a temperature somewhat less than the boiler. Then it flows across underneath the floor, and loses more heat, until it comes to rise again near the stove, where it forms an *up-leg* again, which leg is cooler than an equal perpendicular height in its corresponding down-leg just mentioned, because it has traveled further. This, then, gives a greater weight in the up-leg than in the down one, and a preponderance against the circulation. If, now, the factor in favor of the circulation in the down-leg of the flow-pipe outweighs the factor against the circulation in the up-leg of the return-pipe, there will be a circulation going on in the right direction. If, on the other hand, the factor against the circulation in the up-leg of the return circulation is the greater, the circulation will stop, or be extremely slow, until such time as the water in the down-legs of the flow and return can cool sufficient to overcome the resistance of the up-leg of the return, when there will be an intermittent circulation, or a *mean* (average) slow circulation established, which will be of no practical use as a means of warming water.

Diagram *k* shows a method for getting equal circulations of practical value in both boilers when one is beyond a doorway. The flow-pipe is carried from the back, of ample size, direct to the height of the doorway, and run to both boilers. The side-coupling connections are then dropped of equal size and distance. The returns from both boilers are dropped to an equal distance below the floor and carried back in a return-pipe to the water-back, as shown, rising underneath the flow-pipe to enter the range. This gives precisely the same piping and circulation to each boiler, and prevents a "short circuit" by way of the first boiler.

To a critical examiner it may now appear that a method is put forward in diagram *k* for the two boilers that is very much the same as for the further boiler in diagram *j*, and the question is very likely to be asked, How is it that it will work on two or more boilers and not in the case of the single one? It does work in the case of the single one, but poorly: first, because the hot water makes a short circuit through the nearer boiler; and, secondly, because of the slow circulation to the further boiler, the rising legs cool more and lessen their power to ascend, and though the down-legs also cool, they do not cool in the same proportion, so as to equally increase the power to descend, for the reason that the hot pipe loses more heat per unit of surface than the cooler one, the loss being about directly as the difference of temperatures between the pipes and the air of the rooms they are in. For this reason the return-pipe beneath the floor should be covered to prevent loss of heat.

With diagram *k* the very hot water from the water-back goes directly to the upper horizontal flow-pipe, which should be of large diameter. In the rarity and lightness of this vertical column, nearly all

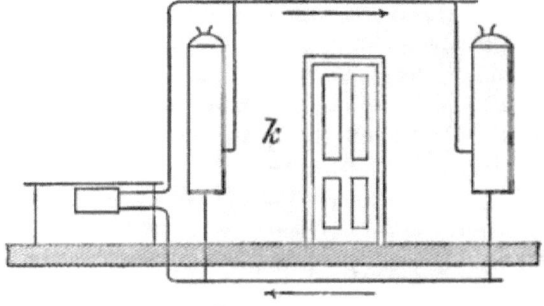

FIGURE 126.

of the power to circulate exists. The quick passage of the water to supply two boilers through this pipe lessens the loss of heat to the water of a single boiler—not meaning that less heat is lost per unit of pipe-surface, as that is a constant, and therefore more nearly maintaining an equal density throughout its length. On the other hand, in the down-legs of the flow-pipes and "return"-pipes, the same quantity of water is divided between two pipes, and consequently it has a slower velocity and more surface and loses more heat; therefore becoming more dense, and adding to the power to move the up-column, or whole circulation. Then, where they merge into a single pipe again, the velocity doubles, and though the loss per unit of surface is the same, the loss from the water is only half what it would be in two upward pipes.

The distance dropped below the floor should be as short as possible and running in a box cut into the floor-joists, or running between them, and nicely packing with a non-conductor of heat, is more likely to insure a good circulation than using exposed pipes in a cellar, as all possible should be done to lighten the upward column in the return-pipe. It is an improvement, also, to cover the flow-pipe up to the point where it turns horizontally.

NEW METHOD OF HEATING TWO BOILERS BY ONE WATER-BACK.

Q. Is there not some arrangement by which two boilers can be heated from one water-back?

A. Figure 127 (page 184) illustrates a new method of warming two boilers from a single water-back, each boiler being under a different pressure.

The arrangement has been devised to overcome the objection to and necessity for *two* water-backs in the same range, where water from a tank or cistern at the top of a house must be warmed to supply the upper stories, while water for kitchen and laundry purposes and the lower stories is obtained directly from the street supply in the usual manner.

The contrivance consists essentially of the high-pressure or "tank" boiler A, the low-pressure or "Croton" boiler B, and, in the absence of any other name, what may be called the "*heater*," C; with, of course, a water-back of ample dimensions in the range.

There are three distinct circulations: (1) The warm water flowing from the back (which in this case is the low-pressure) passes through the pipe c to the heater C, returning through the pipe c'; (2) The warm water in the outside chamber (g) of the heater C, passing through the pipe d into the boiler B, and returning to the heater through the pipe d''; (3) The water from the inner chamber or tubes (f) of the heater C passing through the pipe e into the boiler A, and returning to the inner chamber again through the pipe e'.

It will be seen by this that the *first* and *second* circulations are low-pressure, and that the *third* is high or tank-pressure; but not so of necessity, as the tank-pressure may be used in the water-back, heater, and boiler B, transposing the order of the boilers; but the arrangement shown is, in the opinion of the inventor, the best, as by this order the tank may become empty, by neglect or otherwise, without danger to either boilers, or the tank-water may be shut off without drawing the fire.

The heater is seven inches in diameter by fourteen inches long, outside measurement, and is made of copper. The inner part (f) is a tubular heater, with connecting chambers at the ends. The water of the outer chamber is around and between the tubes, and imparts its

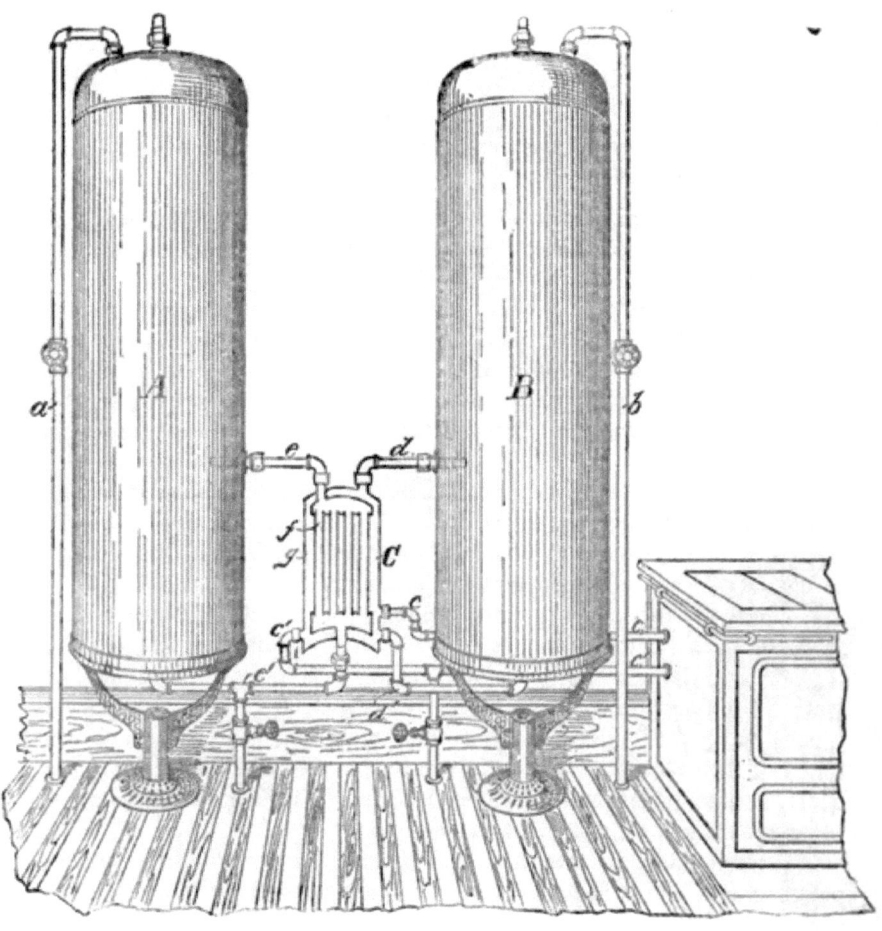

FIGURE 137.

heat to the water within the tubes. The tubes are three-quarters of an inch in diameter by ten inches long, and thirteen in number, and have been found by experiment to give equal temperatures to both boilers.

How much less surface in the inner part of the heater would give good results the inventor does not know, but he points out the fact that an excess of surface can have no other effect than to maintain an equable temperature between the boilers. He also points out that should the fire go down, leaving both boilers full of pretty hot water, and should the warm water in any one boiler be drawn away, exchanges of heat by circulation still go on between the boilers and the heater, warming the cold boiler, and, of course, cooling the warm one, but, nevertheless, giving a greater quantity of warm water from the boiler drawn on than could be gotten if it connected directly with its own water-back.

This was devised by Mr. John Tucker, of New York.

PLAN OF HORIZONTAL HOT-WATER BOILER.

COLONEL JAMES TUCKER, of Boston, furnished us with the plan, Figure 128 (see page 186), and description of the method he adopted in fitting up a horizontal boiler in a house near Boston, which we take from the *Sanitary Engineer* of December 1, 1880.

The construction of the kitchen would not admit of the boiler being placed in the usual upright position; the sink and range occupied all the space between the two doors, there being no other available place to locate the sink, consequently the boiler was made to order and slung horizontally over the range, on two iron bands three inches by one-quarter of an inch, connected on top of boiler by bolts and ¾-inch rods run up through the floor timbers with nuts on top. The water can be drawn off in the usual way and the boiler removed if necessary, the iron rods remaining in place. The cost of the iron rods and bands did not exceed two dollars more than the usual iron stand.

HOT WATER CIRCULATION IN BUILDINGS.

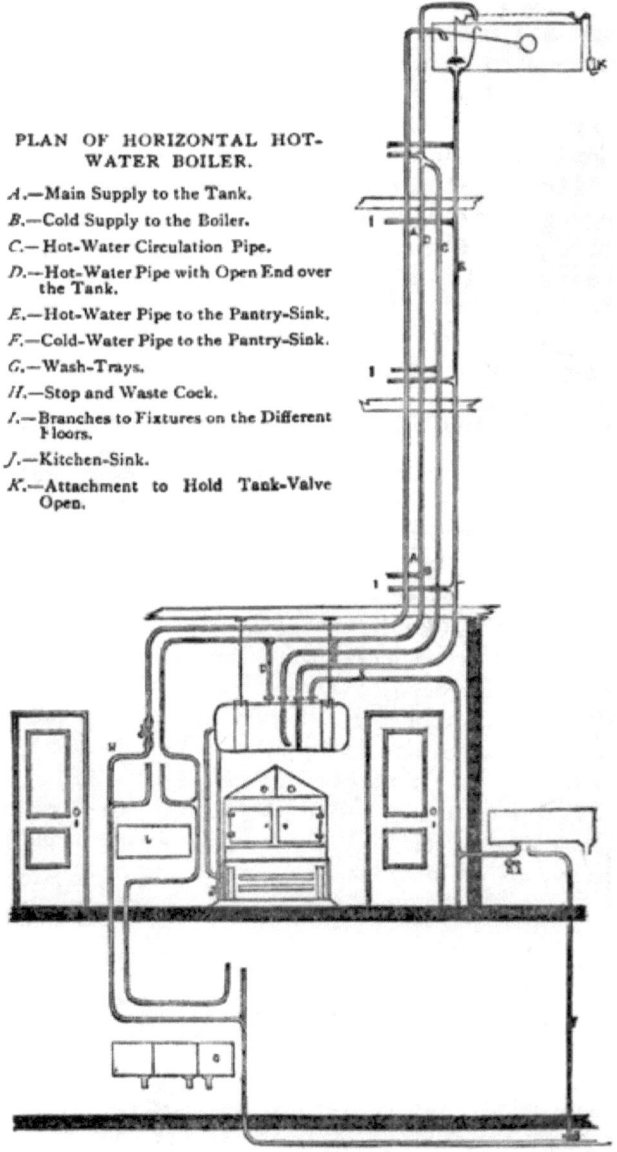

PLAN OF HORIZONTAL HOT-WATER BOILER.

A.—Main Supply to the Tank.
B.—Cold Supply to the Boiler.
C.—Hot-Water Circulation Pipe.
D.—Hot-Water Pipe with Open End over the Tank.
E.—Hot-Water Pipe to the Pantry-Sink.
F.—Cold-Water Pipe to the Pantry-Sink.
G.—Wash-Trays.
H.—Stop and Waste Cock.
I.—Branches to Fixtures on the Different Floors.
J.—Kitchen-Sink.
K.—Attachment to Hold Tank-Valve Open.

FIGURE 129. (See preceding page.)

HOT WATER SUPPLY IN VARIOUS BUILDINGS.

KITCHEN AND HOT WATER SUPPLY IN THE RESIDENCE OF MR. W. K. VANDERBILT, NEW YORK.

The following extract is taken from the articles on the plumbing in this house that appeared in the sixth volume of the *Sanitary Engineer*:

Figure 129 represents a portion of the kitchen, showing the range and boilers, most of the water-pipes, and the sink. The sketch was made before the hood over the range was in place, as it would have hidden the greater part of the boilers. The inside is plastered on a perforated lining of galvanized-iron separated from the outer shell of copper to prevent radiation of heat from the range and boilers into the room. The hood is very heavy and is supported from the floor-beams above by galvanized-iron hangers of an ornamental pattern. Hot air and odors from the range are removed into a chimney-flue through an opening partly seen behind the left-hand boiler.

The range has two fire-boxes, square in horizontal section, and each fire-box has two water-backs, so arranged that either fire-box will heat water for either boiler alone or both together. Each water-back is shaped like a short piece of angle-iron, lining two adjacent sides of the fire-box, while the two opposite sides are lined with the corresponding water-back, so that each fire-box is surrounded on all sides by water-backs.

There are two boilers, as will be seen, hung in a horizontal position over the range. That on the left, marked a, is designed to be supplied from the street-pressure, and the other, a_1, from the tanks in the top of the house. These boilers are made of very heavy copper, weighing about 360 pounds each, and are supported on brass "cradles" attached to the brass rods $b\ b$. It will be noticed that each boiler has four pipes, c, c, c, c, to the range. This is to provide for the heating of water for either boiler by one fire-box; one pair of each set of pipes crosses to the fire-box below the other boiler, or, in other words, each fire-box

FIGURE 109.

has a pair of pipes from each boiler. These pipes are of heavy brass, like all the water-pipes shown, and are one and a half inches in inside diameter. Each has a stop-cock just below the boiler, as shown at d, operated by wrench-handles, put on only when occasion requires their use. The 1-inch pipe e, entering the extreme left-hand c-pipe (being the supply from the street-pressure boiler to one of the water-backs in the fire-box below it), is the return or circulation pipe from the plate-warmer in the butler's pantry, directly over the kitchen. The main circulation-pipe f (also 1-inch), for the street-pressure boiler, enters the third c-pipe from the left, which is the supply from the street-pressure boiler (on the left) to the right-hand fire-box. The 1-inch pipe g (the lowest of those on the right) is a continuation of the lower horizontal part of f, and is for emptying the street-pressure boiler. The $1\frac{1}{4}$-inch pipe h, coming to the extreme right-hand c-pipe, is the circulation for the tank-boiler, a_1. The 1-inch branch i (not shown as large as it is proportionally) is for emptying the tank-boiler. The $1\frac{1}{2}$-inch pipe j, entering the right-hand boiler, is from the tanks, while k is from the street. It is two inches in diameter at its entrance, diminished to one and a half inches after the two 1-inch branches k_3 k_4 have been taken from it to other fixtures. It continues this size, in k_1, to the boiler a. The $1\frac{1}{4}$-inch pipe k_2 goes to fixtures in other rooms. The main hot-water supply l, from the street-pressure boiler, is $1\frac{1}{2}$-inch, diminishing as it sends off branches, l_1 being $1\frac{1}{4}$-inch, l_2 1-inch, and l_3 (to the butler's pantry-sink) $\frac{1}{2}$-inch. In like manner the several pipes marked m, m_1, and m_2 are the hot-water supplies from the tank-boiler, being of the following sizes, respectively: $1\frac{1}{2}$-inch, $1\frac{1}{4}$-inch, and 1-inch. These supply-pipes from the tank-boiler go to all fixtures needing hot water above the first floor, which, with the basement, is supplied from the street-pressure system. This arrangement was necessary from the fact that the public supply is uncertain above the first floor in this house. Though it may never be necessary, an interchange of this system (so far as is possible) is provided through the $1\frac{1}{4}$-inch and $1\frac{1}{2}$-inch pipes n and o, connecting the street supply-pipe k with the tank supply-pipe j. By opening the cock on n water is admitted from the street supply-pipe to the tank-boiler, and by opening that on o water from the tank supplies all street-pressure fixtures, check-valves p p on both n and o preventing the water from flowing the wrong way.

All the stop-cocks have removable handles. They are not kept on as shown in the illustration, but were put on, with the handles at right angles with the pipes, to show them more clearly. From each is a ⅜-inch waste-pipe to empty the part of the pipe beyond the cock when it is closed. These connect with the ¼-inch pipes g g (finally increased to ½-inch) which discharge the waste from all the cocks into the under-drainage.

In the extreme left of the view, the pipe r (of brass, 1-inch) is a safe-waste from a sink, and the large pipe s a steam-heating pipe, canvas-covered.

The range, as is evident from the illustration, is remarkably extensive. It was, of course, made specially for this place, and with great pains. A plate-warmer, t, of iron, stands on the back part. There are two fire-boxes, u u, as already intimated; three baking-ovens, v v; a roasting-oven, w; a broiler, x; and beneath it an ash-bin, y.

The room is very large, and finished in a very substantial and durable, but simple style. The floor is of small, irregular broken chips of white marble rolled in a dark brown cement and afterward rubbed smooth. Around this, next the walls, is a black border five inches wide, made of small (⅝-inch) squares of marble; inside of this is a narrower band (3-inch) of similar white marble blocks, and inside of this a single row of black squares. The walls, to the height of nearly four feet above the base-boards, which are of black marble, are finished in dove-colored marble capped by a border of black marble, and above that in white tiles having a simple blue pattern. All the projecting edges of the wall (as those of the piers at each end of the range) are covered by rounded strips of brass, fitted over the edges of both the intersecting faces of tile, and fastened with brass screws driven into wooden plugs inserted in holes drilled in the brick. All projecting face angles of tiled wall throughout the house are finished in the same way. There are several sets of white marble shelves in the angles of the wall, with backs of the same material, and under the windows, opposite the range, is a single shelf of marble, very large, with marble back and ends. It measures about two feet wide by twenty feet long and is two and a half inches thick. The sink shown on the right is cut from a single block of dove-colored marble.

In the butler's pantry, directly over a part of the kitchen, are two sinks of heavy white porcelain, each measuring about 18 x 30 inches, set in Italian marble slabs, with casings of cherry-wood. They have standing overflows, nickel-plated, with flaring tops to secure a more rapid escape of water. The supplies are ½-inch, and the waste 3-inch with 3-inch trap, from which is 2-inch vent. One sink has counter-cocks and the other "bibs" with long shanks—in both cases heavily nickel-plated and made specially for this place. Within a casing adjoining one of the sinks is a plate-warmer, consisting of a coil of 1-inch brass pipe, through which circulates hot water from the street-pressure kitchen-boiler, having a direct return to the water-back, as already described in explanation of the illustration.

The architect under whose direction the work was done is Mr. Richard M. Hunt; the plumber is Mr. John Toumey.

KITCHEN AND HOT WATER SUPPLY IN THE RESIDENCE OF MR. CORNELIUS VANDERBILT, NEW YORK.

The following extract is from the description of the sanitary arrangements in the residence of Mr. Cornelius Vanderbilt, New York, in the seventh volume of the *Sanitary Engineer:*

The kitchen in this house contains a large amount of plumbing-work. In it, or connected with it, are some features peculiar to this place, or at least such as we have not before described.

The sketch, Figure 130, shows the arrangement of the greater part of the work. One of the most striking peculiarities seen in it is the location of the range. Instead of being placed against the wall between brick piers, under the chimney or very near it, it stands out in the room two feet or more from the wall behind, and at a considerable further distance from the chimney, which is on the right hand beyond the end of the range.

Another novel feature is the method of supporting the horizontal boilers. They are usually suspended from the ceiling, but here they are supported from the floor, resting in nickel-plated iron frames of an ornamental pattern. The boilers—one for street and one for tank pressure service—are of heavy copper, with riveted heads. Each is connected with two water-backs, so arranged that both boilers may be heated from either of two fire-boxes, or either boiler alone heated from either fire-box. The upper boiler is supplied from the street-pressure, and furnishes hot water for all the baths, basins, and sinks below the third floor. The lower boiler is supplied from the tank, and furnishes hot water for fixtures above the third floor. Those on that floor may be supplied from either. The supply-pipe to the street-pressure boiler is connected with that to the tank-boiler by a pipe having in it a valve opening toward the latter, so that if the tank-supply should fail the tank-boiler will fill from the street-pressure; or, by a stop-cock on this

FIGURE 120.

connecting pipe, the tank-boiler may be shut off entirely and the street-supply only used. Vacuum-pipes are connected with the hot supplies from each boiler to prevent any danger of collapse in case the supply fails. These join and enter the sediment-pipe below the stop-cock on it, thus furnishing an air-inlet if there should ever be need of one. A valve on each pipe above their junction, opening inward, prevents loss of water from either under normal conditions.

The following is an explanation of the lettering on the sketch : a, the street-pressure boiler ; b, the tank-pressure boiler, each about 150 gallons capacity ; c, the supply to the street-pressure boiler, $1\frac{1}{4}$-inch, passing around through the outer divisions of three sink grease-traps before entering the boiler ; d (1-inch), from the boiler a to a water-back in the right-hand fire-box ; e ($1\frac{1}{4}$-inch), return from the range to the boiler ; f ($1\frac{1}{4}$-inch), hot supply from the street-pressure boiler, passing both to the upper floors and to the cellar ; g ($\frac{3}{4}$-inch), return circulation to this boiler ; h (1-inch), the cold-water connection from the same boiler with a water-back in the left-hand fire-box ; and i ($1\frac{1}{4}$-inch), the hot-water return to the boiler. The ($1\frac{1}{4}$-inch) pipe k is the supply to the tank-boiler b ; l (1-inch) is the cold-water connection of this boiler with the other water-back in the left-hand re-box ; m ($1\frac{1}{4}$-inch), the hot-water return ; n ($1\frac{1}{4}$-inch), the supply from the tank-boiler going direct to the division-cock on the third floor, and o ($\frac{3}{4}$-inch), the return circulation. The other water-back in the right-hand fire-box is connected with the same boiler by the pipes p (1-inch) and q ($1\frac{1}{4}$-inch). The vacuum-pipes $r\ r$ ($\frac{3}{4}$-inch) join and enter the sediment-pipes below their junction. The latter are behind the range and not seen ; there is one for each boiler, being a $\frac{3}{4}$-inch branch from one of the two pipes leading from each boiler to the range. The combined sediment and vacuum pipe terminates over a sink in the cellar. The connection between the street and tank supplies, spoken of above, is marked s, and is 1-inch.

The remaining letters apply to the pipes under the enameled-iron sink at the left of the range : t is the entrance of the cold-water pipe (supplying boiler a) to the outer part of the grease-trap u, and v its exit ; $w\ w$ is the waste (2-inch), forming a deep trap, and x the air-pipe to prevent syphoning ; y is the hot water-supply to the sink, and z the cold, both $\frac{1}{2}$-inch.

In a corner of the room, in front of the range, is a deep pot-sink, of tinned and planished copper (not seen in the sketch). This has the same kind of grease-trap on the waste. This sink is so deep, and the bottom consequently so near the floor, that there was not room to put the grease-trap above it. Accordingly, a hole was made large enough for it through the brick and concrete floor, and lined with an iron casing or box. The boiler-supply water is passed around the grease-trap in this way: The main line runs along beneath the floor (suspended from the ceiling of the cellar) past the location of the trap above. Directly opposite the trap a stop-cock is placed on the main line, and a branch, taken off on one side, passes through the trap and comes back into the main line on the other side of the stop-cock when the latter is closed. If it is open and those on the branches closed it flows straight past. It may be well to explain here, for the benefit of those who have not seen this grease-trap or a description of it, that the water is thus made to circulate around it (through an annular space entirely separated from the interior), for the purpose of cooling the collected grease and causing it to solidify. The supply to the boiler is chosen to effect this object, because not only is there no objection to thus slightly warming the water, but it is actually so much saving of heat.

All the pipes, with their frames, supports, and fasteners, are nickel-plated. The brass pipes are frequently bent in long curves, like lead, and sharp turns with elbows avoided as much as possible. The piping is all put together with frequent unions, so that it can be easily taken apart. It was all fitted in position while unplated, then taken down and put back after being plated.

Over the range is a very large copper hood for arresting and removing the odors and hot air. As this would have hidden much of the piping if shown in the sketch, it is only indicated in dotted lines. The outline is not strictly correct; the width is considerably greater, projecting in front of the range a foot or two. It is hung from the iron floor-beams overhead. The hot air and odors from cooking are carried off through an opening in one end of the hood into a rectangular duct surrounding the smoke-pipe.

A plate-warmer on the back of the range was left out entirely to avoid confusion in the sketch. Attached to that are several gas-burners to light the range. The gas-pipe comes up through the range into one of the rods supporting the shelves of the plate-warmer, and thence along behind the turned-down front edge of the upper shelf, and is thus entirely hidden.

The architect under whose direction this work was done was Mr. George B. Post; the plumbers were Messrs. Robert Ennever & Son.

KITCHEN AND HOT WATER SUPPLY IN THE RESIDENCE OF MR. HENRY G. MARQUAND, NEW YORK.

The following extract, showing only the kitchen, is from the description of the plumbing in the residence of Mr. H. G. Marquand, New York. Richard M. Hunt was the architect, and Alexander Orr the plumber.

The boilers A and B, Figure 131, are respectively the "Croton" and "tank" boilers shown in diagram Figure 3, page 96, issue of July 3, 1884, which diagram is illustrative of the system of piping used in the distribution of the hot and cold water.

The letters used here to indicate the parts are the same as those used in the diagram, and a comparison with it will familiarize the reader with the system and assist him to compare the disconnected parts.

The position of the kitchen is over A, cellar plan; the chimney-jambs corresponding to the position of the range shown in the cut, from which the position of the boilers and the sinks can be readily ascertained.

The "Croton" water-pipe m, $1\frac{1}{2}$ inches in diameter, is taken from the general cold system in the cellar through the floor at m, passing up and entering the boiler A at m on top. The "tank" water-pipe k, also $1\frac{1}{2}$ inches in diameter, comes through the floor from the tank-main in the cellar, entering the boiler at the top. Between the "Croton" pipe m to the boiler A and the tank-pipe k to the boiler B is a $\frac{3}{4}$-inch pipe, shown by dotted lines, and furnished with a stop-valve and check-valve, a'. The object of this pipe is to allow water to pass from the Croton-pipe m into the tank-pipe k, thence to the tank-boiler, should the water-supply from the tank be interrupted or should the tank be run empty. The passage of the water from the tank-pipe to the Croton-pipe is, of course, prevented by the check-valve, which only opens upward and which is kept to its seat when water is in the tank by the greater pressure. The pipe f is where the hot water leaves the Croton-tank for low distribution. Upward from the boiler it extends into a header (f), composed of $1\frac{1}{2}$-inch nipples and tees, from which the pipes f^3 extend to the different points of distribution, such as butler's pantry, billiard-room, servants' bath, and all points in basement and first floor, and to the "cut-offs" of the different risers to the second floor. In like manner the hot-water pipe l from the tank-boiler B extends into a *header*, l, from which the pipes l^1 either run to the fixtures on the third floor or to the "cut-offs" of the risers for the

second floor. The pipe f^1 is the warm "Croton" supply to the kitchen-sink, and is stopped in the pipe at the *star*. The pipe m^1 is a branch of the pipe m, and is the cold Croton water-supply to the same sink, stopping at the same *star*, the pipes being connected in this manner above the sink for the sake of a symmetrical appearance. In like manner the pipe f^2 conveys warm water to the pantry-sink, the pipe m^2 being the cold supply, the *star* being the dividing point, as before.

The pipe j is the return-circulation pipe to the Croton boiler, while l performs the same functions for the high-pressure circulation to the tank-boiler.

There are separate water-backs to each boiler, as plainly indicated in the illustration, the circulation-pipes being as shown. The pipe p, with its valves, show the "draw-off" connections of both boilers.

All the pipes shown, except the waste-pipes and air-pipes of the sinks, are seamless brass pipes, tinned, and the fittings are mostly special and of brass, the couplings being extra heavy with long threads, and all nickel-plated.

The sinks used are of white porcelain, supported in cast-brass frames, with turned legs. The slabs back of the sinks are of reddish-gray marble, against which the pipes are fastened. The arrangement of the traps and air-pipes are shown and are all plainly, though tastefully, "soiled."

Under the hood over the range is a large register opening into a flue parallel with the range-chimney flue, which latter warms it. This flue is 12″x16″ in its cross-section. The hood is lined inside and out with very light-tinted tiles, as are all the walls of the kitchen. The frame and rail under the lower edge of the hood are of brass, and the arrangement for connecting the range with its chimney-flues is such as to show no pipe.

The kitchen-floor is of encaustic tiles of selected designs, the colors being neutral.

KITCHEN AND HOT WATER SUPPLY IN THE RESIDENCE OF MR. A. J. WHITE.

FIGURE 132 shows another arrangement of a kitchen, and is in use in the residence of Mr. A. J. White, Fifth Avenue, New York City.

The kitchen is situated in a bay fronting on Sixty-sixth Street, the view showing three sides of an octagonal room, and illustrating an arrangement of *two* boilers—one on each side of the range—each being

198 HOT WATER SUPPLY IN BUILDINGS.

warmed by a separate water-back; the one on the *right* being the
"Croton" or low-pressure service boiler, while the other is the "tank"
or high-service boiler. The pipes are all of lead and very heavy, and
the "back-air" pipe from the sink-trap is carried upward after entering
the wall to the right of the sink. The "Croton," or street-supply, is

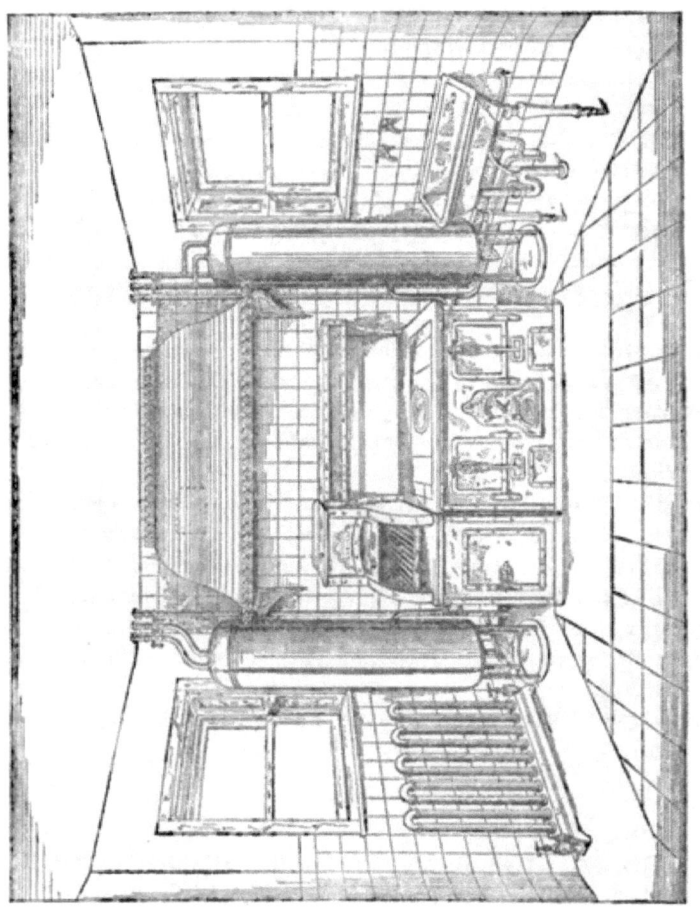

FIGURE 132.

shown coming through the floor just back of the sink-trap. From there
it may be traced under the boiler and up at the side, entering at the
centre "spud" of the boiler, and also continuing into the ceiling, it
being the centre pipe of the three. To the right of it the hot-water
pipe leaves the boiler and branches up and down, the downward pipe

being for the sink-faucet. The pipe which is the left of the three which here enter the ceiling is the return hot-water or "circulation-pipe." Its course can be traced to its junction, with the hot water entering the back, beyond which point it joins the boiler, and continues to become the "draw-off" or sediment-pipe. On the left of the picture is the high-service or "tank-boiler." The pipe to the extreme left conveys the hot water from the boiler; the one in the centre is the cold-water supply from the tank, and the one on the right the circulation-pipe.

The architect of the building is Mr. James E. Ware, of New York, and the master plumber is Mr. John Renehan.

HOT WATER SUPPLY IN AN OFFICE BUILDING.

FROM the article describing the plumbing of the Duncan Office Building, in New York, in the seventh volume of the *Sanitary Engineer*, we take the following, which refers to the hot-water supply:

The former supply of water to the building (which has been considerably increased in size in its reconstruction) was through a 1½-inch pipe from the low-pressure main in Pine Street. This connection remains, and supplies the fixtures in the cellar. All other fixtures are supplied from a new 3-inch pipe from the high-pressure main in Nassau Street—the basement-floor being supplied by the street-pressure direct, and the upper floors from a tank on the roof. Each supply has its own meter, and the two are connected so that either may take the place of the other in case one fails.

The water-pipe is all of galvanized-iron, except in exposed places above the cellar, as the connections with water-closet cisterns, where it is of brass, nickel-plated. All draw-cocks at basins and sinks are self-closing. Besides the fixtures mentioned in the first article are two water-closets, a basin, and two urinals in the basement. These urinals are flushed from a separate cistern; a chain in each stall is connected with the same valve, so that both urinals are flushed together whenever either chain is pulled. This arrangement is expected to secure a more frequent flushing than by the more common method of placing a stop-cock on the pipe to each urinal.

The accompanying drawing, Figure 133, represents the hot-water reservoir or boiler and connecting-pipes in the engineer's room in the cellar. On the right hand are seen the indicators showing the height of the water in the two iron tanks on the roof; the larger of these, having a capacity of about 4,500 gallons, supplies all the fixtures above the basement, except those in the janitor's apartments on the top floor, which are supplied from the smaller tank, which holds about 2,000 gallons. The

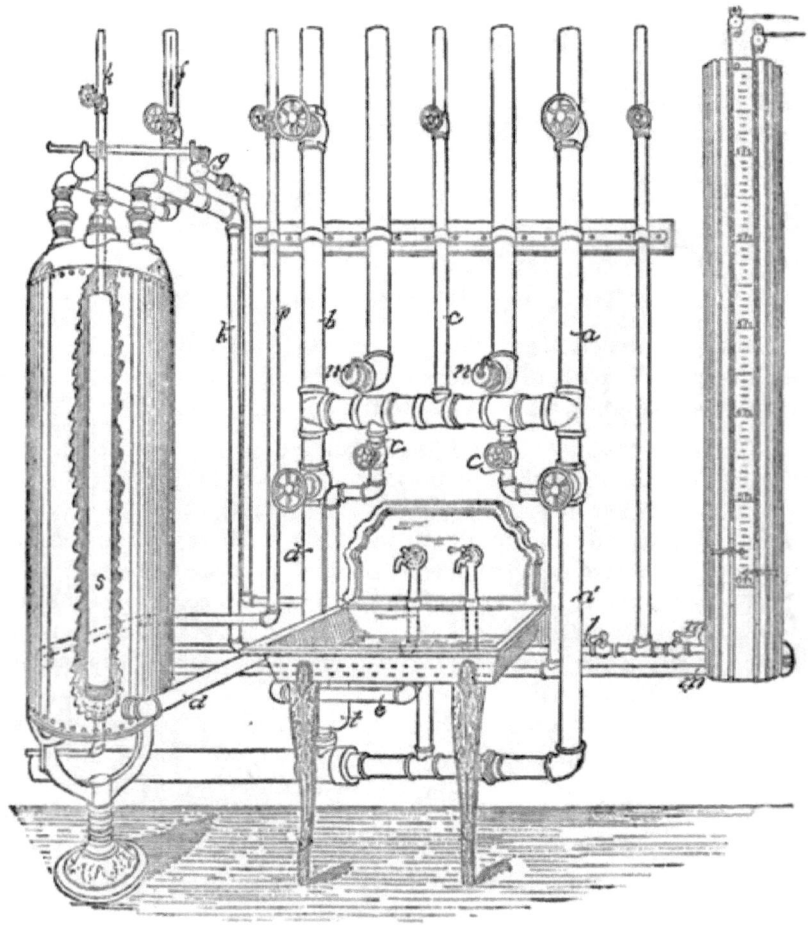

FIGURE 133

whole supply of the larger tank is brought to the cellar by the 2-inch pipe *a*; thence the greater portion is taken by the 2-inch pipe *b*, to supply the line of water-closets, urinals, and slop-sinks described in a preceding article. Other fixtures in different parts of the building are supplied by the 1-inch pipes *c c*. One of these, connected with *m*, supplies basins in the rear, which may also be supplied direct from the street, when the pressure is sufficient, through the pipe *l*, which supplies the sink shown. The 2-inch pipe *d* (reduced to 1½-inch at the turn behind the sink) supplies the boiler; at the junction of the horizontal and vertical parts of *d* a 1½-inch pipe, *e*, is taken to the drain-pipe below the sink for emptying the boiler. The tank may be emptied through *d'* into the same drain.

The water in the boiler shown (which supplies the slop-sinks on all the floors) is heated by steam passing through the 2-inch pipe *s* in the centre. The arrangement is essentially the same as that adopted by the same plumber in the Mills Building, as described in Vol. VI., page 203, of our issue of August 10, 1882. The connections have been somewhat simplified in this job by fittings devised by Mr. John Tucker, the foreman. The essential peculiarity is the provision for the expansion of the pipe inside the boiler. This is accomplished by passing the steam-pipe *k* (½-inch) through a stuffing-box on the top of the boiler, the expansion being taken up by the spring of the horizontal part (not shown) of the same pipe. This small pipe is connected with the larger about six inches below the top of the boiler, by being threaded into an annular disk or circular plate welded into the top of the 2-inch pipe. At the bottom the return steam-pipe is threaded into a hollow nut cast on the bottom of a cap-shaped fitting, which screws into the bottom of the boiler, and into which the 2-inch pipe is threaded. By this arrangement it is claimed that the whole head of steam can be turned on without producing any noise in the boiler, and that the water may be heated very rapidly. It is said to have worked very satisfactorily in the Mills Building during the year it has been in use.

The main hot-water supply from the boiler is 1½-inch (marked *f*); another pipe of the same size has on it a safety-valve, *g*, with a ¾-inch blow-off pipe to the sink this 1½-inch pipe is then reduced to ¾-inch to supply the sink. The circulation-pipe *p* (¾-inch) enters the boiler on the back side, as indicated in dotted lines. The sink-trap is marked *t*. The safe-waste pipes are collected into two 2-inch pipes, *n n*, from opposite portions of the building, which end over the sink as shown, having flap-valves on the ends. These main lines are continued through the roof, there increased to three inches in diameter for ventilation. As they are closed at the bottom, the circulation is between the openings under the fixtures and the outer air. These pipes, like the water-supply pipes, are of galvanized-iron.

The plumber was Mr. T. J. Byrne.

KITCHEN AND HOT WATER SUPPLY IN THE RESIDENCE OF MR. SIDNEY WEBSTER.

The following is taken from the *Sanitary Engineer* of December 4, 1883 :

Our illustration, Figure 134, shows the novel arrangement of high and low pressure boilers in the residence of Mr. Sidney Webster, at 245 East Seventeenth Street, New York. The problem in this case was to utilize the limited space between the door and window for the kitchen-range and boiler paraphernalia. As the length of the space was not sufficient for the usual order of "double boiler" (one within the other), the arrangement shown was devised in preference to placing the boilers at a distance from the water-backs, whereby the question of circulation between the backs and the boilers might be jeopardized by carrying the flow-pipes above windows and door, and the return-pipes underneath the floor.

Little can be said of the arrangement that is not apparent to the plumber in our very accurate drawing of the kitchen, but of the materials used and their sizes we will say a few words. The boilers are 48-ounce copper, each being forty-two inches long by twenty-one inches in diameter. They are encircled by copper bands, which secure them to vertical hangers, which enter the floor-beams, with large iron washers on top. The boiler A Figure 135, is the low-pressure or "Croton" boiler, the other boiler (B) being the tank-boiler. The "Croton" or street-pressure pipe comes through the floor at the right of the range, and is supplied with a check-valve at a in the diagram, thence runs behind the boilers, as shown by the dotted lines, connecting directly with the low-pressure boiler at a, and with the high-pressure boiler through the pipe and check-valve s, which connects with the tank or high-pressure supply-pipe b close to where it enters its boiler. The object of the connection s, which is well known to plumbers, is to provide an auxiliary supply to the high-pressure boiler should the tank in the top of the house be empty through any cause, at which time the low-pressure will press through the check-valve and supply the boiler.

Two water-backs are used, the pipes e forming the primary circulation for the low-pressure boiler, and the pipes f performing the same function for the other. The pipe C is the *warm* low-pressure supply, which goes to the lower stories—first and the basement—the pipe C′ being the return circulation from the same. The pipe d is the *warm*

high-pressure pipe supplying the upper stories, d'' being the return circulation for the same. The pipe used is bright seamless brass, with cast-brass elbows and fittings.

Behind the boiler A is a ventilator-register of one and one-half square feet area, and opening into a chimney parallel with the range-

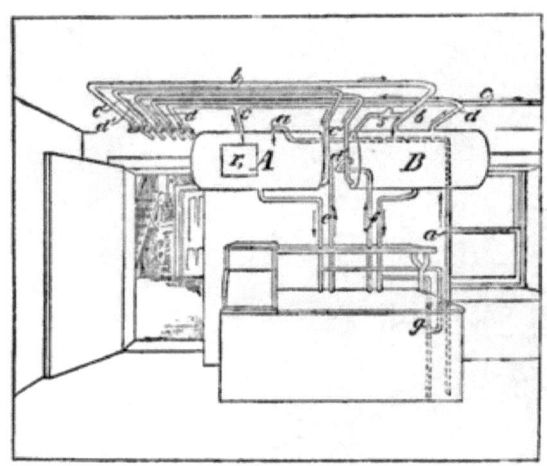

FIGURE 135.

chimney. The chimney-breast, which forms the background to the range and boilers, is of white glazed brick, quoined with glazed chocolate-colored bricks. The floor is of encaustic tiles in warm colors, and, taken altogether, the kitchen is very complete.

The architect was Mr. Richard M. Hunt. The plumber was Mr. John Toumey.

PLUMBING AND WATER-SUPPLY IN THE RESIDENCE OF MR. H. H. COOK.

THE following extracts, referring to features connected with the hot and cold water-supply in the residence of Mr. H. H. Cook, of New York, are taken from Volume X. of the *Sanitary Engineer* :

Figure 136 is a detail of the means provided to reach the hand-holes of the traps of the rain-water leaders and hand-holes of other traps beneath the basement-floors. The rain-water leaders are brought into the house-drains in the positions intended to be the fittest for the flushing of all parts of the drains. There are two fresh-air inlets, one in the outer wall of the Fifth Avenue area and the other in the area at Seventy-eighth Street. The sewers at these points are each six inches in diameter and the air-inlets five inches. All the house-drains and sewer-pipes, as well as such back-air pipes as are not of wrought-iron, are of extra heavy cast-iron. The heads of all the rising-lines, as well as the back-air lines, are run alongside the roof-rafters to one point near the apex, where they are all connected into a copper hood of large area, whose opening to the outer air is turned downward.

The water-supply is taken from both the Fifth Avenue main and from that on Seventy-eighth Street. The object of this is to be able to take water from either streets should the water in the mains of one of the streets be shut off. The pipe from each source of supply, after

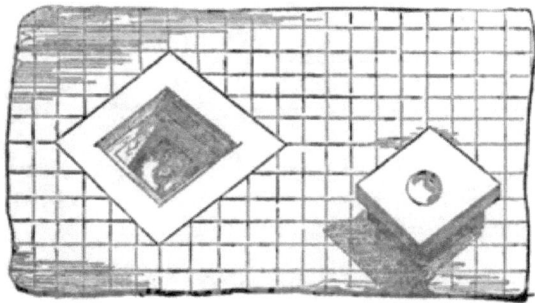

FIGURE 136.

passing the service-cock, is one and a half inches internal diameter, and is AAA lead as far as the position marked A on the plan. Here the different services pass through their respective meters, the mode of distribution from this point being shown by Figure 137, which is a detail at A on the plan.

The water, after passing the meter that may be in use at the time, passes to a 4-inch brass header, as shown; thence it is distributed downward, through brass pipes, to get it underground once more, to join with lead pipes of the same diameters, for distribution to the principal parts of the house; one of the objects of putting it underground being to keep it at a lower *mean temperature* than could be obtained by running it on the ceilings through the basement.

The order of the pipes in the detail corresponds to the order in the plan, and may be traced to their point of delivery thereon. The centre

pipe (one and a half inches) is for the main kitchen boiler-supply only
The basement-supply, as well as supplying water to the basement
fixtures, furnishes a "Riker" gas-pump with water, to be forced to a
tank in the top of the house at times when it will not rise there, for a

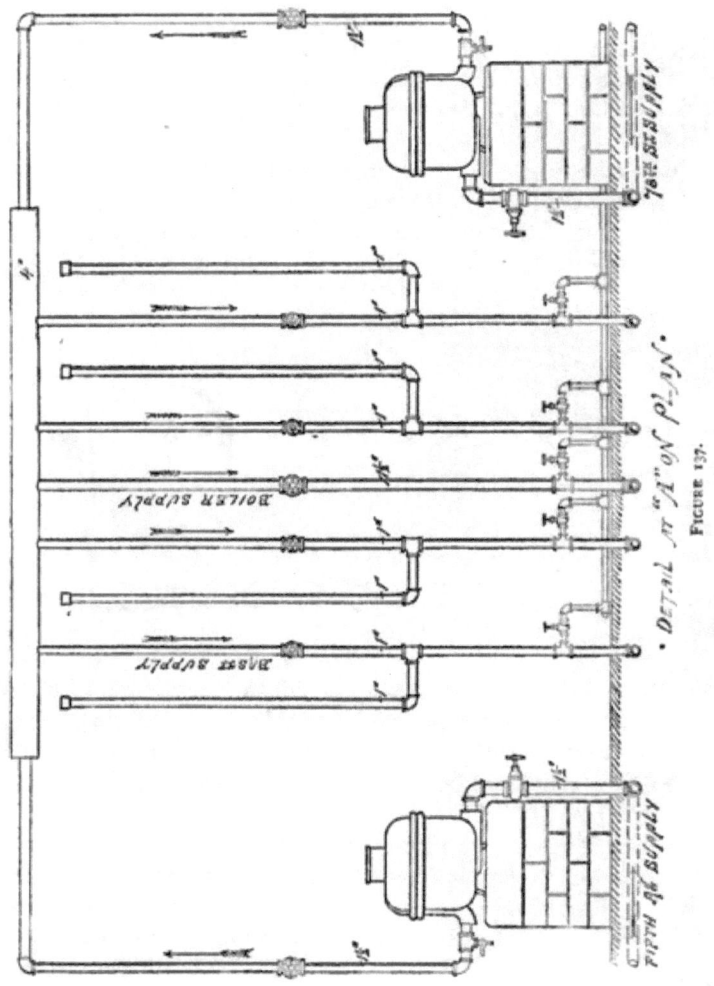

FIGURE 137.

high-pressure or tank supply. The other three pipes run to the principal divisions of the house, to supply the fixtures with cold "Croton" water as high as it will rise. Air-chambers are used on these pipes near the stop-valves in the position shown, their object being to prevent water-hammer at these ends of the pipes as is supposed likely to be caused by the reaction of the flow and column when suddenly checked, although there are air-chambers at the heads of the lines and ends of the principal branches.

The cold "Croton" supply is carried as high as the third-floor fixtures, which it reaches at nearly all times, the pressure in the night being sufficient to fill the tank in the attic without pumping.

The cold tank-supply for the second, third, and fourth floors is carried from the tank downward to the basement, thence it is distributed and run to the different rising-line recesses, up which the cold and hot supplies are also carried to the lines of fixtures.

Figure 138, page 208, shows the hot-water distribution from both the street-pressure and tank-pressure boilers, commonly known as "Croton" boiler and "tank-boiler." These pipes are all carried just beneath the basement-ceiling on specially contrived hangers, and may be seen in the kitchen sketch, Figure 139, page 209. Figure 138 is the fac-simile of a sketch made by Mr. Alexander Farmer, foreman for Mr. Muir, before the work was commenced, for the purpose of illustrating the principle to be followed by the workmen, and a comparison of the same with the finished work as shown in the kitchen (which is drawn from a photograph) will go to show how closely the original plan was carried out.

A double boiler is used, as shown in the diagram, the high-pressure or tank-boiler being inside the low-pressure or street-supply boiler, from which it receives heat in the usual manner. To a plumber it is not necessary to analyze the diagram, but for other readers who take a general interest we will outline the course of the water through the different pipes. The "street-supply" in diagram Figure 138 is the continuation of the "boiler-supply" in Figure 137, and is the (cold) street-supply to the low-pressure or outer boiler. It enters the boiler at the upper end, the water being carried down within it through a supply-tube. A branch of the street-supply is also carried to the inside or tank-boiler, but does not enter it direct, connecting with the tank-supply at the nearest point. The object of this connection is to insure the filling of the inside boiler with water from the street service, should the tank become empty from any cause. To prevent the tank-water from running backward through this connection the *check-valve* shown is provided, which valve will open upward and let the water pass when the pressure in the tank-pipe is less than in the street-pipes. A check-valve is also used in the street-supply to the outer boiler, to prevent the emptying of this boiler through an empty main should the latter be drawn out. The two stub-pipes shown at the left are the pipes which maintain the primary circulation between the outer boiler and the water-back of the range. The second circulation is through the "Croton hot" main pipe (see diagram) from the top of the outer boiler to the different branches, and the lines of fixtures to a point just below the "cut-off" in a line.

From this point it returns through the "Croton circulation" to enter the water-back and boiler again, as may be seen by tracing downward in the direction of the arrows. The third circulation is through the "tank hot" main, whose branches are carried to the higher stories, from which the "tank circulation" returns from a point above the "cut-off," and enters the inner boiler again by passing through the bottom of the outer one, as shown.

Figure 139 shows the interior of the kitchen. The walls and ceiling are white marble slabs, about four feet square, set with plaster of Paris, and held in position with brass rosettes, which form heads or nuts to tap-bolts which fasten with the iron joists and to expansion-bolts in the walls. The floor is of small white ceramic tiles, laid in cement upon a concrete bottom, as before mentioned.

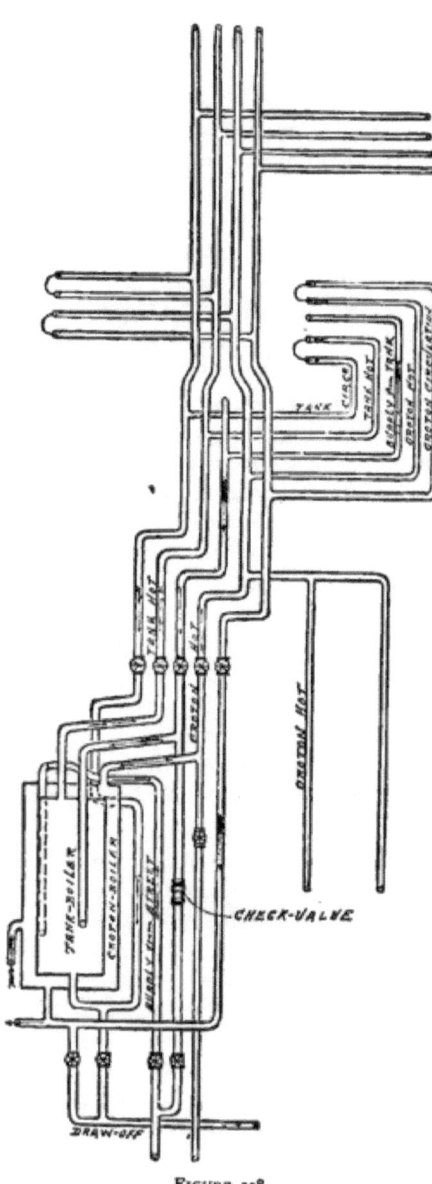

FIGURE 138.

HOT WATER SUPPLY IN BUILDINGS.   209

Between the boiler and the range, and also under the sink, will be noticed positions in the floor where hand or peep hole covers to the house-drain are placed, such as are shown in detail in Figure 136. The sink is of very heavy white earthenware, with the back supported on a

FIGURE 134.

marble cleat, and the front resting on nickel-plated brass legs. Otherwise it is as plain as possible, with no place for lodgment of dirt. All the pipes shown are seamless brass and tinned, with nickel-plated fittings, valves, and hangers.

Under the hood of the range are two vent-registers, aggregating four square feet of area in the clear. They open into two chimneys, 12″x20″ each, which run parallel with and at each side of the range-chimney, which is of cast-iron, that the latter may communicate some of its heat to them.

One point worthy of special mention is the warming of a plate-closet in the butler's pantry by a branch from the primary or water-back circulation. It will be noticed that between the hood of the range and the boiler are two pipes, one starting from a *tee* close to the side of the boiler and the other returning into the circulation-pipe as it flows backward to the water-back. These pipes are the "flow" and "return" from a hot-water coil of about thirty feet lineal of ¾-inch pipe which is placed within the plate-closet. It was the intention of the master plumber to take the flow-pipe from the head of the boiler instead of from the primary circulation-pipes; but fearing that should any considerable quantity of water be drawn from the boiler it would cool the coil also, he changed it to the *tee* in the pipe, as shown, in which position it warms the coil shortly after the fire is started and before the boiler is very warm, giving a constant temperature of about 180° at the coil.

The architect was Mr. W. Wheeler Smith; the plumber Mr. James Muir.

THE CONSTRUCTION OF TURKISH AND RUSSIAN BATHS.

The following description of the Turkish baths at Nos. 16 and 18 Lafayette Place, New York, designed by Mr. Paul J. Schoen, architect, is taken from the *Sanitary Engineer* of October 18, 1883:

The buildings are 165 feet deep, by 53 feet front, the principal floor and basement being devoted to bath purposes. The principal floor is reached from the street by a flight of stone steps; the level of the basement-floor, where the baths proper are, being two or three feet below the sidewalk.

"The baths" consist of Turco-Russian, Russian, and Turkish, with sitz-bath, needle-baths, douche, and warm and cold showers in the different departments. Figure 140 is a section through the Turco-Russian and Russian, and Figure 141 is a section on the line A B through the Turkish.

The Turco-Russian chamber is a seasoning-room, in which the temperature is kept at 118° to 120° Fah., and is hot air laden with moisture

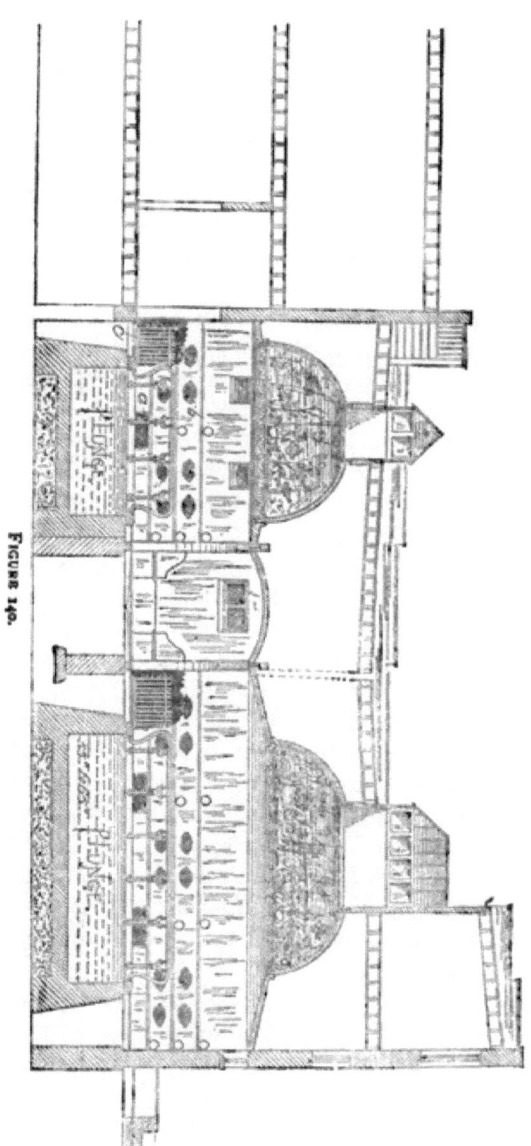

Figure 140.

to the point of saturation. It is warmed by direct radiation; the steam-coils (C) being placed under the marble terraces at the sides, as shown. Two circulations of the air are established; one, which may be called a local circulation, is the revolution of the air of the chamber in through the large register *a* to the coils to be warmed, returning again to the room through the small round register *b*. The other circulation is for the renewal of the air, and is in at the arrow under the terrace, where it comes in contact with a coil, and diffusing with the air under the terrace, escapes with it. At the same time a portion of the air which has been through the chamber and which enters the terrace at *a* escapes through the vent-flues V V.

The Russian bath is similarly arranged with regard to the "local circulation"—*i. e.*, the warming circulation—the coils being under the terrace, with the exception of the circulation for the change of air. The inlets are Z-shaped openings through the walls under the windows, and shown by the arrows, the vents or air-outlets being at the floors under the terraces, and escaping through the flues in the walls marked V V V V. The air here is laden with all the moisture that can be held in suspension at a temperature of 120°, a supply being constantly kept up by an escaping steam-jet within the terrace. The amount of steam-pipe under the terraces in these two chambers could not be obtained with any accuracy, as Dr. Ryan was his own engineer in the matter, and had added surface in many sections until he obtained the desired heat necessary to maintain the temperature when moving air as fast as his flues would remove it.

In the Turkish bath the temperature varies from 135° to 140° Fah., and is dry heat. The warming is by direct radiation, exposed in the rooms, the quantity of 1-inch steam-pipe being 4,500 feet, lineal. Air enters through the radiators from the outside, and is drawn off through the vent flues V V, high up in the fire-place chimney, and a large register over the plunge, near the apex of the roof. In addition to the vent-flues skylights above the domes over the plunges can be opened when required. The walls are made double and the windows small, to prevent an unnecessary loss of heat.

The plunge-baths, 7 x 12 feet and 7 x 22 feet, are supplied with Croton water and the large plunge of the Turkish bath from an artesian well. The method of renewing the water is to draw them off entirely every night and sponge them out, then fill them with fresh water, and let a comparatively small stream flow through them all day, the surplus running off through an overflow in the manner usual to plumbing fixtures. The temperature in the mineral-water plunge is thus maintained at 55° to 60° Fah.

HOT WATER SUPPLY IN BUILDINGS. 213

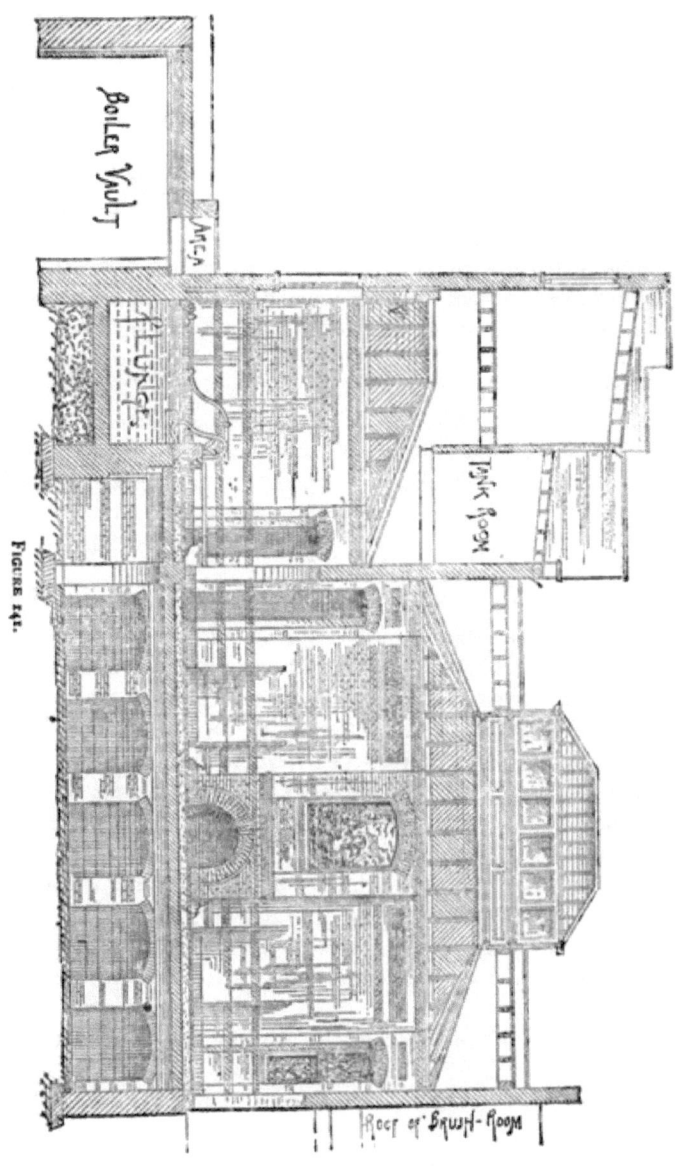

FIGURE 141.

There are five tanks of 11,000 gallons capacity for the storage of Croton and artesian well water, and one tank 4 x 6 x 9 feet for warm water, to guard against an interruption in the supply from temporary causes.

Croton water is supplied to the building through a 2-inch pipe, with a meter, for the boilers and all purposes for which the artesian water cannot be used. The capacity for pumping artesian water is 240 gallons per minute, and a little less than 100,000 gallons is used in the 24 hours.

A prominent feature of the appointments is the "needle-bath," shown in Figure 142. It is all brass pipe, nickel-plated, with ornamental fittings. The horizontal arms are perforated with fine openings, to discharge a fine spray on the body of the bather. The central vertical pipe is connected with the warm and cold pipes K and N by the cocks A and B, which admit of variable degrees of temperature in the spray. The cocks C and H regulate the shower and control the supply in the same manner. F and G are the liver-sprays, being metallic pads perforated with minute openings, one being cold and the other tepid, and are controlled by the cocks D and E. A douche, L, is in the floor-slab, and is regulated by the cocks J and I.

The floors and walls in the vapor-baths are marble, and the ceilings and domes wood, painted and ornamented in oil. Around the domes slight condensation takes place, and would drop on the bathers were it not that an internal eaves-trough, that is nicely arranged to harmonize with the finish, carries this drip to a convenient down pipe.

Steam is supplied to the building by a boiler 16 feet long by 5 feet 6 inches diameter, with fifty 4-inch tubes, and the water of condensation is returned by an "Albany" trap. A smaller boiler, 14 feet by 48 inches diameter, is kept in reserve.

The principal or parlor floor of the building is for the use of the guests after bathing and resting, preparatory to going into the street. The reception-room is 24 x 60 feet, beyond which is a parlor 22 x 21, in the rear of which is a billiard-room 24 x 30. Adjoining the billiard-room is a café 16 x 24.

For those not acquainted with the routine of baths we append the following short description: The bather pays at one desk, passes to another and leaves his valuables, is assigned a dressing-room, and after disrobing is shown to the Turco-Russian bath, a seasoning-chamber in which all bathers remain awhile before entering either Russian or Turkish baths. When his skin is slightly moist, he is led to a couch and soaped, scrubbed, and rinsed off with a tepid shower, when he passes to either of the baths. The rest of that time in the bath (which may vary from twenty to forty-five minutes, according to his strength or the doctor's orders) he spends in alternately sweating and showering, finally finishing with a cold plunge or shower bath. He is then passed into

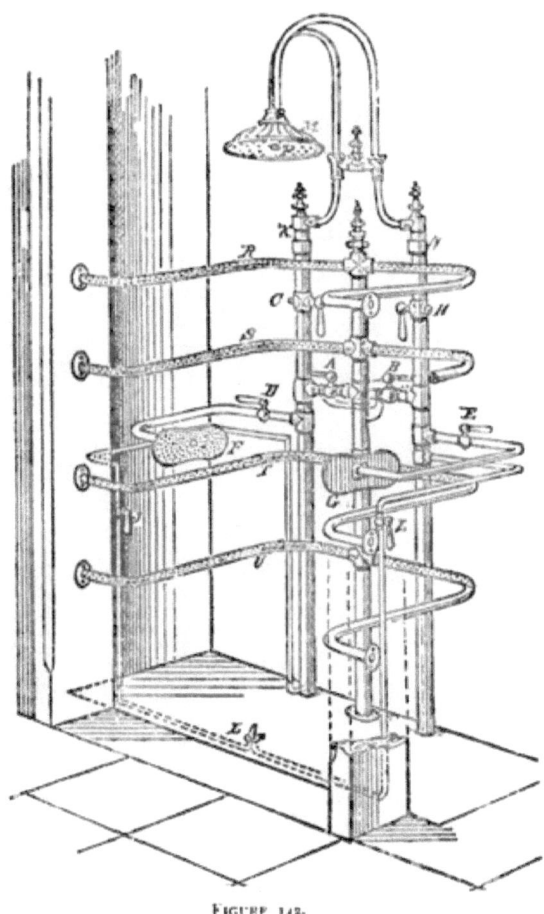

FIGURE 142.

the cooling-room and dried with towels, from thence to the rubbing-room, where he is rubbed and manipulated with the bare hand of the attendant until his body is all aglow. He is then placed on a couch in another chamber with a sheet spread over him, and there takes his ease until he feels like resuming his clothing.

FORM OF PLUMBING SPECIFICATION

FOR

AN ISOLATED COUNTRY HOUSE.

PLUMBING SPECIFICATION FOR AN ISOLATED COUNTRY HOUSE IN A POPULOUS DISTRICT, VALUED AT $20,000; SUPPLIED WITH WATER FROM CORPORATION PIPES AND DISCHARGING HOUSE-WASTE INTO A FLUSH-TANK AND SUBSURFACE IRRIGATION SYSTEM, OR INTO A STREET-SEWER.

It is not intended that the following form of specification shall be suitable for every house such as indicated, but only to suggest points that require consideration. No general specification can be drawn that will meet the requirements of any job.

Earthen Drain.—From end of iron house-drain (to flush-tank or to street-sewer), and at a depth of —— feet, lay a 4-inch salt-glazed earthen-pipe, with a fall of not less than —— inch to the foot.

House-Drain.—From house end of earthen-drain, not less than five feet outside of foundation-wall, carry a 4-inch cast-iron pipe, with grade not less than —— inch to the foot, to foot of soil-pipe as shown, and make a thoroughly tight connection between the iron and the earthen pipes with Portland cement.

Trap and Fresh-Air Inlet.—Provide in line of drain a one-half S-trap, of iron, four inches inside diameter, provided with brass cleaning trap-screw as shown, and having a 4-inch iron fresh-air inlet-pipe. (See Figure 143, next page.)

Soil-Pipes.—The vertical soil-pipe to be 4-inch cast-iron pipe, continued as straight as possible full size through the roof, and at least three feet above the highest window.

Waste-Pipes.—Connect, as shown on plan, with house-drain, by 2-inch cast-iron pipe, the wastes from kitchen and pantry sinks and wash-trays and continue the same at least full size through the roof, as shown on section

NOTE.—Two-inch pipes should be enlarged in the Northern States to 4-inch pipes from a point below the roof to prevent clogging of the pipe in winter.

Water-Closet.—Furnish and fit up as shown on plan one water-closet. [Specify the kind and make of closet and cistern, if such is required.] If cistern is to be made by plumber, give size and weight of lead or copper for cistern and service-box, size of valve, and kind of ball-cock. [If closet has its own trap omit following reference to trap.] Provide 4-inch heavy lead trap to be connected with Y-branch of soil-pipe by the necessary 4-inch 8-lb. lead waste-pipe and brass ferrule. [Omit the following where no water-closet cistern is required.] Supply cistern through a ½-inch lead pipe, branched from main supply-pipe and place ½-inch lever-handle stop-cock near cistern. Provide the necessary 1¼-inch pipe from closet-cistern to bowl of water-closet, also, all necessary chain, levers, etc., for the proper working of the closet. [Where receiver of closet is to be ventilated, call for 1½-inch lead pipe to be carried to the open air.]

Also furnish and fit up where shown one water-closet for servants' use. [State details as in previous case.]

Slop-Hopper.—Furnish and fit up as shown on plan one slop-hopper. [Specify the kind and make of hopper, and cistern, if such is required.] If cistern is to be made by plumber give details as above for water-closet. [If slop-hopper has its own trap omit following reference to trap.] Provide —— inch heavy lead trap, to be connected with Y-branch of soil-pipe as elsewhere provided for.

Bath.—Where shown on plans, furnish and fit up one bath. [State the size, kind, fitting, and, if of copper, the weight required, and the maker's name.] Supply with hot† and cold water through ¾-inch lead pipe, and waste through —— inch* lead pipe, with the necessary —— inch lead trap and trap-screw; waste to connect with soil-pipe in manner specified under "General Requirements."

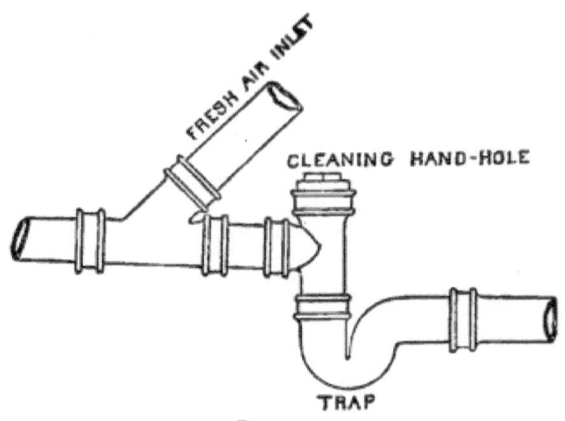

FIGURE 143.

Wash-Basins.—Furnish and fit up where shown 15-inch common overflow wash-basin [if any patent or special kind is required, state which], to be set in a 1¼-inch Italian marble slab of size indicated on plan, countersunk face, molded edges, back, and sides, ⅞-inch thick and twelve inches high. Basin-rim ground so as to make a close joint with the marble, and basin to be fastened to slab by three brass clamps, leaded into marble; joint between basin-rim and slab to be made tight with plaster of Paris. Furnish and fit up two plated basin-cocks [state kind, maker, or patent, and kind of plating required], plated plug, chain, and chain-stay. [State kind, size, and kind of plating; if any special waste arrangement is required, state which.] Supply with hot† and cold water through ½-inch lead pipe, branched from supply-pipe from tank to boiler. Waste through 1½-inch lead pipe, with the necessary 1½-inch lead trap and trap-screw to connect with Y-branch of soil-pipe in manner elsewhere provided for.

---

* Size of waste-pipe to be determined by the kind of bath-tub and by the desired quickness of discharge.

† If brass pipes are preferred for the hot-water pipes, the specification can be modified to call for brass instead of lead.

Wash-Trays.—Furnish and fit up as shown on plans three wash-trays. [Here state the kind and size required, and, in case of wooden tubs, specify whether plumber or owner is to furnish them.] Supply each with hot† and cold water through ⅝-inch lead pipe, and ⅝-inch flange and thimble bibb-cocks. [State kind and make; also, if to be of brass or plated; if porcelain or soapstone tubs are used, call for flange and bent coupling-cocks; state if tubs are to have holes for faucets in back or to be supplied over top of tub.] Furnish the necessary 1½-inch plugs, couplings, and chains. [State if brass or plated.] Waste through 2-inch lead pipe, with 2-inch trap and trap-screw, to connect with 2-inch iron waste-pipe, as elsewhere provided for.

Kitchen-Sinks.—Furnish and fit up one sink [state the kind and size, whether to be placed on brackets or on legs, and state if back is required] as indicated on plan. Supply with hot† and cold water through ⅝-inch lead pipe, and two ⅝-inch flange bibb-cocks, one to have hose-screw for filter. Waste through 1½-inch lead pipe and the necessary 1½-inch lead trap with trap-screw; to connect with a 2-inch iron waste-pipe, as described before. Outlet in sink to be protected by a strong metallic strainer [state kind] securely fastened to the sink.

NOTE.—If grease-trap is used, the waste from sink to be connected to grease-trap and not to the iron waste-pipe.

Grease-Trap.—Furnish and set where shown on plan grease-trap. [Here state whether it is to be attached to sink, placed in kitchen or basement, or built of masonry outside the house.] Make all necessary connections between sinks, grease-trap, and waste-pipe.

Pantry-Sink.—As shown on plans, furnish and fit up one butler's sink [state size and whether of copper or porcelain], and set the same in wood [or, if preferred, in 1¼-inch marble slab, with countersunk face, molded edges, and back of ⅞-inch marble, twelve inches high.] Supply with hot† and cold water through ½-inch lead pipe and two upright pantry-cocks [state kind or make, and kind of plating], with the necessary plug, chain, and chain-stay [or state special waste arrangement, if any is preferred]. Waste through 1½-inch lead pipe, and 1½-inch lead trap and trap-screw, to connect with iron waste-pipe, as elsewhere provided for, or if grease-trap is used with the latter.

Safes.—Place safes of 4-lb. sheet-lead under all fixtures above the kitchen-floor, the sizes of the spaces occupied by said fixtures, edges to be turned up at least two inches all round. Carry a 1-inch lead drip-pipe from safe under tank, and connect each safe-waste with it; carry down to cellar and discharge where leakage will be readily noticed, the end of drip-pipe being suitably protected [here state manner of protection] to prevent odor from cellar or kitchen being carried into the upper part of the house. Provide 1½-inch convex strainer for each safe, securely soldered to the lead.

Cold-Water Supply.—Pay corporation charges and insert a tap in street-main (if not done by Water Department), and from that point furnish and connect with corporation-tap a ¾-inch pipe of weight as specified under "General Requirements." Run this pipe in cellar to a point as near directly under tank as practicable, and continue pipe to above and over the tank. Place a ¾-inch round-way lever-handle stop and waste cock just inside cellar-wall, to shut off water from house and to empty all house-pipes when necessary. Run a special line of ¾-inch lead pipe, as shown, from

---

† If brass pipes are preferred for the hot-water pipes, the specification can be modified to call for brass instead of lead.

inside stop and waste cock, to supply the kitchen and pantry sinks. All other branches to fixtures to be taken, not from rising main, but from down pipe from tank to boiler, as shown.

Tank.—Line a tank holding 200 gallons [tank to be furnished ready for lining by the owner] with copper [or lead ; state size of sheet and weight required]. Supply

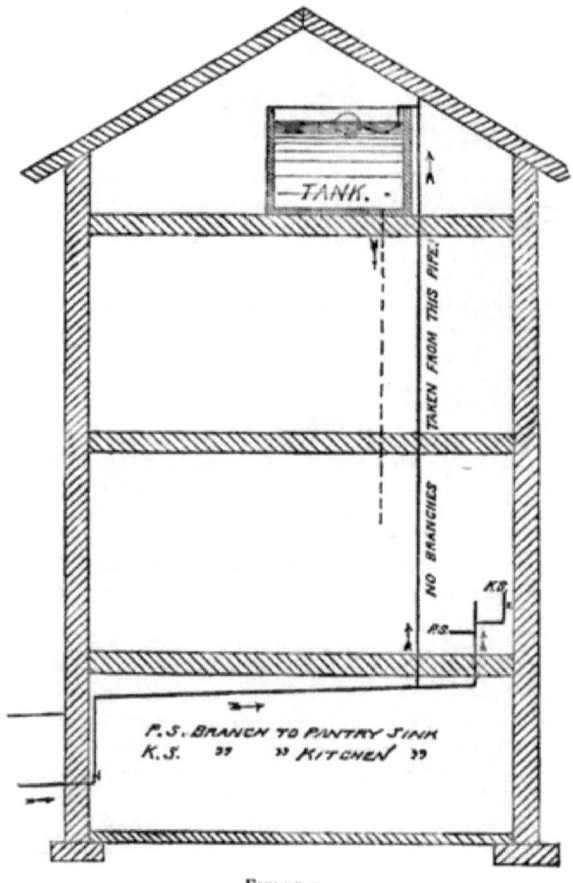

FIGURE 148.

tank from rising main, as described heretofore, through a ¾-inch ball-cock [state kind and make required], and provide a tank-valve, with air-tube carried above water-level in tank, placed at bottom of tank, and from it run ¾-inch lead pipe to boiler and fixtures as shown. Provide 2-inch lead overflow-pipe for tank, and run same to nearest roof-gutter or to a roof lower than tank. Provide brass flap-valve at outlet end to keep out cold air. [If discharge into gutter or on some roof is impracticable, carry overflow-pipe down to kitchen and discharge over sink.] From bottom of tank carry a 1½-inch lead pipe provided with a 1½-inch round-way stop-cock, placed just under the tank, and connect pipe with overflow-pipe for emptying the tank to permit of frequent cleansing. (See Figure 144.)

NOTE.—This tank is not intended as a storage-reservoir, but is used principally to supply boiler and fixtures [except kitchen and pantry sinks] at a steady, moderate pressure.

Boiler.—Furnish and fit up one —— gallon heavy dome-head boiler [here state kind and strength of boiler, and make required, number of couplings required in top of boiler, etc.], set on boiler-stand [state kind and pattern], and supply with water through a ¾-inch lead pipe† from tank. Boiler-connections to water-back to be brazed —— inch copper pipes. Provide the necessary ¾-inch sediment-pipe and stop-cock, this pipe to connect with the house side of the nearest convenient trap, to permit the emptying of the boiler at pleasure. Place a ¾-inch stop-cock on supply-pipe to boiler near top of same.

Hot-Water Supply.—Carry a ¾-inch lead pipe,† provided with a stop-cock near the top of boiler, to bath, taking off the necessary branches as shown, and continue with ¾-inch lead pipe to over and above tank, to act as vent or relief pipe for boiler. Carry a ½-inch lead pipe† from sediment-pipe just inside of sediment-cock to top of hot-water service-pipe in bath-room, for keeping up a constant circulation of hot water. From top of boiler carry also another line of ¾-inch lead pipe to supply hot water to kitchen and pantry sinks and wash-trays,

All lines of hot and cold water pipes must have a constant grade to allow proper circulation and the perfect draining of the whole supply-system from its lowest point.

Range.—Furnish and set complete one range with water-back. [State kind and size required, or state if owner furnishes range, and the plumber is only required to make water-back connections.]

List of Fixtures.—The house to contain the following fixtures : In first story, one kitchen-sink, one range, one bath-boiler, one pantry-sink, one servants' water-closet, three wash-trays ; in second story, one bath, one wash-basin, one water-closet, one slop-hopper ; in attic, one tank ; al[1] to be as heretofore described.

Rain-Leader.—Rain-water leaders to be [state kind] properly secured with iron hooks, and connecting with house-drain, preferably outside main trap if rain-water is admitted to sewer. Each leader to be trapped by a trap located below frost-level. If house-drain delivers into flush-tank, rain-water is to be conducted by a vitrified pipe to storage-cistern, or discharged into gutter, creek, or nearest stream or other convenient place.

NOTE.—Never allow rain-water from roof to saturate ground in the vicinity of the house.

GENERAL REQUIREMENTS.

Earthen Drain.—Earthen pipe to be without hubs or bells ; pipe lengths to be perfectly straight, truly cylindrical, hard-burnt, and not less than three-fourths inch thick. Pipe to be laid with a fall of not less than —— inch to the foot. Joints to be made with loose rings or collars, set in mortar. Mortar to consist of one part hydraulic cement and two parts clean, sharp sand. Sand and cement to be mixed dry, and to be wetted up only in small quantities as used. No tempered-up cement to be

---

† If brass pipes are preferred for the hot-water pipes, the specification can be modified to call for brass instead of lead.

used. Pipe to be laid in a trench, carefully excavated, with bottom trimmed to a perfect grade, and having depressions for joints of pipes, so that each length of pipe shall be evenly supported throughout the entire drain. The interior of each length to be made perfectly clean before the next length is laid down. Drain to be laid with perfect alignment, and deviations from straight run to be made with special curves. Back-filling to be first hand-packed with care, and then well rammed to prevent the slightest settling of the drain. Connections with flush-tank to be as shown on plan, and with street-sewer as required by corporation.

Before refilling trench, earthen sewer to be tested by at least two feet head of water at its upper end.

If earthen pipe with sockets is used, joints to be made by filling the space between spigot end and bell with hydraulic mortar, which should be applied with particular care at the bottom of the joint. The inside of each pipe-joint to be thoroughly cleaned from any projecting cement. Rubber gaskets to be used on spigot end, and the workmen to wear rubber mittens in putting in the cement.

If the bottom of the trench is not firm a bed of gravel or sand or a concrete foundation must be provided.

Flush-Tank and Subsurface-Irrigation System.—Flush-tanks and subsurface-irrigation system to be arranged as described in the *Sanitary Engineer*, pp. 530 and 554, Vol. VII. Connection between drain and flush-tank to be arranged as shown. When the drain connects with the street-sewer the trap should be on the iron pipe just inside the cellar-wall, and the fresh-air inlet should open at a point. [Here indicate location.]

Iron Pipes.—All iron pipes to be sound, free from holes, flaws, or other defects, of a *uniform* thickness of at least one-fourth of an inch, and to be thoroughly coated inside and outside with coal-tar pitch, applied hot, or its equivalent. The weight of pipe to be as follows :

    2-inch pipe $5\frac{1}{2}$ lbs. per foot.
    3   " $9\frac{1}{2}$ "   "
    4   "   13   "   "

Pipe-Joints.—All joints of iron pipe to be thoroughly calked with oakum and molten lead. Joints between cast-iron and lead pipe to be made with brass or copper ferrules. If of brass, ferrules to be calked into hub of iron pipe, and lead pipe soldered to it by a wiped-joint. If of copper, inside diameter of ferrule to be larger than outside diameter of lead pipe to permit of drawing the lead pipe through the inside of the ferrule, and lapping it over the flange as shown. After being thus protected against corrosion, copper ferrule is to be calked into hub, and the wiped-joint to be made in the usual manner. (See Figure 145.)

Iron pipe lengths, when vertical, to be supported under each hub by strong iron hooks, and when hung from ceiling to be held in place by strong iron hangers, securely fastened to the beams, or, better, to be supported at intervals by brick piers. All changes in direction to be by bends, and all branches to be Y-branches. At intervals of not more than twenty feet insert into the line of drain Y-branches, with brass trap-screws, for cleaning and inspection purposes. Mouths of any soil, waste, or vent pipe above the roof to be located remote from chimney-tops or ventilating-shafts. Wherever any pipe passes through the roof a water-tight joint must be made by providing a

PLUMBING SPECIFICATION.

flashing of sheet-lead, tin, or copper, eighteen inches square, with a funnel around pipe, the flashing to be securely fastened to the roof, and the funnel turned over and calked into hub of pipe.

Testing Pipes.—After completion of the piping, and before any fixtures are connected, all openings of waste, soil, and vent pipes to be plugged, and the whole system of piping filled with water, and allowed to stand twenty-four hours, if required by the architect. [This important test is not, however, practicable in winter time, and some other test is in that case to be substituted.] If any leak is shown, the defect to be made good, and pipes again tested until the system is proved gas and water tight to the satisfaction of the architect or superintendent.

The weight of the lead pipes is to be as follows:

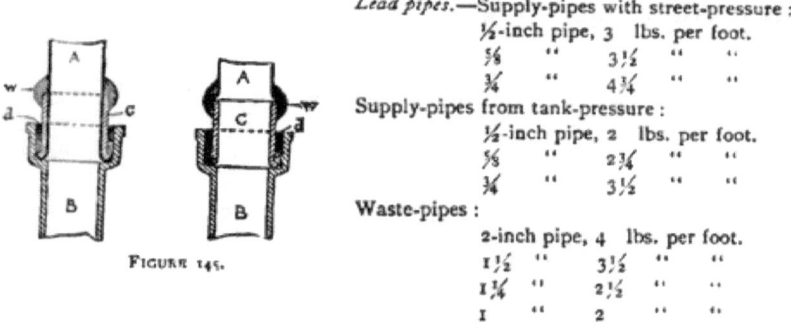

FIGURE 145.

Lead pipes.—Supply-pipes with street-pressure:
½-inch pipe, 3 lbs. per foot.
⅝   "   3½ "   "
¾   "   4¾ "   "

Supply-pipes from tank-pressure:
½-inch pipe, 2 lbs. per foot.
⅝   "   2¾ "   "
¾   "   3½ "   "

Waste-pipes:
2-inch pipe, 4 lbs. per foot.
1½ "   3½ "   "
1¼ "   2½ "   "
1   "   2   "   "

All joints between lead pipes to be wiped-joints. All vertical lead pipes to be supported by metal tacks, soldered to the pipe, and fastened with screws to boards put up by carpenter; tacks to be not less than three feet apart. Horizontal lead pipes must be supported throughout their length on boards, to prevent trapping, and be fastened by brass bands and screws. No hooks to be used in fastening lead pipe. Hot-water pipes must not be fastened with tacks; brass bands only should be used to allow for expansion and contraction. Hot and cold water pipes to be kept at least one-half inch apart everywhere. All stop-cocks on supply-pipes to be arranged easy of access.

No supply-pipes to run on outside walls unless absolutely necessary, and in this case pipes to be securely protected in all exposed places. [Here state kind of protection required.]

Air-Chambers.—No cock to be placed at the end of a line of pipe, but the supply-pipe to be extended so as to provide an air-chamber in each case. (See Figure 146.)

Traps.—All traps for fixtures to be arranged so as to be easily accessible.

Back-air Pipes.—Every trap under fixtures to be provided with a ventilating-pipe taken from just beyond crown of trap to prevent syphonage, and secure a circulation of air through the branch-pipes, as hereinafter provided for. Water-closet traps to have 2-inch lead vent-pipes, and all other traps to have vents of same area as the trap, except when vent-pipe does not require to exceed twenty feet in length to reach a point above the roof. No vent-pipe to be smaller than 1¼-inch. Each lead vent must connect with vertical pipe of not less than 2-inch external area, said vertical pipe to be placed alongside the nearest vertical soil or waste pipe. If back-air pipes are carried through the roof they must be enlarged to four inches to prevent clogging in winter time in colder latitudes.

Overflows.—Overflow-pipes from basins, bath, and pantry-sink to be branched into dip of trap under the fixtures.

All soil, waste, vent, or supply pipes must be exposed to view or be cased in wood, fastened with screws, so that they are readily accessible.

No pipe or fitting shall be boxed in or otherwise hidden till it be passed upon by the architect or superintendent.

During construction **all** pipe ends must be covered to prevent the entrance of sticks or other materials that might cause obstructions.

The architect or superintendent may reject any pipe, fixture, appliance, or piece of work which, in his opinion, does not meet the requirements of this specification, and his decision in all matters shall be regarded as final.

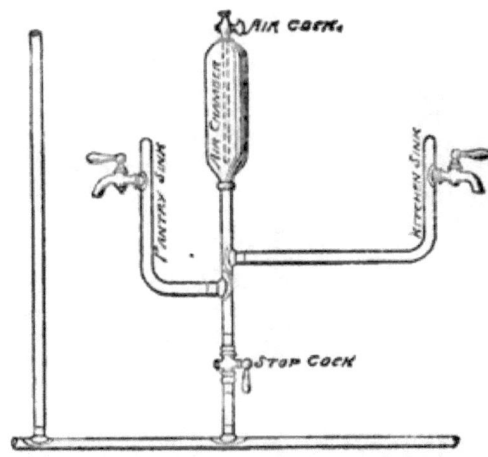

FIGURE 146.—DETAIL OF BRANCH OF WATER-SUPPLY TO PANTRY AND KITCHEN SINKS.

The plumber must not do any cutting; this will be done for him, wherever necessary, by the carpenter.

The plumber shall do all his work promptly, as the progress of the building requires.

Plumber to furnish all materials and implements, and to perform all labor requisite to complete all the work in a workmanlike manner, according to the drawings and specifications, including any material or labor not specifically described or mentioned, but which are necessary for the proper carrying out of these specifications.

Where the specifications vary or conflict with the drawings the contractor to be governed by the specifications.

All the work to be tested after completion by turning the water on everywhere, and any defects found to be at once repaired and all left in perfect order.

APPENDIX.

TEXT OF PLUMBING LAWS AND REGULATIONS IN FORCE IN NEW YORK, BROOKLYN, AND BOSTON, MAY, 1885.

NEW YORK.

THE REGISTRATION OF PLUMBERS, AND THE LAW AND REGULATIONS GOVERNING THE PLUMBING AND DRAINAGE OF ALL BUILDINGS HEREAFTER ERECTED.

CHAPTER 450, LAWS OF 1881.

AN ACT to secure the Registration of Plumbers, and the Supervision of Plumbing and Drainage, in the Cities of New York and Brooklyn.

Passed June 4, 1881.

The People of the State of New York, represented in Senate and Assembly, do enact as follows :

SECTION 1. On or before the first day of March, eighteen hundred and eighty-two, every master or journeyman plumber, carrying on his trade in the cities of New York and Brooklyn, shall, under such rules and regulations as the respective Boards of Health of the Health Departments of said cities shall respectively prescribe, register his name and address at the Health Department of the said city; and after the said date, it shall not be lawful for any person to carry on the trade of plumbing in the said cities unless his name and address be registered as above provided.

SEC. 2. A list of the registered plumbers of the city of New York shall be published in the *City Record* at least once in each year.

SEC. 3. The drainage and plumbing of all buildings, both public and private, hereafter erected in the city of New York, or in the city of Brooklyn, shall be executed in accordance with plans previously approved in writing by the Board of Health of the said Health Departments of said cities respectively. Suitable drawings and descriptions of the said plumbing and drainage shall in each case be submitted and placed on file in the Health Department. The said Boards of Health are also authorized to receive and place on file drawings and descriptions of the plumbing and drainage of buildings erected prior to the passage of this act in their respective cities.

SEC. 4. The Board of Estimate and Apportionment of the city of New York shall add six thousand dollars to the apportionment of the Health Department for the year eighteen hundred and eighty-one, and shall insert the same in the tax levy, to provide for carrying out the provisions of this act, so far as it relates to the city of New York.

SEC. 5. Any court of record in said cities respectively, or any judge or justice thereof, shall have power at any time after the service of notice of the violation of any of the provisions of this act, and upon the affidavit of one of the Commissioners of Health of the said cities, to restrain, by injunction order, the further progress of any violation named in this act, or of any work upon or about the building or premises upon which the said violation exists; and no undertaking shall be required as a condition to the granting or issuing of such injunction, or by reason thereof.

SEC. 6. Any person violating any of the provisions of this act shall be deemed guilty of a misdemeanor.

SEC. 7. This act shall take effect immediately.

RULES AND REGULATIONS

For the Registration of Plumbers, and relating to Plans and Specifications for Plumbing and Drainage, Adopted by the Board of Health of the City of New York, in accordance with Chapter 450, Laws of 1881.

I.

The Registration of Plumbers.

RULE 1. Every plumber engaged in business in the city of New York shall appear in person at the Health Department, No. 301 Mott Street, and register his name and address, pursuant to the provisions of Chapter 450, Laws of 1881, upon the forms prescribed by the Health Department.

RULE 2. It shall be the duty of every plumber to give immediate notice of any change in residence or place of business, for the correction of the register.

RULE 3. The list of registered plumbers shall be published in January of each year.

II.

Of Plumbing.

The law requires that the plumbing and drainage of all buildings, public and private, shall be executed in accordance with plans and specifications previously approved in writing by the Board of Health; and that suitable drawings and descriptions of the said plumbing and drainage shall, in each case, be submitted and placed on file in the Health Department.

Drawings and descriptions of the plumbing and drainage of buildings erected prior to the passage of the act may be placed on file in the Health Department.

Blank specifications for plumbing and drainage will be furnished to architects and others on application at this office.

As the law requires that the plumbing and drainage be executed according to a plan approved by the Board of Health, no part of the work shall be covered or concealed in any way until after it has been examined by an inspector of the Board of Health, and notice must be sent to the Board when the work is sufficiently advanced for such inspection.

III.

Plan of Drainage and Plumbing Approved by the Board of Health.

The following plan of construction has been approved by the Board of Health. When the work is completed, and before it is covered from view, the Board must be notified that it may send an inspector:

1. All materials must be of good quality and free from defects ; the work must be executed in a thorough and workmanlike manner.

2. The arrangement of soil and waste pipes must be as direct as possible.

3. The drain, soil, and waste pipes, and the traps, must, if practicable, be exposed to view for ready inspection at all times, and for convenience in repairing. When necessarily placed within partitions or in recesses in walls, soil and waste pipes must be covered with wood-work so fastened with screws as to be readily removed. In no case shall they be absolutely inaccessible.

4. It is recommended to place the soil and other vertical pipes in a special shaft, between or adjacent to the water-closet and the bath-room, and serving as a ventilating-shaft for them. This shaft should be at least two and a half feet square. It should extend from the cellar through the roof, and should be covered by a louvered skylight. It should be accessible at every story, and should have a very open but strong grating at each floor to stand upon.

Shafts not less than three square feet in area are required in tenement-houses, to ventilate interior water-closets.

5. Every house or building must be separately and independently connected with the street-sewer.

6. Where the ground is made or filled in, the house-sewer —that is to say, the portion of the drain extending from the public sewer to the front wall—must be of cast-iron, with the joints properly calked with lead.

7. Where the soil consists of a natural bed of loam, sand, or rock, the house-sewer may be of hard, salt-glazed, and cylindrical earthenware pipe, laid on a smooth bottom free from all projections of rock, and with the soil well rammed to prevent any settling of the pipe. Each section must be wetted before applying the cement, and the space between each hub and the small end of the next section must be completely and uniformly filled with the best hydraulic cement. Care must be taken to prevent any cement being forced into the drain to become an obstruction. No tempered-up cement shall be used. A straight-edge must be used inside the pipe, and the different sections must be laid in perfect line on the bottom and sides.

8. Where there is no sewer in the street, and it is necessary to construct a private sewer to connect with a sewer on an adjacent street or avenue, it must be laid under the roadway of the street on which the houses front, and not through the yards or under the houses.

9. The house-drain must be of iron, with a fall of at least one-quarter inch to the foot, if possible, and not more than one inch to the foot.

10. Where water-closets or a school-sink discharge into it, the drain must be at least four inches in diameter.

11. It must be hung on the cellar wall or ceiling, unless this is impracticable, in which case it must be laid in a trench cut at a uniform grade, walled up on the sides with brick laid in hydraulic cement, and provided with movable covers, and with a hydraulic concrete base of four inches in thickness on which the pipe is to rest.

12. It must be laid in a straight line, if possible. All changes in direction must be made with curved pipes, and all connections with Y-branch pipes and one-eighth bends.

13. Any house-drain or house-sewer put in and covered without due notice to the Health Department must be uncovered for inspection at the direction of the inspector.

14. A running or half-S trap must be placed on the house-drain at an accessible point near the front of the house. This trap must be furnished with a hand-hole for convenience in cleaning, the cover of which must be properly fitted and made gas and air tight with some proper cement.

15. There must be an inlet for fresh air entering the drain just inside the trap, of at least four inches in diameter, leading to the outer air and opening at or near the street curb, or at a convenient place not less than four feet from the nearest window. No cold-air box for a furnace shall be so placed that it can by any possibility draw air from this inlet-pipe. The inlet-pipe should never be carried up to the roof inside or outside the house.

16. No brick, sheet-metal, earthenware, or chimney-flue shall be used as a sewer-ventilator, nor to ventilate any trap, drain, soil, or waste pipe.

17. Every vertical soil-pipe and waste-pipe must be of iron, and where it receives the discharge of fixtures on two or more floors it must be extended at least two feet above the highest part of the roof or coping, of undiminished size, with a return-bend or cowl. It must not open near a window, nor an air-shaft which ventilates living-rooms.

18. Soil, waste, and vent pipes in an extension must be extended above the roof of the main building, when otherwise they would open within twenty feet of the windows of the main house or the adjoining house.

19. Horizontal soil and waste pipes are prohibited.

20. The minimum diameter of soil-pipe permitted is four inches. A vertical waste-pipe, into which a line of kitchen-sinks discharge, must be at least two inches in diameter with one inch and a half branches.

21. Where lead-pipe is used to connect fixtures with vertical soil or waste pipes, or to connect traps with vertical vent-pipes, it must not be lighter than D pipe.

22. There shall be no traps on vertical soil-pipes or vertical waste-pipes.

23. All iron pipes must be sound, free from holes, and of a uniform thickness of not less than one-eighth of an inch for a diameter of two, three, or four inches, or five-thirty-seconds of an inch for a diameter of five or six inches, and in case the building is over sixty-five feet in height above the curb the use of what is known as extra heavy pipe and corresponding fittings are required, which weigh as follows:

2 inches,	5½	pounds per lineal foot.	
3 "	9½	"	"
4 "	13	"	"
5 "	17	"	"
6 "	20	"	"
7 "	27	"	"
8 "	33½	"	"
10 "	45	"	"
12 "	54	"	"

24. Before they are connected they must be thoroughly coated inside and outside with coal-tar pitch, applied hot, or some other equivalent substance.

25. When required by the inspector from the Board of Health, the plumbing must be tested with the peppermint or the water test by the plumber, in the presence of the inspector, and all defective joints made tight, and other openings made impermeable to gases. Defective pipe discovered must be removed and replaced by sound pipe.

26. All joints in the iron drain-pipes, soil-pipes, and waste-pipes must be so calked with oakum and lead, or with cement made of iron filings and sal-ammoniac, as to make them impermeable to gas.

27. All connections of lead with iron pipes must be made with a brass sleeve or ferrule, of the same size as the lead pipe, put in the hub of the branch of the iron pipe and calked in with lead. The lead pipe must be attached to the ferrule by a wiped joint.

28. All connections of lead pipe should be by wiped joints.

29. Every water-closet, urinal, sink, basin, wash-tray, bath, and every tub or set of tubs, must be separately and effectively trapped, except where a sink and wash-tubs immediately adjoin each other, in which case the waste-pipe from the tubs may be connected with the inlet side of the sink-trap; in such a case the tub waste-pipe is not required to be separately trapped.

30. Traps must be placed as near the fixtures as practicable, and in no case shall a trap be more than two feet from the fixture.

31. All exit-pipes must be provided with strong metallic strainers.

32. In no case shall the waste from a bath-tub or other fixture be connected with a water-closet trap.

33. Traps must be protected from syphonage, and the waste-pipe leading from them ventilated, by a special air-pipe, in no case less than two inches in diameter for water-closet traps, and one inch and a half for other traps. Except in private dwellings, the vertical vent-pipes for traps of water-closets in buildings more than four stories in height must be at least three inches in diameter, with two-inch branches to each trap, and for traps of other fixtures not less than two inches in diameter, with branches one and a half inches in diameter, unless the trap is smaller, in which case the diameter of branch vent-pipe must be at least equal to the diameter of the trap. In all cases vertical vent-pipes must be of cast or wrought iron.

34. These pipes must either extend two feet above the highest part of the roof or coping, the extension to be not less than four inches in diameter to avoid obstruction from frost, or they may be branched into a soil-pipe above the inlet from the highest fixture. They may be combined by branching together those which serve several traps. These air-pipes must always have a continuous slope, to avoid collecting water by condensation.

35. Traps of fixtures near the fresh-air inlet may be ventilated by being connected with it.

36. No trap vent-pipe shall be used as a waste or soil pipe.

37. Overflow-pipes from fixtures must, in each case, be connected on the inlet side of the trap.

38. Every safe under a wash-basin, bath, urinal, water-closet or other fixture must be drained by a special pipe not directly connected with any soil-pipe, waste-pipe, drain, or sewer, but discharging into an open sink upon the cellar floor or outside of the house.

39. The waste-pipe from a refrigerator shall not be directly connected with the soil or waste pipe, or with the drain or sewer, or discharge into the soil; it should discharge into an open sink. Such waste-pipes should be so arranged as to admit of frequent flushing, and should be as short as possible, and disconnected from the refrigerator.

40. The sediment-pipe from kitchen-boilers must be connected on the inlet side of the sink-trap.

41. All water-closets within the house must be supplied with water from special tanks or cisterns, the water of which is not used for any other purpose. The closets must never be supplied directly from the Croton supply-pipes. A group of closets may be supplied from one tank. But water-closets on different floors are not permitted to be flushed from one tank.

42. The valves of cisterns must be so fitted and adjusted as to prevent wasting of water, especially where cisterns are supplied from a tank on the roof.

43. The overflow-pipes from water-closet cisterns must discharge into an open sink, or where its discharge will attract attention and indicate that waste of water is occurring, but not into the bowl of the water-closet, not into the soil or waste pipe nor into the drain or sewer. When the pressure of the Croton is not sufficient to supply these tanks, a pump must be provided.

44. Tanks for drinking-water are objectionable; if indispensable, they must never be lined with lead, galvanized iron, or zinc. They should be constructed of iron, or wood lined with tinned and planished copper. The overflow should discharge upon the roof, or be trapped and discharge into an open sink, never into any soil or waste pipe or water-closet trap, nor into the drain or sewer.

45. Rain-water leaders must never be used as soil, waste, or vent pipes, nor shall any soil, waste, or vent pipe be used as a leader.

46. When within the house, the leader must be of cast-iron, with leaded joints; when outside of the house and connected with the house-drain it must be trapped beneath the ground or just inside of the wall, the trap being arranged in either case so as to prevent freezing. In every case where a leader opens near a window or a light-shaft it must be properly trapped at its base.

47. No steam-exhaust or blow-off pipe from a steam-boiler will be allowed to connect with any soil or waste pipe, or directly with the house-drain. They should discharge into a tank or condenser the waste from which, if to be discharged into the sewer through the house-drain, must be connected on the sewer side of the running trap.

48. Subsoil drains must be provided whenever necessary.

49. Yards and areas should always be properly graded, cemented, flagged, or well paved, and properly drained; when the drain is connected with the house-drain, it must be effectively trapped. Front-area drains must, where practicable, be connected with the house-drain inside of the running trap.

50. Cellar and foundation walls must, where possible, be rendered impervious to dampness, and the use of asphaltum or coal-tar pitch in addition to hydraulic-cement is recommended for that purpose.

51. No privy-vault or school-sink will be allowed in any cellar or basement; nor shall the general privy accommodation of a tenement or lodging house be allowed to be in the cellar or basement.

52. No privy-vault, or cesspool for sewage, will be permitted in any part of the city where water-closets or a school-sink can be connected with a public sewer in the street.

53. School-sinks must be of cast-iron, not more than two feet in depth, connected at the upper end with the Croton supply, and at the lower end with a drain leading to the street-sewer, and provided with an outlet at the lowest point and on the bottom so as to admit of a complete discharge of the contents whenever the outlet is opened and the sink flushed with water.

54. The sink must be set so that the flange will be at least two feet below the yard surface, to prevent freezing. It must be at least ten feet from any window or as near that distance as practicable.

55. The waste-pipe from a hydrant-sink in the yard must be properly trapped, especially where it discharges into a school-sink, a privy-vault, or cesspool, or the house-drain.

56. Open light and air courts must be properly drained.

57. When a privy-vault or cesspool must necessarily be used, and the water-supply of the premises is from a well, they must be at least fifty feet from the well; and the privy-vault must be absolutely tight.

By order of the Board,

CHARLES F. CHANDLER,
President.

EMMONS CLARK,
Secretary.

BROOKLYN.

CONSTRUCTION OF DRAINS, SOIL-PIPES, AND PLUMBING OF NEW BUILDINGS.

PLANS AND DRAWINGS.

25—I. There must be a separate plan for each house, giving the exact location of the same in the manner specified on the plan, including the ward, block number, lot number, and street number, when possible.

II. Every plan must contain a clear description of the plumbing, on a blank prescribed and supplied for this purpose, showing size, kind, and weight of pipes and kind of traps, closets, and fixtures to be used.

III. Plans will be approved or rejected within ten days from the time of filing.

IV. All drawings must be legibly drawn in ink on heavy white paper, or on tracing linen.

V. The size of the paper or linen must be 8 by 12½ inches, or 12½ by 15 inches, and the drawing so made as to leave not less than an inch of margin outside thereof. The former size is preferred, and should be used whenever practicable.

VI. One vertical drawing will be sufficient for a building when it can be made to show all the work. If the work is intricate, and cannot be shown by one drawing, two or more should be made.

VII. This Department (Department of Health) must be notified when any work is ready for inspection, and all work must be left uncovered and convenient for examination until inspected and approved. All notifications of this nature must be in writing, specifying the plan number.

VIII. After a plan has once been approved, no alteration of the same will be allowed except on the written application of the owner. All applications for information or rulings from this Department (Department of Health) must be made in writing, addressed to the Commissioner.

CONSTRUCTION OF WORK.

SOIL-PIPE.

IX. The main sewer-pipe must have a fall of at least one-half inch to the foot. When practicable it must be run on the cellar-wall, securely fastened thereto, and must in such case be of iron. When it is impracticable to run the sewer-pipe on the cellar-wall, it may be laid in a trench beneath the basement or cellar floor, and may in such case be either of iron or earthenware, as hereafter specified. This trench must remain open until this Department gives permission to close it.

X. That where sewer-pipes are to be placed in the ground, cast-iron pipes one-half inch in thickness, or glazed earthenware pipes one and a quarter inches in thickness, and with hubs three inches deep, will be required; that joints on earthen pipes must be made with Portland cement, sand, and iron filings, thoroughly mixed before wetting with a weak sal-ammoniac solution; that all pipes laid beneath the ground, whether iron or earthen, must be filled with water, and shown so filled to the inspector.

XI. The main sewer must be trapped with a running trap of the same material and size as the sewer-pipe, and must be located inside the front wall of the building. No connection with the house-sewer for the discharge of sewage or rain-water shall be made on the street side of said trap. The trap must be provided with a hand-hole, for convenience in cleaning. There must be a fresh-air inlet-pipe entering the sewer-pipe inside and close to the said trap, of a diameter not less than three inches, leading to the outer air, and opening at any convenient place away from windows.

XII. Hand-hole openings, four inches in diameter, must be provided on all pipes laid beneath the ground; said openings to be closed with brass ferrule and screw-cap, and one such opening be required at each branch, and one at each end of the cellar in the main line; said screw-caps to project above the level of the cellar-floor; or, if they do not project above the cellar-floor, manholes must be provided in order to give access to them.

XIII. An opening must be provided in the cellar-walls of all buildings for the entrance of the sewer-pipe; said opening to be two inches clear of the pipe on the top and both sides, to avoid injury by settlement.

WASTE-PIPES.

XIV. All waste or soil pipes must be continued, full bore, above the roof, without return bend, and provided with a wire screen at top. Lead pipe may be used for horizontal lines two inches or less in diameter. All other waste-pipes, two or more inches in diameter, must be of iron. The term waste-pipe or soil-pipe includes all branches taken off the main lines and continued, vertically or horizontally, seven or more feet. The size of waste-pipes shall be as follows: Those that receive the discharge from eight sinks or basins shall be 3 inches in diameter at least; those that receive the discharge from three to seven sinks or basins shall be 2 inches in diameter at least, and those that receive the discharge from one or two sinks shall be not less than 1½ inch. Waste-pipes from safes under wash-basins or other fixtures must not connect directly with any sewer, soil-pipe, or other waste-pipe. Waste-pipes from refrigerators, if carried to the sewer, must first discharge into a drip-pan, and be provided with a trap and stop-cock between said drip-pan and sewer.

XV. All main pipes receiving the discharge from water-closets and other fixtures must be of cast-iron; must be sound, free from holes, and of a uniform thickness, and what is known as extra heavy pipe, weighing as follows:

2 inches,	5½	pounds per lineal foot.	
3 "	9½	"	"
4 "	13	"	"
5 "	17	"	"
6 "	20	"	"
7 "	27	"	"
8 "	33½	"	"
10 "	45	"	"
12 "	54	"	"

Corresponding fittings will be required. All branches or deviations from straight lines must be made with proper fittings. Soil and waste pipes must in all cases be continued, of undiminished size, at least two feet above the roof, without return bend, and provided with a cap, grating, or screen at the top.

XVI. Air-pipes must be of iron or lead (sheet metal will not be permitted), and must not terminate in chimney-flues. They must be carried up inside of the house. When more than one water-closet discharges in the same vertical line of soil-pipe, a separate air-pipe connection, not less than two inches in diameter, must be provided for the trap of each, which pipe may connect with the soil-pipe above the upper water-closet. When the trap of the water-closet is set two or more feet from the vertical line of the soil-pipe, a return connection must in all cases be provided, even where there is but one water-closet on the line. Air-pipes from several traps may be combined by branching together and then carried into a soil-pipe above the inlet from the highest fixture, or continued above the roof. The weight of material for air-pipes shall be the same as that specified in the case of soil and waste pipes.

XVII. All rain-water conductors which are carried up within the walls of a building must be of iron, as required for soil-pipe. Connections with such rain-water conductors along their vertical course for the discharge of sewage or waste-water therein will not be permitted.

TRAPS.

XVIII. Every wash-basin, bath-tub, sink, urinal, water-closet, or other fixture connected with the sewer-pipe of any building shall be separately trapped as close to the fixture as possible. Water-sealing traps of any pattern may be used when separate air-pipe connections from the top of the same are provided; where separate air-pipe connections are not provided, traps which will not unseal must be used. A trap will be considered as unsealed if, when syphoned, it shows a water-seal less than three-quarters of an inch in depth. This rule does not apply to traps of water-closets.

XIX. No overflow connection shall be made with any part of a trap, except into the inlet-pipe thereof, and above the body of the trap; and no connection of any waste-pipe—other than that from the fixture to be trapped—will be permitted to enter the body of the trap.

WATER-CLOSETS, PRIVIES, ETC.

XX. *On Streets that are Sewered.*—All buildings that are located upon a street in which a public sewer exists must be provided with water-closets, either in the house or yard; privy-vaults will not be permitted when a public sewer exists in the street.

Water-closets will not be permitted in any room or apartment that has not a window, having an area of at least four square feet, opening directly to the external air; they will, however, be permitted in rooms or apartments having no windows communicating directly with the external air, provided that there is an air-shaft extending up to or above the roof, having an area of not less than four feet, with an opening to the external air of an equal area; this opening, at the top of the air-shaft, can be arranged by extending the shaft above the roof and providing a sash, of an area equal to that of the shaft, which can be controlled by cord and pulley from below.

In no class of buildings, whether public, private, or tenement, will water-closets be permitted in cellars. [A "cellar" shall be taken to mean and include the lower story of any building or house of which one-half or more of the height from the floor to the ceiling is below the level of the curb of the street adjoining.] In tenement-houses gangs of water-closets will not be permitted in the basement, unless a ventilating-shaft (as above described) of an area of not less than four square feet is provided.

Iron privy-sinks will only be permitted when located in the yard, under the same conditions as privy-vaults; they must be set on the surface of the ground, and no masonry will be permitted on top of the casting.

All water-closets must be furnished with a sufficient supply of water to keep them at all times clean and well flushed.

All water-closets located above the first story must be supplied from a tank, which must hold not less than ten gallons of water for each water-closet which it supplies.

XXI. *On Streets that are not Sewered.*—Water-closets will not be permitted in any building situated upon a street that is not sewered; in such cases water-tight privy-vaults must be provided.

Waste-water from houses situated on unsewered streets must be conveyed to cesspools that are water-tight; into these cesspools rain-water must not be conducted; rain-water must be conveyed to cisterns that are water-tight or to the street gutter.

No privy-vault, sink, cistern, or cesspool shall hereafter be made or rebuilt in the city of Brooklyn within twenty-feet of any dwelling or factory, without a special permit in writing from this board. All vaults, sinks, cisterns, and cesspools shall be made and kept water-tight. This must be done in one of the following ways: By the use of a crock or vessel of glazed earthenware, not less than one and a quarter inches in thickness; or by a cast or wrought iron vessel one-half inch in thickness; or by brick mason-work, constructed as follows: The inner four inches of the bottom and sides must be of hard brick, soaked in tar, or dipped and laid in hot roofing-cement; if tar-soaked bricks are used, the inner surface of the vault, cesspool, etc., must in all cases be covered over with roofing-cement, applied hot.

XXII. All water-closets located above the first story must be supplied from a tank.

XXIII. All joints in iron pipe must be filled with lead and securely calked. Cement and putty joints will not be permitted. All connections of lead with iron pipe must be made by soldering the lead pipe to a brass thimble or ferrule, with wiped or overcast bolted joints. All ferrules must be of brass, either cast or drawn, and be not less than one-eighth of an inch thickness.

XXIV. No opening shall be provided in the sewer-pipe of any building for the purpose of receiving the surface-drainage of the cellar, unless special permission is granted, and any opening so made must be immediately and permanently closed when directed by this department.   J. H. RAYMOND, M. D., *Commissioner*.

Attest: R. M. WYCKOFF, M. D., *Secretary*.

CITY OF BOSTON.

ORDINANCE FOR THE REGULATION OF PLUMBING.

Be it ordained by the City Council of the City of Boston as follows :

SECTION 1. No person shall carry on the business of plumbing unless he shall have first registered his name and place of business in the office of the Inspector of Buildings, and notice of any change in the place of business of a registered plumber shall be immediately given to said inspector.

SEC. 2. Every plumber, before doing any work in a building, shall, except in the case of the repair of leaks, file at the office of the inspector, upon blanks to be provided for the purpose, a notice of the work to be performed; and no such work shall be done in any building without the approval of said inspector.

SEC. 3. Every building shall be separately and independently connected with the public sewer, when such sewer is provided; and, if such sewer is not provided, with a brick and cement cesspool, of a capacity to be approved by the said inspector.

SEC. 4. Drains and soil-pipes through which water and sewage is used and carried shall be of iron, when within a building and for a distance of not less than five feet outside of the foundation-walls thereof. They shall be sound, free from holes and other defects, of a uniform thickness of not less than one-eighth of an inch for a diameter of four inches or less, or five thirty-seconds of an inch for a diameter of five or six inches, with a proportional increase of thickness for a greater diameter. They shall be securely ironed to walls, laid in trenches of uniform grade, or suspended to floor-timbers by strong iron hangers, as the said inspector may direct. They shall be supplied with a suitable trap, placed, with an accessible clean-out, either outside or inside the foundation-wall of the building. They shall have a proper fall toward the drain or sewer, and soil-pipes shall be carried out through the roof, open and undiminished in size, to such height as may be directed by the said inspector; but no soil-pipe shall be carried to a height less than two feet above the roof. Changes in direction shall be made with curved pipes, and connections with horizontal pipes shall be made with Y-branches.

SEC. 5. Rain-water leaders, when connected with soil or drain pipes, shall be suitably trapped.

SEC. 6. Sewer, soil-pipe, or waste-pipe ventilators, shall not be constructed of brick, sheet-metal, or earthenware, and chimney-flues shall not be used as such ventilators.

SEC. 7. Iron pipes, before being put in place, shall be first tested by the water or kerosene test, and then coated inside and out with coal-tar pitch, applied hot, or with paint, or with some equivalent substance. Joints shall be run with molten lead and thoroughly calked and made tight. Connections of lead pipes with iron pipes shall be made with brass ferrules, properly soldered and calked to the iron.

SEC. 8. Every sink, basin, bath-tub, water-closet, slop-hopper, and each set of trays, and every fixture having a waste-pipe, shall be furnished with a trap, which shall be placed as near as practicable to the fixture that it serves. Traps shall be protected from syphonage or air-pressure by special air-pipes, of a size not less than the waste-pipe; but air-pipes for water-closet traps shall not be of less than 2-inch bore for thirty feet or less, and of not less than 3-inch bore for more than thirty feet. Air-pipes shall be run as direct as practicable, and shall be of not less than 4-inch bore where they pass through the roof. Two or more air-pipes may be connected together or with a soil-pipe; but in every case of connection with a soil-pipe such connection shall be above the upper fixture of the building.

Sec. 9. Drip or overflow pipes from safes under water-closets and other fixtures, or from tanks or cisterns, shall be run to some place in open sight, and in no case shall any such pipe be connected directly with a drain, waste-pipe, or soil-pipe.

Sec. 10. Waste-pipes from refrigerators, or other receptacles in which provisions are stored, shall not be connected with a drain, soil-pipe, or other waste-pipe, unless such waste-pipes are provided with traps, suitably ventilated, and in every case there shall be an open tray between the trap and refrigerator.

Sec. 11. Every water-closet or line of water-closets, on the same floor, shall be supplied with water from a tank or cistern, and the flushing-pipe shall not be less than one inch in diameter.

Sec. 12. Pipes and other fixtures shall not be covered or concealed from view until after the work has been examined by the said inspector, and he shall be notified by the plumber when the work is sufficiently advanced for inspection.

Sec. 13. Plumbing-work shall not be used unless the same has first been tested by the said inspector with the peppermint, ether, or water test, and by him found satisfactory.

Sec. 14. No steam-exhaust shall be connected with any soil or waste pipe, or drain which communicates with a public sewer.

Sec. 15. Water-pipes in places exposed to frost shall be packed with mineral wool, or other substance equally good, and they shall be cased to the satisfaction of the said inspector.

Sec. 16. A grease-trap shall be constructed under the sink of every hotel, eating-house, restaurant, or other public cooking establishment.

Sec. 17. The provisions of Sections 3–13, inclusive, and of Section 15 of this ordinance, shall apply only to buildings erected, or to work performed, after its passage.

MARCH, 17, 1883.
Approved.

ALBERT PALMER, *Mayor.*

PENALTY.

Revised Ordinances, Chapter I.

Section 5. Whoever violates a provision of any ordinance of the city, whether included in these Revised Ordinances, or hereafter enacted, shall, unless other provision is expressly made, be liable to a penalty of not less than two nor more than fifty dollars for each offense.

Sec. 6. When anything is prohibited in an ordinance, not only the persons actually doing the prohibited thing, but also the employers and all other persons concerned therein, shall be liable to the penalty prescribed.

Note.—All plumbing shafts shall be constructed of non-combustible material. Packing must be of mineral wool or other non-combustible material satisfactory to the inspector; all cutting of timber, headers, trimmers, or walls, must first be approved by the inspector.

INDEX.

ABSORPTION of light by gas-globes, 118.
Accidental discharge from fixtures into vent-pipes, and how to detect it, 70.
Admission to the New York Trade-Schools, 78.
Air in water-pipes, 93.
Air-binding caused by using too many traps, 34.
Air-inlets to drains, advantages *versus* disadvantages of, 48, 49.
Air-inlets, how to arrange, 57, 58.
Air-inlets, typical, locations of in cities, 50 to 53, 53 to 57.
Air-supply of furnaces taken from the sewer, 23, 24, 25.
Apartment-house boilers cause trouble from giving out of expansion-pipes, 170 to 172.
Automatic cistern-filter, 122 to 125.
Automatic shut-off for gas (hot-air) pumping-engine, 86.
Auxiliary heater for boilers, 143.
Auxiliary heater for use when two boilers are connected with a single water-back, 183.

BACK-LOG boilers, 138, 141.
Bad taste of water in cooler, cause of, 107.
Basin and bath waste water, should it be run into cesspools, or how disposed of, 81.
Basin and bath wastes, what should the size of be, 83.
Basin, how fixed to marble slabs, 120.
Basin-trap rendered of no use by improper overflow connection, 22; by improper outlet, 36.
Bath and basin wastes, how to dispose of, 81.
Bath and basin waste-pipes, what should the size of be, 83.
Bath and kitchen boilers, forms of in use in England and America, 135 to 153.
Bath-boilers, forms of used in England and America, 135 to 186.
Bath-boilers used in Great Britain, 137.
Bath-boiler used with gas-stove in Europe, 137.
Baths, needle, 214, 215.
Baths, Russian and Turkish, construction of, 210 to 215.

Bath-supply at the bottom and the risk of syphonage through it, 73.
Bath-wastes connected improperly with water-closet traps, 21, 66, 95.
Bathing-pool, how to heat, 84.
Bidets, 115.
Boilers and their appurtenances as arranged in various buildings, 187 to 215.
Boilers and water-backs, how to arrange for summer kitchens, 160.
Boilers, action of discussed, 168, 169.
Boilers bursting, cause of, 167, 168.
Boiler-circulations discussed, 161, 162, 168 to 170.
Boiler-circulations below level of boiler and water-back, 155; below level of floors, 161.
Boiler-circulation clumsily arranged without the return-pipe, 156, 157.
Boiler-circulations interrupted, causes of, 158.
Boiler-circulations returning into hot-water pipe, 158.
Boilers and gas-stoves used in Europe, 137.
Boilers, back-log, 138, 141.
Boilers, collapse of, causes of and how to prevent, 164, 165.
Boilers, conical, 143.
Boilers, double, 145 to 148.
Boilers, expansion or vent-pipes of give out, causes of, 170 to 172.
Boilers fitted up in Montreal, 139.
Boilers fail to furnish hot water, cause of, 156.
Boilers, forms of in use in England and America, 135 to 153.
Boilers heated by exhaust steam, 150.
Boilers, horizontal, as used in Boston, 185, 186.
Boilers, horizontal, setting and connections of, 151, 152.
Boilers in the residence of W. R. Vanderbilt, 187 to 191; in the residence of Cornelius Vanderbilt, 191 to 194; in the residence of Henry G. Marquand, 195 to 199; in the residence of A. J. White, 197 to 199; in the Duncan Office Building, 199 to 201; in the residence of Sidney Webster, 202 to 204; in the residence of H. H. Cook, 207 to 209.

Boilers in flats, how arranged, 150; in hotels, 150.
Boilers, noise in and its causes, 136.
Boilers, open, for heating water, how to be arranged, 157.
Boilers placed one at each side of range and connected with separate water-backs, 197, 198.
Boilers, single, with two ranges or water-backs, 153, 154, 173-74-75-76-77.
Boilers, single, with three or more ranges or water-backs, 177.
Boilers, two, heated by a single water-back, with the aid of an auxiliary heater, 183.
Boilers, two, in residence of Henry G. Marquand, 195.
Boilers, two separate used, sizes of, 149.
Boilers, two with one range, 153, 178 to 181.
Boilers, vent or expansion pipes of give out, causes of, 170, 172.
Boilers, preventing collapse of, 87.
Boilers used in Great Britain, 137, 138; in Canada, 139, 140; in the United States, 141 to 143; in Boston, 144; in New England, 149, 150.
Boilers, reverse attachments for, 148, 149.
Boilers, vacuum-valves on not reliable, 87.
Boilers with auxiliary heaters, 143.
Boilers with three couplings on top, 144.
Boilers, wrought-iron, 141.
Boston boilers, 144.
Boston plumbing, examples of bad, 30, 31.
Botch plumbing of reckless character, 32.
Box-castings in water-backs, manner of their explosion, 167.
Bottle-traps, proper position of inlets and outlets of, 67.
Bottle-traps rendered of no use by improper arrangement of inlet and outlet, 36.
Buildings of great height, tanks for, 121.
Burnishing wiped joints, 77.
Bursting of boilers and connecting-pipes, 167, 168.
Bursting of water-backs, causes and prevention of, 136, 137, 166 and 167.
Butler's pantry in the residence of W. K. Vanderbilt, 190.
By-passes, several cases of discussed and illustrated, 17 to 21, 35, 63.
By-passes, around traps of basin and bath, 17; around trap of basin, bath, and water-closet, 18, 19, 21, 34, 35; around traps of wash-trays and sink, 19; around traps of two basins, 19; around trap of water-closet and urinal, and also around trap of urinal and wash-basin, 19.

CAPILLARY attraction removing water from traps, 76.
Carving-tables, how to fit up, 111.
Cellar-floors, how to make impervious to air, 94.
Cellar-floors, pollution of how to be removed, 84.
Cement floors not impervious to air, 94.
Cesspools, construction and management of, 99.
Cesspools, disinfection of, 98.
Cesspools, faulty plan of, 126.
Cesspools, leaching, objectionable, 97.
Cesspools, partitions in clog up, 126.
Cesspools should be ventilated, 97.
Cesspools used for privy-vaults, 101.
Cesspools, will the contents of freeze, 106.
Chimney-flue connected improperly with soil-pipe, 29, 30, 37, 62, 125.
Chimney-flue converted into a cesspool, 30.
Chimney-flue unreliable when used as a vent-pipe for plumbing systems, 37, 62, 125.
Circulation of hot-water boilers, below boiler and water-back level, 155; below floor level, 161.
Circulation of hot water, causes of, 161, 162, 168 to 170.
Circulation of hot-water boilers, discussion of, 135 to 186.
Circulation of hot-water boilers interrupted, causes and remedies, 158.
Circulation of hot-water boilers, used in Montreal, 139, 140; used in the United States, 141, 144.
Circulation-pipes, single, with several flow-pipes in the same system, 159.
"Cistern plan" of boiler used in Montreal, 139.
Cisterns for filtering rain-water, 122 to 125.
Cisterns, bush-pipes of, how to arrange to prevent syphonage, 114.
Cisterns under houses, how to construct, 104.
Cisterns. See also tanks.
City house, ground-water drainage of, 46 to 48.
Coils for water-coolers, construction of, 107.
Collapse of boilers, causes of, and how to prevent, 164, 165.
Condensation in vent-pipes, 69.
Connecting refrigerator waste-pipes with drains, 127, 128.
Conical boilers, 143.
Cook's, H. H., residence, plumbing, water-supply, boilers, etc., in, 204, 210.

INDEX.

Copper hood over range in residence of Cornelius Vanderbilt, 194.
Copperas for cesspools, 98.
Copley's, S. F., filtering-cistern, 122 to 125
Corrosion of tank-linings, 82, 87, 101.
Corrosion of tank-linings, how to prevent, 82, 87.
Country house, ground-water drainage of, 45.
Country house, plumbing blunders in, 34, 35.
Country house, plumbing specification for, 217 to 224.
Couplings for two boilers acting together, 152, 153.
Couplings on horizontal boilers, 152, 153.
Coverings for water-pipes, 88.
Cowls and hoods on soil-pipes objectionable on account of their freezing, 65.
Croton bugs, how to get rid of, 98.

DANGEROUS blunders in plumbing, illustrated by typical examples, 17 to 38.
Depth of trap-seals and the resistance to syphonage action, 67.
Details of the construction of a house-tank, 102.
Direct water-supply to water-closets, dangers of illustrated, 128 to 130
Disconnecting safe-wastes from soil-pipes, 130 and 131.
Disinfection of cesspools, 98.
Dome-top boilers, 138.
Double boilers, 145 to 148.
Double boilers in residence of H. H. Cook, 207, 209.
Drainage and plumbing of an office building defective, 119.
Drainage of ground-water in a country house, 45 ; in a city house, 46.
Drainage of houses. See house-drainage.
Drainage of a Saratoga house, 41 to 45.
Drains, broken, admit sewer-gas into cellars, 26.
Drains, depth of below foundations to prevent dampness, 115.
Drains, how to connect with refrigerator waste-pipes, 127, 128.
Drains improperly arranged turn sewer-gas on to the furnace, 23, 24, 25.
Drains of stoneware, specification for the laying of, 59 to 61.
Drawing water from deep wells, 117.
Duncan Building, hot-water supply boilers, etc., in, 199 to 201.

EARTHEN drains. See stoneware drains.
Elliot, W. G., describes foot-vents, 53.
Exhaust-steam for heating boilers, 150.
Expansion-pipes of boilers give out, cause of, 170, 171, 172.

Expenses and losses of plumbers, 133.
Explosions of water-backs, causes and prevention, 136, 137, 166.
Explosions of water-backs, safety-cock to prevent, 167.

FACTORY, number of water-closets required in, 82.
Faucet for cold water delivers hot water, how to prevent this, 80.
Faucets, irregular flow of water from, 78.
Field's automatic syphon, theory of, 97.
Filtering cistern, construction of, 122.
Fire-boxes in the residence of W. K. Vanderbilt, 187.
Fitting sheet-lead to a large tank, 108.
Fixing basins to marble slabs, 120.
Flats, boilers in, 150.
Flues, heated, dangers of when used to ventilate plumbing-work, 29, 30, 37, 62.
Flushes, "light," of no use, 114.
Flush-tank, size of, for small hospital, 101.
Foot-vents, advantages *versus* disadvantages of, 48.
Foot-vents, how to arrange, 57.
Foot-vents needed to prevent breaking of seals of traps, 31.
Foot-vents, typical locations of in cities, 50 to 53, 53 to 57.
Freezing of contents of cesspools, 106.
Freezing of water-backs, 136, 137.
Fresh-air inlets. See air-inlets and foot-vents.
Furnaces derive their air-supply from the public sewer, 23, 24, 25.

GALVANIZED-IRON pipe, is it dangerous with soft waters, 112, 114.
Galvanized sheet-iron not proper for soil-pipes, 85.
Gas-burners, position of for ventilating flues, 90, 91.
Gas-engines, automatic shut-off for, 86.
Gas-globes, to what extent do they absorb light, 118.
Ground-water drainage of a country house, 45; of a city house, 46, 48.

HAND-HOLE openings in floors to give access to traps, 205.
Heated flues unreliable when used as ventilating pipes for plumbing, 29, 30, 37, 62, 125.
Heaters for use with one water-back and two boilers, 183.
Heating a bathing-pool, 84.
Heating a room from a water-back, 163.

High buildings, tanks for, 121.
Hospital, size of flush-tank required by, 101.
Hood over range in residence of Cornelius Vanderbilt, 194; over range in residence of Henry G. Marquand, 197; over range in residence of H. H. Cook, 209, 210.
Hoods and cowls on soil-pipes objectionable on account of their freezing, 65.
Hooper, L. M., describes arrangements of foot-vents, 50.
Horizontal-boilers in the residence of W. K. Vanderbilt, 187 to 189; in the residence of Cornelius Vanderbilt, 191 to 194; in the residence of Sidney Webster, 202, 203.
Horizontal boilers, plan of used in Boston, 185, 186.
Horizontal boilers, setting of, 151, 152.
Hot-air engine. See gas-engine.
Hot-water circulation in buildings, queries, apparatus, etc., 135 to 186.
Hot-water circulations when pipes pass below the floor level, 161, cf. 155.
Hot water flowing irregularly, cause of, 78, 80.
Hot water flowing from cold faucet, cause and cure of, 80.
Hot-water pipes, should stop-cocks be placed on, 77.
Hot-water pipes, causes of wearing out of, 151, 169, and 170.
Hot-water pipes, flow and return, taken below floor level, 161.
Hot-water supply as arranged in various buildings, 187 to 215.
Hot-water supply in residence of W. K. Vanderbilt, 187 to 191; in the residence of Cornelius Vanderbilt, 191 to 194; in the residence of Henry G. Marquand, 194 to 197; in the residence of A. J. White, 197 to 199; in an office building, 199 to 201, in the residence of Sidney Webster, 202 to 204; in the residence of H. H. Cook, 207, 208, 209.
Hotels, boilers in, 150.
House-drainage, discussion of features of, 39 to 72.
House-drainage, requirements of, 39.
House-tanks, details of construction of, 102.
How to construct a sunken reservoir to hold 2,000 gallons, 89.
How to run pipes between boiler and water-back for a summer-kitchen, 160.
Hughes, J. W., describes the boiler used in Montreal, 139, 140.
Hush-pipes in cisterns, how to arrange, 114

Hydraulic-ram, why it would not work, 92.

ICE should never be stored under a dwelling, 70.
Ignorant way of dealing with a kitchen boiler, 156, 157.
Intermediate tanks for high buildings, 121.
Irregular flow of water from hot and cold faucets, 78, 80.

JOINTS between lead and cast-iron pipes recklessly made, 33.
Joints, rust, how made, 88.

KIND of men who do not like the *Sanitary Engineer*, 131, 132.
Kirkbridge, Dr., adopts a system of ventilating plumbing by heated flues, 62.
Kitchen and hot-water supply in the residence of Mr. W. K. Vanderbilt, 187 to 191; in the residence of Cornelius Vanderbilt, 191 to 194; in the residence of Henry G. Marquand, 195 to 197; in the residence of A. J. White, 197 to 199; in the residence of Sidney Webster, 202 to 204; in the residence of H. H. Cook, 207, 208, 209.
Kitchen-boilers, forms of, in use in England and America, 135 to 153.
Kitchen-boilers. See further under boilers.

LAFAYETTE Place Russian and Turkish baths, 210 to 215.
Leaching cesspools objectionable, 97.
Lead linings, fitting to tanks, 108 to 110.
Lead lining of tanks, corrosion of, 101.
Lead lining of tanks, how to protect, 82, 105.
Lead vent or expansion pipes giving out, cause of, 170, 171, 172.
Light absorbed by gas-globes, 118.
Lightning, is it likely to strike soil-pipes, 106.
Linings of tanks, how to prevent corrosion of, 82, 105.

MANCHESTER Steam Users' Association on the bursting of water-backs (boilers), 138.
Marble slabs, how to fix basins to, 120.
Marble slabs, stains on, 105.
Marquand's, Henry G., residence, boilers, etc., in, 195 to 197.
Marquand's, Henry G., residence, safe-wastes in, 131.
Materials for water-pipes, 110.
Meeker's, James, plan for a horizontal boiler, 185, 186.

INDEX.

Men who do not like the *Sanitary Engineer*, 131, 132.
Meters in the residence of H. H. Cook, 205, 206.
Miscellaneous queries, apparatus, etc., 73 to 134.
Montreal, Can., style of boiler used in, 139, 140.

NEEDLE-BATHS, 214, 215.
New method of heating two boilers from one water-back by the use of an auxiliary heater, 183.
New England boiler arrangements, 149, 150.
New York Trade-Schools, admission to, 78.
Nichols, Prof. W. R., discusses the use of galvanized-iron water-pipe, 112 to 114.
Noise in boilers, 136.
Non-explosive water-backs wanted, 167.
Number of water-closets required in a factory, 82.

OFFICE building, plumbing defective in, 119.
Office building, hot-water supply of, 199 to 201.
Outlets of water-closets, size of, 93.
Overflow-pipes from tanks should not be connected directly with soil-pipes, 130.
Overflow-pipes improperly placed invalidate traps, 22.
Overflow-pipes, when foul, cause bad smells, 95, 96.

PAINT for tank-linings, 87.
Pantry-sink slabs, material for, 99, 100.
Pasco & Palmer's automatic shut-off for gas pumping-engines, 86.
Pipe-coils might lessen liability of range explosions, 167.
Pipe of galvanized-iron, should it be used with soft waters, 112 to 114.
Piping about the boilers in the residence of W. K. Vanderbilt, 189; in the residence of Cornelius Vanderbilt, 193; in the residence of Henry G. Marquand, 195; in the Duncan office building, 201; in the residence of Sidney Webster, 202; in the residence of H. H. Cook, 205, 208.
Plan of cesspool, faulty, 126.
Plans are needed in doing plumbing-work, 38.
Plate-closet in residence of H. H. Cook, 210.
Pennsylvania prison, plumbing is arranged on faulty principle, 62.

Philadelphia, Pa., back-log boilers in, 138, 141.
Plumbers' expenses and losses, 133.
Plumbers' profits, what are reasonable, 133, 135.
Plumbing and water-supply in the residence of H. H. Cook, 204 to 210.
Plumbing blunders, dangerous, typical cases of, 17 to 38.
Plumbing blunders in a country residence, 34, 35.
Plumbing, general requirements of stated, 39.
Plumbing of an office building defective, 119.
Plumbing of a Pennsylvania prison arranged on faulty principles, 62.
Plumbing of a Saratoga house, 41 to 45.
Plumbing specification for an isolated country house, 217 to 224.
Plumbing should be done on carefully prepared plans, 38.
Pollution of cellar-floor, how remedied, 84.
Pollution of wells, test for, 100.
Portable ranges for boilers, 156.
Princeton College drains, specification for, 59 to 61.
Privy-vaults, cesspool used for, 101.
Profits of plumbers, what are reasonable, 133, 134.
Pumping air from water-closets into tea-kettles, 128, 129.

RAHT, E. E., puts an intermediate tank in high buildings, 121.
Rain-leaders, how to connect with soil-pipes and drains, 115.
Rain-leaders improperly connected with drains, 26, 27.
Rain-water cistern-filter, 122 to 125.
Rand system of ventilating plumbing discussed, 62.
Ranges in residence of W. K. Vanderbilt, 187 to 191; in residence of Cornelius Vanderbilt, 191, 192.
Ranges, single, with two boilers, 153, 178 to 182.
Ranges, two, with single boiler, 153, 154, 173 to 177.
Ranges, three or more, with single boiler, 177.
Reasonable plumbers' profits, 133, 134.
Receivers of water-closets, when improperly ventilated, may admit sewer-gas, 27 and 28, 30 and 31.
Reckless botching, 32.
Refrigerator waste-pipes, how to be connected with drains, 127, 128.
Reservoir to hold 2,000 gallons, how to construct, 89.

Residences of W. K. Vanderbilt, of Cornelius Vanderbilt, of H. G. Marquand, etc., etc. See Vanderbilt, W. K.; Vanderbilt, Cornelius; Marquand, Henry G., etc., etc.
Return circulations below level of boilers and water-backs, 155, cf. 161.
Return circulation omitted by mistake, 156, 157.
Return circulation taken into hot-water pipe, 158.
Return-pipe, single, with several flow-pipes on the same system, 159.
Reverse attachments for boilers, 148, 149.
Russian and Turkish baths, construction of, 210 to 215.
Rust in a suction-pipe, how to prevent, 85.
Rust joints, how made, 88.

SAFE-WASTES, methods of disconnecting from soil-pipes, 130, 131.
Safe-wastes from water-closet become passageways for foul matters, 23; become inlets for sewer-gas, 23.
Safety-valves, operation of, 163.
Sanitary Engineer, The, not liked by certain kinds of men, 131, 132.
Saratoga house, drainage and plumbing, plans of, 41 to 45.
Sediment-pipes of boilers, should they be connected with waste-pipes, 158.
Self-acting water-closets, how arranged, 116.
Separate water-backs in residence of Henry G. Marquand, 197.
Setting horizontal boilers, 151, 152.
Several flow-pipes and one return in the same system, 159.
Shut-off for automatic gas-engine (hot-air engine), 86.
Sinks for pantries. See pantry-sinks.
Size of bath and basin waste-pipes, 83.
Size of flush-tank for hospital, 101.
Size of soil-pipes in an ordinary house, 89.
Size of water-pipes. 88, 125.
Slabs for pantry-sinks, should they be of wood or marble, 99, 100.
Smell of well-water, cause of, 118.
Soil-pipes, are they likely to be struck by lightning, 106.
Soil-pipes, galvanized sheet-iron should not be used for, 85.
Soil-pipes should not be connected directly with tank overflows, 130.
Soil-pipe, size of, in an ordinary house, 89.
Soil-pipes, should they be ventilated through the roof or into a heated flue, 69.

Soil-pipe terminals, danger of freezing unless they are without hoods or cowls, 65.
Soil-pipe vents, opening into water-closet room, 25; opening into chimney-flue, 29, 30, 37, 125.
Specification for laying stoneware-drains, 59 to 61.
Specification for the plumbing of an isolated country house, 217 to 224.
Stains on marble slabs, 105.
Steam carving-tables, how to fit up, 111.
Stoneware drains, how to secure tightness of, 64.
Stoneware drains, specification for laying, 59 to 61.
Stop-cocks on hot-water pipes, are they safe, 77.
Sub-surface disposal of bath and basin waste-water, 81.
Suction-pipes, how to prevent the formation of rust in, 85.
Summer-kitchens, how to arrange boilers and water-backs for, 153, 160.
Sunken reservoir to hold 2,000 gallons, how to construct, 89.
Sweating of tanks, cause of, 105.
Syphon, Field's, theory of, 97, 98.
Syphoning water through the bottom supply of a bath, 73 to 75.

TABLES for carving, how to fit up, 111.
Tanks, fitting sheet-lead to, 108 to 110.
Tanks for a house, details of the construction of, 102.
Tanks for high buildings, 121.
Tanks, lining of, corrosion of, 101.
Tanks, lining of, how to prevent corrosion of, 82, 87, 105.
Tanks, lining of, paint for, 87.
Tanks, location of to give good discharge at faucet, 115.
Tank-overflows should not be connected directly with soil-pipes, 130.
Tanks, sweating, cause of, 105.
Tar-coated water-pipe, does it affect taste of water, 83.
Tenement-house plumbing, examples of bad, 29.
Terra-cotta pipe, will it affect drinking-water, 105.
Terry, Stephen, describes his experience with the syphoning of water through the bath-supply, 73 and 74, 75.
Tests for pollution of wells, 100.
Tightness of stoneware drains, how secured, 64.
Tile drains. See stoneware drains.
Trade-schools in New York, terms of admission to, 78.

Traps, hand-hole openings in the residence of H. H. Cook, 204, 205.
Traps, dangers from omission of and reliance on heated flues, 62.
Traps, how to protect from syphonage when soil-pipe is used as rain-leader, 68.
Traps, inlets and outlets of and their relation to each other, 67.
Traps, multiplication of produces air-binding, 34.
Traps of basins rendered of no use by improper overflow connections, 22, 36
Traps of wash-trays made of no use by improper connection of waste-pipe, 28
Traps of water-closets improperly connected with waste-pipes from other fixtures, 21, 66.
Trap-seals broken for want of foot-vents, 32.
Trap-seals, depth of and syphonage action, 67.
Trap-seals disturbed by the wind, 117.
Trap-seals lost on account of capillary attraction, 76.
Traps, two to one water-closet objectionable, 94.
Traps, vent-pipes, and by-passes, 17 to 21, 34, 63.
Trap vent-pipes, how to prevent condensation from stopping, 69.
Trap vent-pipes, sizes of, 68.
Trap vent-pipes, wrongly connected inside the seal, 119.
Traps, why they should be ventilated, 70 to 72.
Tucker's, John, auxiliary heater for use when two boilers are connected with a single water-back, 183.
Tucker's, John, boiler in the Duncan building, 201.
Turkish and Russian baths, construction of, 210 to 215.
Two boilers connected with a single range, 178 to 182.
Two ranges connected with a single boiler, 153, 154, 173 to 177.

VACUUM-VALVES on boilers not reliable, 87, 151.
Vacuum-valves, operation of, 163.
Valve-supply to water-closets, dangers of, 128, 129.
Vanderbilt's, W. K., residence, boilers, etc., in, 187 to 191.
Vanderbilt's, Cornelius, residence, boilers, etc., in, 191 to 194.
Vanderbilt's, W. H., residence, safe-wastes in, 132.
Ventilating-flues, gas-jets for, 90, 91.

Ventilation of cesspools necessary, 97.
Ventilation of traps, why it is necessary, 70 to 72.
Ventilating plumbing by hot flues, dangers of illustrated, 29, 30, 37, 125.
Vent-pipes, accidental discharge from fixtures into, and how to dectect it, 70.
Vent-pipes, combination of several into one, 95.
Vent-pipes from traps, sizes of, 68.
Vent-pipes not to be run into heated flues, 29, 30, 37, 125.
Vent-pipes from traps, when added to old work may produce by-passes, 17 to 21.
Vent-pipes from water-closets serve as inlets for sewer-gas, 22, 25, 27, 28.
Vent-pipes, how to prevent condensation from the stopping of them, 69.

WASH-TRAYS, waste-pipe of so connected with trap as to admit sewer-gas, 28.
Waste-pipes of baths and basins, what should the size be, 83.
Waste-pipes of refrigerators, how to connect with drains, 127, 128.
Waste water from baths and basins, can it be safely run into a cesspool, 81.
Water, is the taste of, affected by tar-coated pipe, 83.
Water, why it is milky when first drawn, 110.
Water-backs, bursting of, the causes and prevention, 136, 137, 138, 166.
Water-backs arranged to heat a room, 163.
Water-backs, explosions of, causes and prevention, 136, 137, 138, 166.
Water-backs, explosions of, safety-cock to prevent, 166.
Water-backs in residence of Henry G. Marquand, 197; in residence of A. J. White, 197, 198.
Water-back, one arranged to heat two boilers with the aid of an auxiliary heater, 183.
Water-backs, non-explosive, wanted, 167.
Water-backs with horizontal boilers in the residence of Sidney Webster, 202, 203.
Water-closets, dangers of connecting directly with water-supply, 128 to 130.
Water-closets, number of, required in a factory, 82.
Water-closet receiver vent-pipes admit sewer-gas, 27, 28.
Water-closets, size of outlets of, 93.

Water-closets, safe-wastes of become passageways for foul matters, 23; become inlets for sewer-gas, 23.
Water-closets, self-acting, how arranged, 116.
Water-closet traps improperly connected with waste-pipes from other fixtures, 21, 66, 95.
Water-closet traps, two of them for one closet objectionable, 94.
Water-closet, ventilating openings take sewer-gas from soil-pipe, 25, 27.
Water-closets, ventilating openings in casings of admit sewer-gas, 22; ventilating openings in receivers admit sewer-gas, 27, 28, 31, 33.
Water-closet ventilation, 115.
Water-cooler, cause of bad taste of water in, 107.
Water-hammer, how to prevent, 92.

Water-meters in the residence of H. H. Cook, 205, 206.
Water-pipes in the Duncan building, 199.
Water-pipes, air in, 93.
Water-pipes, coverings for, 88.
Water-pipes in a house, proper size of, 88, 125.
Water-pipes, materials for, 110.
Water-supply from hot and cold faucets irregular, 78, 80.
Water-supply of high buildings, how arranged, 121.
Wells, deep, drawing water from, 117.
Wells, tests for pollution of, 100.
Wells, cause of smell of water of, 118.
White's, A. J., residence, boilers, etc., in, 197 to 199.
Why water is milky when first drawn, 110.
Wind disturbing seals of traps, 117.
Wiped-joints, burnishing, 77.
Wrought-iron boilers, 142.

APPENDIX.

PLUMBING law of New York City and Brooklyn, 225.
Plumbing regulations of Boston, Mass., 235.

Plumbing regulations of Brooklyn, N. Y., 231.
Plumbing regulations of New York City 226.

www.ingramcontent.com/pod-product-compliance
Lightning Source LLC
Chambersburg PA
CBHW031746230426
43669CB00007B/508